Egyptian History and Mythology

An Enthralling Overview of the History of Egypt, and Egyptian Myths of Gods, and Goddesses

Free limited time bonus

Stop for a moment. We have a free bonus set up for you. The problem is this: we forget 90% of everything that we read after 7 days. Crazy fact, right? Here's the solution: we've created a printable, 1-page pdf summary for this book that you're reading now. All you have to do to get your free pdf summary is to go to the following website: **https://livetolearn.lpages.co/enthrallinghistory/**

Once you do, it will be intuitive. Enjoy, and thank you!

Table of Contents

Part 1: History of Egypt

An Enthralling Overview of Egyptian History

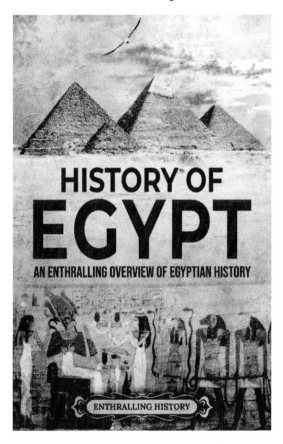

Introduction

Egypt is a vibrant country that draws millions of visitors every year. People from all over the world flock to the home of the pharaohs to tour the Nile and visit its historic landmarks. While it is a beautiful country with a fascinating blend of cultures, much of its allure is due to its illustrious and enigmatic history. From magnificent palaces to towering pyramids, Egypt's history is part of the landscape, which allows it to fit seamlessly into Egypt's bright present and future. However, the country is so much more than a handful of old pyramids and temples. This book will take the reader on a comprehensive tour of Egypt's ancient, medieval, and modern history, which will deepen your appreciation for this magnificent country.

Part one of this book provides a brief but comprehensive overview of ancient Egypt and the powerful dynasties that ruled over it. Discover how Lower and Upper Egypt became a country that produced stunning works of art. These dynasties formed an integral part of the Egyptian empire. The kings were associated with the divine and ruled with iron fists. Learn about some of the most important kings and what they did with their godly kingships.

The second part of this book leaves pharaohs and pyramids behind. It picks up from the Greek and Roman takeover, which ended independent Egyptian rule and introduced new ruling dynasties and cultures. For example, the Ptolemaic kingdom was a unique Greco-Egyptian ruling family with a dramatic history that has been the subject of books, films, and art for centuries. However, there's more to this period than over-the-top rulers, as the Nile became a key port that generated trade for the country. During this time, Egypt became a center of philosophy and attracted famous scholars. In time, Egypt became a Muslim country and had to fight fiercely for its independence.

The next section will discuss Egyptian society through the ages. From ancient to modern times, the structure of society has contributed to how the country functioned. This section will examine factors like the Nile River and how it impacted society and the economy. It will also take a look at religion, art, architecture, and language, which all had an immeasurable impact on the country as a whole.

Finally, the last chapters of the book will be dedicated to taking a look at some of the most important figures in Egyptian history. Find out about the boy king, Tutankhamun, who ruled for a few short years and whose unexpected death ensured his lasting legacy. The story of his cursed tomb has been a subject of fascination for years and opened up a larger conversation about the preservation of Egyptian treasures. While Egypt was mostly ruled by men, there were women who managed to rule in their own right, such as Hatshepsut and Cleopatra.

In time, the Age of Pharaohs passed, and the Greeks and Romans lost control of the area, which allowed sultans to take power. Discover the story of Saladin, Egypt's first sultan who ushered in a period of great change for the country. Ancient Egypt's political system was larger than life and fraught with danger, but modern Egypt's politics are no less intriguing. Find out more about Hosni Mubarak and Mohammed Morsi, who were both Egyptian presidents who faced monumental challenges during their time in office.

Egyptian history is so much more than its ancient period, and that's something this book sets out to prove. Some of the most fundamental events in Egypt's illustrious history have been laid out in a simple format that allows the reader to discover Egypt's secrets without causing them to lose interest or get lost in a maze of scholarly descriptions. Reading this book is like taking a leisurely tour through Egypt's glittering history and will provide an overview of Egypt's impact on the world in general.

Egypt is one of the most beautiful countries in the world, and its history only adds to its allure. Allow this book to deepen your understanding and appreciation for the home of the pharaohs.

SECTION ONE:
An Overview of Ancient Egypt
(3150–330 BCE)

Chapter 1: The Start of Ancient Egypt (3150–2180 BCE)

The Egyptian empire was around for centuries and experienced several periods of significant changes. This makes it difficult to keep track of Egypt's history, which is why historians group ancient Egyptian history into different kingdoms and intermediate periods. A dynasty in ancient Egyptian history refers to rulers who shared ancestors or origins. There were thirty-two commonly accepted pharaonic dynasties. The earliest of these periods was the Early Dynastic Period, which began soon after Upper and Lower Egypt were united. Next came the Old Kingdom, which is also known as the Age of Pyramids. During this era, the great Egyptian kings built the famous pyramids that still draw visitors to Egypt.

Before Egypt was a prosperous empire, the region consisted of various Neolithic societies that settled along the banks of the Nile. The river provided these communities with everything they needed to thrive. In time, these societies formed kingdoms that became known as Upper and Lower Egypt. These two kingdoms frequently fought each other. Their rivalry became legendary and may have formed the basis of one of Egypt's most enduring myths. However, the kingdoms were eventually united under one ruler, the legendary Menes, who formed the foundation of the Egyptian empire.

Neolithic Egyptian Societies

For thousands of years, Neolithic communities lived along the banks of the Nile and built a comfortable life for themselves. During the period between 9300 and 4000 BCE, Egypt was the home to a diverse group of people who aren't well known because evidence of their existence has been covered by floodplains or the surrounding desert. Thousands of years ago, the regions that are now arid desert plains were once lush and fertile lands. Those conditions attracted Neolithic farmers to raise their crops and flocks in Egypt. Not much is known about these people since they haven't been studied as extensively as their successors, but some burial and ancient sites have shed light on these mysterious tribes.

Egyptian Paleolithic and Neolithic stone weapons and tools.
Gary Todd from Xinzheng, China, CC0, via Wikimedia Commons;
https://commons.wikimedia.org/wiki/File:Ancient_Egypt_Paleolithic_%26_Neolithic_Sto
ne_Weapons_%26_Tools_(28426678975).jpg

Historians have found evidence of megaliths, calendar circles, and shrines, which indicate that the Neolithic people practiced elaborate and distinct religions. In time, these Neolithic tribes began developing funerary rites and buried their dead in dedicated cemeteries. Archaeologists found pottery, shells, jewelry, tools, and weapons buried with the dead. Some of these cemeteries revealed surprising secrets. A few cemeteries were found with people in their fifties, which was an impressive age for the time, but Egypt is also home to the world's oldest discovered infant cemetery, which contained women with their infants, late-term fetuses, and babies.

These grave sites have allowed historians to pull back the curtains of time, as they contain numerous clues about the people buried in them. For example, it is clear that these Neolithic communities had rigid social structures since the grave sites containing older people likely belonged to the elite, while the graves containing younger people might have belonged to poorer workers. These cultures may have practiced polygamy, and families were likely buried together. Great respect was shown to the dead, which may have contributed to later beliefs about the dead. It's clear that while the early Neolithic settlers of ancient Egypt are mostly lost to history, they had a clear impact on the people who later populated Egypt. In time, these tribes formed into two distinct kingdoms: Upper and Lower Egypt.

Upper Egypt

The region that made up the area of Upper Egypt spanned from Cairo to Lake Nasser. It was also known as the Land of Reeds and included all the lands between the Nile and Nubia. For hundreds of years, the capital city of Upper Egypt was Nekhen, which was the patron city of the vulture-like goddess Nekhbet. When the two kingdoms were united, she became the patron goddess of the entire region, elevating her status from a local goddess to a more influential deity.

The people who lived in Upper Egypt before the unification were mostly farmers and herders. They grew emmer, lentils, sesame, wheat, barley, and papyrus. In time, Upper Egypt produced crops like garlic, sugarcane, onions, lettuce, and chickpeas. The land was fertile thanks to the Nile, which meant that the people had more than enough to eat. The Nile was an integral part of their lives, as its flooding allowed the land to remain fertile and prevented their lands from turning into desert plains.

During this time, people began developing distinctive pottery and worked with copper. They also began making mudbricks similar to the ones used in Mesopotamia and used recessed walls and arches in their buildings. These decorative elements were impressive for the time and would have led to the development of more decorative architectural techniques. The people of Upper Egypt were accustomed to warfare since they frequently engaged in battles against Lower Egypt.

Lower Egypt

Lower Egypt was made up of the Nile River delta region that ran to the Mediterranean Sea. You might have figured this out already, but the Nile runs south to north, unlike most rivers. The delta region was famously well watered thanks to several channels and canals that branched off from the Nile, making vast pieces of land incredibly fertile. The capital city of Lower Egypt was the city of Memphis, which was the patron city of the goddess Wadjet. This goddess was often represented as a cobra. Eventually, the two kingdoms were unified, and the two goddesses, Wadjet and Nekhbet, were often pictured together and became known as the Two Ladies.

While the two kingdoms were eventually unified, they still had distinct cultures that shared some similarities but were ultimately unique. These distinct cultures were represented by the Pschent or double crown of Egypt, which the ruler wore. The crown consisted of the Hedjet, which was the white crown that represented Upper Egypt, and the Deshret, which was the red crown that represented Lower Egypt. The union of the two kingdoms became a common theme in Egyptian iconography. Some of these images depicted the goddesses Wadjet and Nekhbet, while others showed the gods Horus and Seth knotting papyrus and reed plants, which represented the two kingdoms. The two separate kingdoms rose to prominence during the last stage of prehistoric Egypt, and their unification would mark a new era. The ancient Egyptians accredited the unification of the two kingdoms to Menes, who has been identified by historians as King Narmer.

King Narmer

The unification of Upper and Lower Egypt was a triumphant feat that had long been accredited to a man named Menes. For years, historians accepted that Menes rose to the challenge of unifying the two kingdoms, but this became difficult since they couldn't locate his rule in the historical record. Another problem was that Menes was simply an honorific, meaning "he who endures." Eventually, historians concluded that Menes was likely King Narmer, whom historians believed ruled shortly before the unification. They surmised that Narmer was known as Menes after he unified the regions, and there is evidence of him wearing the crowns of both Upper and Lower Egypt, which gives credence to this theory.

King Narmer carved into a slate palette.
https://commons.wikimedia.org/wiki/File:EB1911_Egypt_-_Early_Art_-_King_Narmer,_Slate_Palette.jpg

If this is true, then Narmer was the first king of Egypt. Historians believe that Narmer originated in Upper Egypt and came from the city of Thinis. He began conquering the states around his kingdom before moving on to Lower Egypt. Some believe that he peacefully took over Lower Egypt, although the

Narmer Palette, an artifact containing some of the earliest hieroglyphs in the region, depicts Narmer as a mighty warrior. Whatever means were used, Narmer managed to unify Upper and Lower Egypt around 3150 BCE.

For years, Upper Egypt had been rapidly developing into a more urban civilization that traded with other cultures, while Lower Egypt was somewhat more rural, which may have helped the unification. Narmer seems to have been a good king who ruled peacefully. When he died, it's possible that his wife, Neithhotep, may have ruled for some time since her tomb was elaborate and showed that she enjoyed significant status during her life.

The Rivalry between Horus and Seth

In the ancient Egyptian religion, Horus was a god who was represented by a falcon. His right eye represented the sun and power, while the left eye represented the moon and healing. He was often mentioned in connection with the god Seth, with the two being presented as mortal enemies. Seth was a trickster god with various animal features. He was known as the god of the desert, warfare, and chaos. Seth and Horus's reconciliation provided the mythical basis for the unification of Lower and Upper Egypt. Pharaohs were eventually thought to be the living representations of Horus and wore dual crowns that symbolized the unity between the two regions.

Carving depicting Horus defeating Seth.

The myth centers on Osiris, Isis, Horus, and Seth. According to the myth, Osiris was the king of Egypt and a descendant of the creator god Ra. His queen was Isis, who gave the women of Egypt the gifts of weaving, beer brewing, and baking. The couple was very happy and ruled Egypt in harmony. Osiris was also associated with power and rightful rulership, which contrasted sharply with Seth's powers. In time, Osiris's brother, Seth, became jealous of him and wanted to claim the kingship for himself. Seth built an ornate wooden chest and coated it in lead. The trickster managed to trap Osiris in the chest and threw it into the Nile.

Osiris died, and in his absence, Seth became king. However, Isis wasn't willing to forget her husband. She searched everywhere for his body. Eventually, she found the wooden chest in the Nile and brought it home. When Seth discovered what Isis had done, he hacked Osiris's body into pieces and scattered them all over the world. Isis and her sister, Nephthys, tracked down all the pieces and put Osiris back together with bandages. Unfortunately, Osiris's penis was missing, but Isis used magic to make her husband whole again. However, he was neither living nor dead and became the first mummy. Nine months later, Isis bore a son and named him Horus.

When Horus was old enough, he challenged Seth since he was the rightful ruler of Egypt. Seth and Horus fought, and in the bloody battle, Horus's left eye became damaged. This formed an explanation for the phases of the moon. Horus and Seth fought on multiple occasions, but in time, they were reconciled.

King Djoser and Imhotep

King Djoser became the king of Egypt around 2650 BCE and is known for his great building projects, including Egypt's first pyramid. He was the first king of the Third Dynasty (although some sources claim that he was the second) and began commissioning building projects almost as soon as he took the throne. His reign saw great innovations in architecture, including the advancement of designs, symbolism, and ornamentations. Djoser secured Egypt's borders, and Egypt was stable for most of his reign, which lasted about two decades. His tomb, the Step Pyramid of Saqqara, was built under the direction of his vizier, Imhotep, and was the tallest building in the world at that time.

Statue of Imhotep.

While Djoser was a good king, much of his success stemmed from the capabilities of his vizier, the famed Imhotep. After Imhotep died, he was deified and became the god of medicine and wisdom. During his lifetime, Imhotep was an accomplished poet, polymath, physician, architect, and astronomer. While he is best known for overseeing Djoser's Step Pyramid, he also wrote treatises about disease and injury that advanced the field of medicine at the time. He may have started out as a priest but quickly rose through the ranks to become one of the most important men in Egypt.

Under his direction, the Step Pyramid rose to about sixty-two meters high and included a complex that housed a temple, shrines, courtyards, and a living space for the priests. It included many important religious symbols and drew travelers from all over.

King Sneferu

King Sneferu was the first king of the Fourth Dynasty and began ruling around 2575 BCE. His reign proved to be the peak of the Old Kingdom, and he refined the art of pyramid-building. Sneferu

---

ushered in a golden age and built two pyramids at Dahshur. His pyramid at Meidum is referred to as the "false pyramid" because it rests on a huge heap of soil and resembles a tower instead of a pyramid. While the pyramid was undoubtedly impressive, it eventually collapsed sometime after it was built since its foundation was made out of sand instead of rock. It's likely that the builders used Imhotep's original design but made a few modifications that led to its collapse.

Sneferu was known for being a competent king who managed to stabilize his country and win many battles against Nubia and Libya. He built several pyramids, including the Red Pyramid, which is Egypt's first true pyramid. (A "true" pyramid is one with smooth sides, not stepped sides.) Sneferu's earlier attempts fell short of his goal, but he didn't stop until he created the perfect pyramid. While he commissioned many projects, his country didn't suffer because of his ambitions, and Egypt remained stable under his reign.

The Pyramids of Giza

Thanks to King Sneferu's efforts, his successors had the blueprints to build true and lasting pyramids. As a result, the next three kings built the famous Pyramids of Giza. Khufu succeeded Sneferu on the throne. The Greeks considered him a tyrant who abused his power. According to their records, he forced his people into slavery. Herodotus claimed that Khufu introduced various evils to his kingdom and conscripted hundreds of thousands of men to work without pay on his pyramid. He also claimed that the unscrupulous ruler forced his own daughter to work in brothels to raise money for his project. However, Egyptian sources state that he was a good king who took care of his workers and only hired men during times when farming wasn't possible due to the Nile flooding.

Khafre later built his pyramid alongside Khufu's and may have commissioned the Sphinx since the Sphinx's face closely resembles his own. Like Khufu, the Greeks remembered Khafre as an oppressive tyrant, but there isn't much evidence left from his reign to refute the claims. He was succeeded by his son, Menkaure, who built his own temple complex at Giza and was praised by both the Greeks and Egyptians. Unfortunately, it seems that Egypt's abundant resources had begun to dwindle under the weight of such massive building projects, and Menkaure's complex was somewhat smaller than his predecessors' tombs.

The Fifth and Sixth Dynasties

One of King Sneferu's lasting acts was to ally his kingship with the cult of the god Ra. One of his successors, Djedefre, claimed that Egyptian kings were the sons of Ra instead of the living embodiment of Ra. This act allowed Egyptian priests to become increasingly powerful, which diminished the kingship considerably. During the Fifth Dynasty, a woman named Khentkaus became incredibly important, and her tomb is the fourth pyramid at Giza, although no one is quite sure why she received such a high honor. The kings of the Fifth Dynasty are known as the Sun Kings because many of them had names that were derived from the sun god Ra.

Unfortunately, the kingship was slowly losing power as administrators became increasingly more powerful. The Sixth Dynasty began with the rule of Teti, who was murdered by his own men. Government officials dared to build grand tombs that rivaled those of the noble classes. Pepi II Neferkare was a notable king during this period; the texts from the time say he ruled for almost a hundred years and was a capable king at first. However, the longer Pepi II ruled, the more unstable the kingdom became. Egypt needed a powerful and energetic king, but Pepi II grew old and lacked the zeal to make a difference. The central government became increasingly destabilized, and he outlived many of his possible successors. Soon after he died, the Sixth Dynasty ended, as did the Old Kingdom.

The First Intermediate Period

In ancient Egyptian history, there were many periods of prosperity and stability, as well as times of instability. The times of stability are known as kingdoms, while the times of instability are known as intermediate periods. The Old Kingdom ended around 2181 BCE, and the First Intermediate Period began. During this time, Egypt's central government collapsed and was almost completely ineffectual. This allowed local administrators to take care of their own areas. For many years, those officials had been gathering power at the government's expense. Egyptian districts had been divided into nomes by previous kings, and these administrators were known as nomarchs. The nomarchs became incredibly rich and built lavish homes and tombs for themselves.

A terrible drought caused conditions to worsen, and the royal family struggled to come up with a suitable heir when Pepi II died. The First Intermediate Period was characterized by disunity, including friction between Upper and Lower Egypt. It was a time of immense change. There aren't any significant monuments from this era, and art suffered somewhat. There are few written records from this period, which led many to believe that it was a time of chaos. However, it appears that rural areas became richer and more complex during this time. Without a king to use their resources on monuments, the people were able to redirect their resources to other pursuits.

It was certainly a dark age for the social elite of Egypt, as the old order simply didn't matter anymore. However, the lower classes were able to afford more luxury goods, which led to the mass production of many items that had previously been reserved for the higher classes. In time, the kings of Egypt were able to bring the First Intermediate Period to an end and introduced the Middle Kingdom. The First Intermediate Period had a definite effect on Egyptian history, and the Middle Kingdom differed from the Old Kingdom in a few significant ways. For example, the kings of the Middle Kingdom worked with the nomarchs, which stabilized Egypt and turned it into one of the most impressive empires in history.

Chapter 2:
The Middle Kingdom Emerges
(2180–1550 BCE)

The Middle Kingdom is also known as the Period of Reunification. The First Intermediate Period was a time characterized by political division, as local nomarchs gathered power for themselves. During this time, the monarchy suffered greatly and often didn't have the resources to care for the rest of the kingdom. As a result, local nomarchs (government officials in charge of nomes or territorial divisions within Egypt) stepped up to take care of their territories, which increased their influence. While the aristocracy saw this time as a period of chaos and lawlessness, ordinary people began making more money, and mass production became widespread.

However, fewer significant strides were made in art and architecture. When the First Intermediate Period ended, it was followed by the Middle Kingdom, which is known as Egypt's Classical Age due to the art that was produced during the era. Historians disagree about when the Middle Kingdom began. Some consider the Eleventh Dynasty as the beginning of the Middle Kingdom, while others regard the Twelfth Dynasty as the founders. One thing is for certain, Mentuhotep II of the Eleventh Dynasty laid the foundation for Egypt's classical period, which would raise

Egypt to new heights.

Mentuhotep II

During the First Intermediate Period, Egypt was divided into Upper and Lower Egypt again. Herakleopolis was the most important city in Lower Egypt, while Thebes rose to become the most powerful city in Upper Egypt. Once again, the two kingdoms fought each other for supreme control. The old kings of Egypt tried to retain control from their place of power in Memphis, but their efforts were futile once the priests and nomarchs gathered power for themselves. In time, the monarchy moved to Herakleopolis in an effort to consolidate its power, but it was too little, too late.

Mentuhotep II.
https://commons.wikimedia.org/wiki/File:Mentuhotep_II_(detail).jpg

The depth to which the Egyptian monarchy had sunk became clear when a nomarch named Intef rebelled against traditional authority around 2125 BCE. The monarchy was unable to subdue him, and he set up Thebes as an important power in the region. Egypt was on track for reunification, with Intef's successors building up Theban prestige and power. One of Intef's successors, Wahankh Intef (Intef II), claimed the title of "King of Upper and Lower Egypt." However, it was Mentuhotep II who would unify Egypt. Mentuhotep II conquered other nomes and brought them under his rule. He then conquered Herakleopolis and rival nomarchs who were a threat. As a result, he reunited Upper and Lower Egypt into one kingdom.

Finally, Egypt had a strong central government again, which led to more building projects, art, and military expeditions. During the First Intermediate Period, Egypt's nomes developed distinct cultures and unique traits that would eventually influence Egyptian culture as a whole. Mentuhotep was a competent ruler who focused on strengthening his government, expanding trade, and commissioning various building projects. Mentuhotep built a grand temple and mortuary complex (where he was buried) close to his beloved city of Thebes and died around 1957 BCE. Thanks to his efforts, he left Egypt as a strong and wealthy country and was given the honor of being known as the second "Menes" of Egypt.

The Eleventh Dynasty

Mentuhotep II was a strong king who focused much of his attention on reconquering old territories that had been lost to Egypt since the fall of the Old Kingdom. He also reestablished the idea that Egyptian kings were extensions of the gods. He often wore the headdresses of Amun-Ra (god of the sun and air) and Min (god of fertility and harvest and the Egyptian masculine ideal). These would have been extremely effective ways to strengthen his own power since the people were less likely to question the authority of a god. Mentuhotep ruled for about fifty-one years and passed the throne to his son, Mentuhotep III.

Mentuhotep III ruled for a little over a decade and adopted many of his father's policies, which further strengthened Egypt. He built various forts in an effort to protect Egypt from invasions from the east. When Mentuhotep died, he was succeeded by

Mentuhotep IV.

Much of the information about the Eleventh Dynasty comes from the Turin List of Kings, which is a papyrus manuscript from the reign of Ramesses II of the Nineteenth Dynasty. It is one of the most detailed records of Egyptian kingship. Not only does it contain the names of the Egyptian kings but also their regnal dates. The papyrus separates the kings into their appropriate dynasties. According to the Turin List, Mentuhotep III was succeeded by seven kingless years. There is little to no evidence about Mentuhotep IV's reign, and his name hasn't been found in several Egyptian king lists. A few inscriptions have been found bearing his name, detailing how he sent his vizier, Amenemhat, to a quarry to retrieve stones for a royal monument.

It appears as though there may have been a civil war during this period and that Amenemhat was victorious since he became Amenemhet I. There isn't a clear record of how Amenemhet became king, but since he wasn't a royal, it is easy to lean toward the theory of a civil war or coup.

Thebes

Thebes was built on the banks of the Nile River and was located in the middle of Upper Egypt, south of the delta. At its peak, the city housed about seventy-five thousand people, which made it the largest city in the world during its time. It was a wealthy city that was the seat of royal power for many years, which likely attracted more inhabitants as well as the social elite. It was also an important religious city since it was the center of worship for Amun-Ra. The Eleventh Dynasty's kings ruled from Thebes, but when Mentuhotep IV was replaced by Amenemhet I, the Egyptian capital was moved to Iti-tawi. This move may have signaled Amenemhet's desire to distance himself from the previous dynasty.

While Thebes was no longer the capital of the kingdom, it still enjoyed significant influence as a religious center. Senusret I, a king from the Twelfth Dynasty, built a temple dedicated to Amun, which shows that the city still received plenty of attention from the monarchy. During the Middle Kingdom, the city was quite large and had at least two palaces within its boundaries. While Thebes enjoyed significant influence during the Middle Kingdom, it only reached its peak during the New Kingdom when Amun became the principal god.

Amenemhet I

While not much is known about Amenemhet's rise to the throne, it is clear that he was a strong and capable leader. Under his rule, Egypt flourished and interacted with other countries. Amenemhet founded the Twelfth Dynasty, which would rule Egypt for the next two centuries and brought about the distinct culture for which the Middle Kingdom is known. It's possible that Amenemhet moved his capital from Thebes to Iti-tawi to distance himself from the Eleventh Dynasty. However, the new capital was located close to Lisht, which was close to the old capital of Herakleopolis. Iti-tawi was built on fertile plains, which would have allowed it to flourish. This suggests that Amenemhet moved the capital in order to establish his dynasty as completely Egyptian instead of just Theban. The new capital was also placed in a central position, which would have allowed him to rule more effectively and consolidate his power in the country.

Amenemhet also made sure to honor the old capital at Thebes by contributing to Amun's temple. He commissioned various building projects, including fortresses to ward off foreign invaders and a massive pyramid and mortuary complex at Lisht. These buildings resembled the Pyramids of Giza, which shows that Amenemhet wanted to associate himself with the glory of the Old Kingdom kings and their prosperous reigns.

Around the twentieth year of his reign, around 1918 BCE, Amenemhet I appointed his son, Senusret I, as co-regent. Senusret conducted several military campaigns in the south. It would appear as though Amenemhet I faced political unrest during the end of his reign and may have been assassinated.

Art, Culture, and Government during the Middle Kingdom

During the Old Kingdom, art was commissioned to honor the gods, and literary works were usually reserved for Pyramid Texts, inscriptions, and theological stories. However, literature flourished during the Middle Kingdom, and stories about ordinary people became popular. For example, the "Tale of Sinuhe" tells the story of a man who served Amenemhet I but ran away to become a Bedouin after the assassination of the king. He lived among the Bedouin for years since he feared reprisal from Amenemhet's heir,

Senusret, even though Sinuhe was not involved in the king's death. In time, Sinuhe longed to return to his home. He eventually received a pardon from the king, which allowed him to live out his final years among his own people.

Other works posed important questions, such as whether or not there was life after death. Poetry and prose became popular, and stories such as the "Tale of the Shipwrecked Sailor" were developed. Sculptures and paintings focused on depicting daily scenes. Grand buildings were designed to highlight the surrounding landscape, such as Mentuhotep II's mortuary complex.

Middle Kingdom boat carving.
Infrogmation of New Orleans, CC BY 2.0 https://creativecommons.org/licenses/by/2.0 via Wikimedia Commons; https://commons.wikimedia.org/wiki/File:Middle_Kingdom_Ancient_Egyptian_boat_artwork_at_New_Orleans_Museum_of_Art.jpg

During the Middle Kingdom, many kings had double dates on their cartouches, which means it's possible that the kings allowed their chosen successors to rule as co-regents in their final years so there would be no disruption when the king died. It also allowed the successor to learn to be an effective king. This theory hasn't been confirmed, but it seems that quite a few kings appointed their successors during their final years and then appointed these successors to be co-regents. When Mentuhotep II reunited Egypt, he appointed members of his own family to high positions within the government and took considerable power away from the nomarchs. Later kings would follow this example, but many of these kings had good relationships with their nomarchs. In fact, during Senusret II's reign, the nomarchs enjoyed as much prosperity as they had during the First Intermediate Period but at no cost to the monarchy's influence. As a result, the nomarchs were fiercely loyal to their king, which helped Egypt prosper.

The Twelfth Dynasty

Like his father before him, Senusret I wanted to associate his kingship with the Old Kingdom rulers. As soon as he took the throne, he began commissioning building projects that closely resembled the monuments of the Old Kingdom. He also built infrastructure that benefited the whole kingdom. Senusret I managed to increase Egypt's prosperity and awarded officials for their loyalty. He curbed the power of the nomarchs but allowed them to grow wealthier without taking power from the monarchy. As a result, Senusret was able to strengthen his own government without alienating the nomarchs. This peace between the monarchy and the nomarchs allowed Senusret to focus on the military, building projects, agriculture, and art.

It would appear as though Senusret I allowed his successor, Amenemhat II, to rule as co-regent alongside him during the last years of his reign. Not much is known about Amenemhat II except that he was succeeded by Senusret II around 1897 BCE. Senusret II had an extremely good relationship with the nomarchs. He was succeeded by Senusret III, who would lead Egypt into one of its golden ages.

Senusret III

Egyptian kings were usually associated with the gods, but some kings were so great that they were actively worshiped as gods. Senusret III was such a king. Not only was he worshiped as a god in Egypt and had his own cult that was on the same level as the great gods of the Egyptian pantheon, but he was also worshiped in Nubia. He was the son of Senusret II and had a privileged upbringing that included a royal education in Thebes. Senusret III took the throne around 1878 BCE. One of his first acts was to reorganize the government, thereby reducing the number of nomarchs. Strangely, there seems to have been little resistance to this reorganization. It's possible that Senusret III gave the disenfranchised nomarchs positions within his government.

Once his position was secure, he looked toward expanding Egypt's borders and came into conflict with Nubia, Syria, and Palestine. Senusret III was an extremely capable military leader, and many of his expeditions ended in success. In the past, nomarchs had standing armies that the king could call upon for aid, but Senusret absorbed those armies into his own large force. His actions also led to the development of the middle class in Egypt. During his reign, art became more elaborate and realistic. Some of the most famous pieces of art from his reign were his statues, which depicted the king during different times in his life.

Senusret III worked with the cult of Amun, which had historically struggled with the monarchy for power. This peaceful relationship benefited Egypt greatly. Few kings would ever live up to his enduring legacy. Senusret III died around 1839 BCE and was succeeded by his son, Amenemhet III.

Amenemhet III

Amenemhet III had the unenviable task of living up to the example of his father, who was the ideal Egyptian king. Amenemhet didn't leave behind many records of his military victories, which means that he probably didn't go to war as much as his father. He more than likely inherited a peaceful kingdom and didn't feel the need to defend his kingdom. It is also possible that he didn't feel the same need to expand Egypt's borders as his father did. Amenemhet did seem to enjoy initiating building projects, which led to the construction of many important monuments. Herodotus accredited Amenemhet III with building the legendary mortuary temple known as the Labyrinth. The ancient Greek historian claimed that Amenemhet III's mortuary temple at Hawara was one of the most impressive monuments in the ancient world.

Perhaps Amenemhet III's greatest achievement was creating a system that regulated the flow of water into Lake Moeris by draining the marshes surrounding the lake. He increased work at the turquoise mines located in Sinai and used quarries throughout Nubia and Egypt that provided necessary funds for his various building projects. Amenemhet III may not have had the same stellar reign as his father, but he was a capable king who increased Egypt's prosperity in his own right. He was succeeded by

Amenemhat IV around 1815 BCE.

Sobekneferu

Amenemhat IV continued many of his father's policies and launched many of his own initiatives, which included building projects and military campaigns. Unfortunately, he seems to have had a short reign and died without a male heir. This would have been disastrous, as the previous kings seem to have appointed co-regents during their lifetime, which ensured a smooth transition of power. Since Amenemhet IV had no viable heir, there was no co-regent, and the transfer of power wouldn't have been easy. When Amenemhet IV died, the throne went to his wife or sister (or possibly both), Sobekneferu, around 1807 BCE. Not much is known about her reign except that she likely wasn't the first Egyptian queen to rule in her own right. An earlier queen, Nitiqret, is thought to have ruled for a short period during the Old Kingdom, but few records exist from her time.

Statue of Queen Sobekneferu.
https://commons.wikimedia.org/wiki/File:Statue_of_Sobekneferu_(Berlin_Egyptian_Mus eum_14475).jpg

Whether or not Sobekneferu was the first queen of her kind, her reign was certainly remarkable. She reigned several hundred years before Hatshepsut, and she always ruled as a woman and never depicted herself as a man. She commissioned several important building projects, such as the city of Crocodilopolis, which she either founded or repaired. Unfortunately, she wasn't able to provide an heir and died around 1802 BCE, which effectively ended the Twelfth Dynasty.

The Decline of the Middle Kingdom

When Queen Sobekneferu died, the throne passed to Sobekhotep I, who began the Thirteenth Dynasty. While the Thirteenth Dynasty inherited a prosperous and strong country, the kings of this dynasty didn't seem to have the same drive and power as the kings of the Twelfth. Records during this time are rare and fragmented, which means it's difficult to know exactly what led to the decline of the Middle Kingdom. It seems the Thirteenth Dynasty kings were somewhat weaker than those of the Twelfth. While they kept many of the same policies, factions began to develop within Egypt. In time, Hyksos rose to become a powerful political power that rivaled the power of Iti-tawi.

As the Thirteenth Dynasty declined in power, the Hyksos came to rule Egypt. They showed great respect for the Egyptian culture and ruled during the Second Intermediate Period. In the past, the Second Intermediate Period had been characterized as a lawless time, but it seems that most people in Egypt enjoyed relative stability. The change in power would only have impacted Egypt's social elite.

There is no denying that the Middle Kingdom was a time of great prosperity for Egypt, and the achievements of the Twelfth Dynasty elevated Egypt to one of the most powerful and wealthy states in the world. Unfortunately, their successors were unable to keep up that prestige and buckled under the weight of their impressive empire, which led to the rise of a different power in the region.

While the Second Intermediate Period likely wasn't a time of complete chaos, it certainly was a far cry from the heights achieved by the Middle Kingdom. However, the Second Intermediate Period would lead to the New Kingdom and even greater heights for ancient Egypt.

Chapter 3: The New Kingdom (1550–1070 BCE)

Ancient Egypt enjoyed many golden periods during which great pyramids were built and elaborate art was developed. When the Middle Kingdom declined, a foreign influence, the Hyksos, managed to accrue wealth and political power that allowed them to take control of a significant portion of Egypt. In time, the Egyptian monarchy regained strength and drove the Hyksos out of Egypt. Once they were rid of the foreign power, the Egyptians set up boundaries that were supposed to prevent invasions but became stepping stones that helped future kings turn Egypt into a mighty empire.

The most prosperous Egyptian kingdom was the New Kingdom. During this era, literature, architecture, and trade flourished. Egypt became an international power, as it traded and corresponded with the major world powers of the time. More people were writing than ever before, which makes the New Kingdom one of the best-documented eras in ancient Egyptian history. This wealth of information has given modern people a clear look into one of the most fascinating periods in Egyptian history. The New Kingdom introduced legendary figures like Akhenaten, Hatshepsut, Tutankhamun, and Ramesses II. It would also be the period during which Egyptian kings became known as pharaohs.

Hyksos

The Middle Kingdom was a time of incredible unity and prosperity for Egypt, during which the monarchy had firm control of Egypt. However, that power declined under the Thirteenth Dynasty kings, who couldn't live up to the example left by their predecessors. The kings of the Thirteenth Dynasty struggled to keep Egypt unified, and as a result, the Hyksos settled in Avaris, which was located in Lower Egypt. The Kingdom of Kush also gained power close to Upper Egypt, which presented another problem.

While the Hyksos were foreign, their rule wasn't completely unpopular. Later records would paint the Second Intermediate Period as a time of utter chaos, but this could have been a result of propaganda meant to highlight the rule of the New Kingdom kings against the rule of the Hyksos. The foreign rulers seemed to have had a relatively peaceful relationship with the rulers of Egypt and had a definite impact on Egyptian history. For example, the Hyksos influenced Egyptian warfare by introducing chariots and horses. They also brought bronze to Egypt, which allowed for stronger weapons and armor. The Hyksos may have originated from the north, which drew Egypt's attention to the Middle East and inspired future Egyptian kings to expand their empire northward.

Relations between the Hyksos and the Egyptian monarchy soured during the reign of King Seqenenra Taa of Egypt. He went to war against the Hyksos but was killed in battle. His son, Kamose of Thebes, continued his father's war and defeated the Hyksos, but it was Ahmose I who drove the Hyksos out of the kingdom and reunified Egypt.

Ahmose I

Ahmose I took the throne around 1550 BCE during a tumultuous time. He faced incredible odds yet managed to bring peace and stability to Egypt. The Hyksos were infamous for exacting tribute from the Egyptian kings and marrying Egyptian princesses, which may have indicated their intent to join themselves to the Egyptian monarchy. Ahmose I used horses, chariots, and bronze weapons to destroy Avaris and drive the Hyksos to Palestine and later to Syria. Once the Hyksos were driven out of the country, Ahmose reestablished Thebes as the capital of his kingdom and conquered Nubia again. This allowed him to plunder vast amounts of gold from Nubia, which increased Egypt's wealth. Ahmose I realized he had to take firm steps to prevent the Hyksos or others from invading his borders. As a result, he built forts in previously neglected areas and established buffer zones around the borders to protect Egypt from invasion.

Both sides of a ceremonial ax that belonged to Ahmose I.
Color photograph: Heidi Kontkanen (cc-by-sa-2.0 per original uploaded photograph)Black and white photograph: Mariette, Auguste (1821-1881) (Public Domain), CC BY-SA 2.0 https://creativecommons.org/licenses/by-sa/2.0 via Wikimedia Commons; https://commons.wikimedia.org/wiki/File:Ceremonial_axe_of_Ahmose_I_(both_sides).jpg

The Egyptian people venerated Ahmose I like a god, which was an honor that was only reserved for legendary kings. In an effort to boost the Egyptian economy, Ahmose reopened several mines, generating more trade for the country. His efforts established the New Kingdom, which would last for almost five centuries and bring increasing prosperity and fame to the empire. Ahmose I also fought against the Kushites and prevented them from invading Egypt, which was something his predecessors hadn't been able to do. For the first time in centuries, Egypt was united, and the central government was stable again. Ahmose I left a secure kingdom for his son, Amenhotep I, and was venerated along with Narmer as one of Egypt's great unifiers.

Hatshepsut

Amenhotep I was a competent king who made great contributions to art and left a stable throne for his son, Thutmose I, around 1520 BCE. Thutmose I was a warrior like his grandfather, Ahmose I. He expanded Egypt's hold on Nubia and set his sights on more territory and building projects. When he died, his designated heir was apparently his legitimate daughter, Hatshepsut (according to her inscriptions), but the throne went to his son, Thutmose II, who was born by a lesser queen. The siblings were married, as was the tradition at the time. Hatshepsut was the real power behind the throne and became one of the most influential kings of the New Kingdom. For the first seven years, she was depicted as a woman, but she later chose to be depicted as a male ruler.

Statue of Queen Hatshepsut.
Credit: Metropolitan Museum of Art, CC0, via Wikimedia Commons;
https://commons.wikimedia.org/wiki/File:Seated_Statue_of_Hatshepsut_MET_Hatshepsut2012.jpg

Her reign brought great prosperity and stability to Egypt. She was appointed as the wife of the god Amun, which was an influential and powerful role in Egypt. In time, Thutmose II died, leaving behind his son by a lesser wife, Thutmose III. Hatshepsut retained her power and ruled as regent. Around the same time that she began presenting herself as a man, she also declared herself pharaoh. Like her predecessors, she initiated military campaigns and building projects. She also built a temple at Deir el-Bahari, which is one of the most impressive in all of Egypt, and made a lavish campaign to Punt. Hatshepsut commissioned more building projects than any other Egyptian monarch besides Ramesses the Great.

All throughout Hatshepsut's reign, Thutmose III proved his worth by acting as one of her generals. Around 1457 BCE, Thutmose III was sent to subdue a rebellion in Kadesh, and it was around that time Hatshepsut disappeared from history. It's possible that she died from an abscess in her tooth. Whatever the true cause of her death was, Thutmose III was made king and quickly began destroying records of his stepmother's reign. Her accomplishments were erased, and she remained a mystery until historians discovered evidence of her existence in the 19th century CE.

Thutmose III

It is unclear why Thutmose III decided to erase his stepmother's name from history, but a few theories prevail. Some historians think that Thutmose III wanted to restore the balance of Egyptian rulership since Egypt was usually ruled by males, while some think that Thutmose III wanted to prevent women from becoming too ambitious. Thanks to his stepmother's efforts, Thutmose III inherited a stable kingdom, which allowed him to set his sights on expanding Egypt's borders. In fact, Thutmose III was responsible for numerous successful military campaigns that stretched Egypt's borders farther than ever before.

Thutmose completed seventeen military campaigns in two decades and left ample inscriptions detailing his victories. He left so many inscriptions behind that he is one of the most well-known pharaohs in Egypt. When he died, he left the throne to his son Amenhotep II around 1425 BCE. Amenhotep wasn't as eager to go to war as his father and proved to be a capable ruler. He forged a peace treaty with the Mitanni and others. He left the throne to his son, Thutmose IV, around 1400 BCE. Thutmose imitated his father in many ways and restored the Great Sphinx.

Amenhotep III

Amenhotep III ascended to the throne when he was only twelve years old, but he had inherited one of the wealthiest kingdoms in the world. As soon as he was crowned, he married Tiye and elevated her to the rank of "Great Royal Wife," which meant she outranked every other female at court. He proved to be a capable diplomat who used his great wealth to foster good relationships with surrounding nations, usually buying their favor or paying them to do whatever he wanted. Amenhotep III was a good military leader, and some of his inscriptions detail his military campaigns, including a campaign to Nubia. However, his greatest interests lay in art, architecture, and religion.

Statue of Amenhotep III.
IGallic, CC BY-SA 4.0 https://creativecommons.org/licenses/by-sa/4.0 via Wikimedia Commons; https://commons.wikimedia.org/wiki/File:Amenhotep_III.jpg

He commissioned over 250 building projects during his lifetime, most of which were massive and elaborate. Amenhotep III also granted his wife extraordinary powers, allowing her to govern the state while he was preoccupied. The two were often depicted together in carvings or statues. However, while the king continued to grow in wealth, so did the cult of Amun. When Amenhotep III took the throne, the priests of Amun owned as much land as the pharaoh. He saw the danger in this and allied himself with the god Aten, but this did little to curb the priests' power. His son, Amenhotep IV (later known as Akhenaten), would take more drastic measures. Amenhotep III died around 1353 BCE after an extremely successful reign.

Akhenaten

Akhenaten's reign began peacefully enough. He imitated many of his father's policies, but after a few years, he underwent a religious conversion and forced Egypt to go through several reforms. He made the ancient religion illegal and made Aten Egypt's principal deity. Akhenaten moved the capital to his new city, Akhetaten, and claimed that Aten was the supreme ruler of the universe. The king was the human embodiment of Aten. It's possible that his efforts reflected a sincere devotion to this god, but it's also possible that he wanted to reduce the cult of Amun's power. His reforms forced the cult to give up its vast wealth, but the changes also caused serious consequences for the country as a whole.

Akhenaten neglected foreign and state affairs, which resulted in the loss of vassal states and a general breakdown in the local government. His wife, Nefertiti, took over many of his duties and tried to rule the country in his stead as he became increasingly obsessed with his religion. Queen Nefertiti was a capable queen, but the country suffered from the king's neglect. Her power only went so far, and the royal treasury quickly became depleted. The religious reforms resulted in the loss of income for many artisans, which affected the economy. In addition, foreign affairs worsened as his reign continued. Akhenaten died in 1336 BCE, having undone much of his predecessors' efforts.

Tutankhamun

A few years later, Akhenaten's young son, Tutankhamun, took the throne. The eight-year-old king (some sources say nine-year-old king) tried his best to undo the damage done by his father and quickly reversed the religious reforms, restoring the ancient religion. He reopened temples and helped return some of Egypt's former glory. The ordinary people had suffered during the reformation, and Tutankhamun brought stability back to their lives. He married his wife and half-sister, Ankhesenamun, sometime during his reign but died before he could father any heirs. It is believed he died around 1327 BCE.

Statue of Tutankhamun.

Ankhesenamun may have tried to take the throne for herself and famously wrote to King Suppiluliuma I of the Hittites to ask for one of his sons in marriage. The Hittite king sent his son to marry the Egyptian queen, but the prince disappeared during the journey. Tutankhamun's vizier, Ay, became the next pharaoh. Ay continued Tutankhamun's efforts to restore Egypt back to its former glory, but it was Ay's successor, Horemheb, who succeeded in completely reversing the religious reforms initiated by Akhenaten. Horemheb also died without an heir, leaving the throne to his vizier, Paramesse, who became Pharaoh Ramesses I around 1292 BCE.

Ramesses I

Ramesses was the first king of the Nineteenth Dynasty and was likely a close friend of Horemheb. Historians have theorized that Ramesses was part of a military family, which was how he became acquainted with Horemheb. Since Horemheb had no heirs, he appointed Ramesses as his heir, even though Ramesses was advanced in age by the time Horemheb died. It's possible that Horemheb appointed Ramesses since he had an heir. Ramesses took the throne around 1292 BCE and appointed his son, Seti I, as his co-regent. It's likely that Ramesses found it difficult to keep up with his kingly responsibilities or wanted his son to learn how to be a capable king.

Seti I immediately began military campaigns and aimed to regain Egypt's former lands in Syria. In the meantime, Ramesses I busied himself with numerous building projects in Egypt. Ramesses I died after a short reign, which lasted fewer than two years, and left the throne to Seti I. Like his predecessors, Seti poured much of his energy into returning Egypt to its former glory. Seti I commissioned various building projects and began teaching his son how to be a good king. He proved to be a capable ruler. While he did his best to return to the prosperity Egypt had enjoyed under Amenhotep III, it would be his son, Ramesses II, who would become one of the greatest pharaohs in Egyptian history.

Ramesses II

Ramesses II took the throne around 1279 BCE and lived to be almost a hundred years old. When he died, many of his subjects could not remember living under a different ruler, which caused the people to panic. From a young age, Ramesses joined his father on military campaigns and soon began leading his own military expeditions. He fought against the Hittites and secured Egypt's borders while expanding trade routes. Ramesses defeated the Sea Peoples, who were allied with the Hittites, and incorporated them into his own army. He also built the city of Per-Ramesses, which is said to have rivaled the ancient city of Thebes.

In 1274, he fought in the Battle of Kadesh, which ended in a draw. However, the king claimed to have won the battle to boost his own reputation. Later, he was part of the world's first peace treaty when he negotiated with the Hittites. He was also a great patron of the arts, and many historians claim that ancient Egyptian art reached its peak during his rule. Ramesses II commissioned many building projects and left behind a large number of inscriptions. He also had the Tomb of Nefertari built. Nefertari was his favorite wife who died early in his reign, and her tomb was magnificently constructed to reflect the king's favor. Ramesses had Nefertari's likeness carved alongside him in many of his carvings long after she died, which shows the depth of his devotion to his first wife.

Temple of Ramesses II at Abu Simbel.

During Ramesses II's reign, he strengthened the borders, increased trade, and replenished Egypt's coffers. His achievements made him one of the greatest pharaohs in history, and he was deeply loved and revered by the ancient Egyptians. He was succeeded by his heir, Merneptah, around 1213 BCE, who was already an old man when he became king. Merneptah was eager to prove himself and launched various successful military campaigns. He was succeeded for a short period by Amenmesse around 1203 BCE, who may have been a usurper since the rightful heir was supposed to be Seti II. Around 1200 BCE, Amenmesse was no longer mentioned in the records. Seti II reigned to about 1197 BCE and was succeeded by Merneptah Siptah, who inherited the throne as a boy and died young. His stepmother, Tausret, ruled as regent until 1190 BCE until she was succeeded by Setnakht, who was likely another usurper.

Ramesses III

Setnakht may have been one of Seti II's sons. He established the Twentieth Dynasty. He was succeeded by Ramesses III, who proved to be a capable king and the last great king of the New Kingdom. He began his reign by driving off the Sea Peoples and strengthening the country's government. During his reign, the Libyans tried to invade the country, but Ramesses III defeated them in battle and secured Egypt's borders, proving his capabilities as a warrior king. He also built his great mortuary temple in between intermittent fighting against would-be invaders. Trade and industry flourished under his reign, and he used many of Egypt's mines to boost the economy.

However, Ramesses III's reign wasn't completely successful, as he experienced one of the first labor strikes in history. Workers on one of his building projects were unsatisfied with working conditions and refused to work until the problems were fixed. Ramesses III faced serious political instability during his reign and was assassinated around 1155 BCE.

The Decline of the New Kingdom

Akhenaten may have brought his country to the edge of decline during his rule in an attempt to curb the power of the priests of Amun. When his religious reforms were reversed, the cult of Amun was restored, and it continued to amass power and wealth at the expense of the crown. By the time Ramesses III took the throne, the pharaoh's power was nowhere near what it had been during the time of Amenhotep III. Ramesses III was succeeded by his son Ramesses IV, with many of his successors also named Ramesses. However, they shared no similarities with Ramesses the Great, as the monarchy declined rapidly during the reign of the Twentieth Dynasty's kings.

The priests of Amun were left unchecked. This allowed them to effectively divide Egypt into two and take power away from the monarchy until the central government was crippled. Ramesses I had left Thebes centuries prior, which allowed the priests to take control of the ancient city and extend their influence. In time, the king came to represent a subordinate of Amun, which, by extension, made him a subordinate of the priests. Soon, the Nubians took much of southern Egypt while the priests governed Upper Egypt, which led to the Third Intermediate Period. Unfortunately, there wouldn't be another great kingdom to drag Egypt out of the chaos. The Third Intermediate Period ended with the Battle of Pelusium in 525 BCE, which led to the Persian invasion.

Chapter 4: The End of Ancient Egypt (1070–330 BCE)

The Third Intermediate Period brought an end to the glory of ancient Egypt. The New Kingdom was defined by remarkable rulers who fostered diplomatic relationships and expanded Egypt's borders while ensuring that Egypt was stable. They brought immense prosperity to Egypt and built magnificent monuments that still attract tourists today. Unfortunately, by the time the New Kingdom's last great pharaoh took the throne, Egypt was a shadow of its former self and riddled with problems due to religious reforms and issues with succession.

When the Twentieth Dynasty came to an end, so did the New Kingdom. During the Third Intermediate Period, the pharaohs would become almost inconsequential as the cult of Amun seized power in Egypt. As time wore on, Egypt became a battleground for Nubia and Assyria as those foreign powers battled for Egypt's wealth. Before long, the Persians invaded Egypt and would rule over the region for several decades before Alexander the Great arrived and claimed the country as his own. While Egypt remained a strong and influential region, the glittering age of pharaohs and pyramids was over.

The Decline of the Pharaohs

For decades, the cult of Amun's power had grown at the expense of the monarchy. While the pharaohs of the New

Kingdom usually managed to keep the cult of Amun in check, the pharaohs of the Twentieth Dynasty were unable to do so, which would have lasting consequences for Egypt as a whole. The Twentieth Dynasty ended with the reign of Pharaoh Ramesses XI, who died around 1077 BCE. For much of Egypt's history, the pharaohs were seen as extensions of the deities, living gods who enacted the will of the gods on Earth. This status made them all-powerful, and their authority was completely accepted by their subjects. The ancient Egyptians were influenced by their religion and did not dare question the will of the gods.

However, as time went on, pharaohs became known as the children of deities, which curbed their power. The priests became the intermediaries between humans and the gods. This placed incredible power in the hands of the priests, who lived at the temples and claimed vast amounts of land and wealth on behalf of the gods. When Ramesses XI died, he was succeeded by Smendes, a government official from Lower Egypt who started the Twenty-first Dynasty. Smendes moved from Per-Ramesses to Tanis, while the cult of Amun ruled from Thebes. Once again, Egypt was divided, but there is no evidence that this separation was caused by a civil war. It would appear as though the monarchy took care of the administrative duties from Tanis, while the priests ruled in Amun's name from Thebes. This would have required remarkable cooperation, and it doesn't seem as though the two parties were enemies.

Cult of Amun

For much of Egypt's history, Thebes was considered the home of the god Amun. During the New Kingdom, Amun became the most important deity in the Egyptian pantheon and had a similar role in Egyptian culture as Zeus had in Greek culture. Sometime during the rule of Ahmose I, Amun was fused with the sun god Ra and became Amun-Ra. As Thebes rose in importance, so did Amun, which may also explain why the god became so important to the Egyptians. His temple was located at the Karnak temple complex, which was built near Luxor. Its construction began during Senusret I's rule, and it became a custom of the pharaohs to add to it during their reign. This allowed Karnak to become the largest religious building in the world and brought great pride to the Egyptians.

Temple Complex at Karnak

Since Amun became such an important god, his cult also grew in importance. The priests, especially the high priests, were thought to have a direct link to the god, which made them extremely important since they would have had contact with every sort of Egyptian citizen. By the end of the New Kingdom, there were as many as eighty thousand priests who lived and worked at Karnak. The cult of Amun also owned more land and wealth than the pharaoh, which had a definite impact on the monarch's influence. During the Third Intermediate Period, Amun was effectively the king of Thebes. The priests used oracles to determine the god's will to solve judicial, domestic, and political issues. By the Third Intermediate Period, Thebes had become a complete theocracy, and the priests regularly communicated with Amun as if he was the pharaoh. The kings in Tanis would oversee what the elusive god couldn't.

Nubian Conquest

During the Middle and New Kingdoms, Egyptian pharaohs pushed their way into Nubia and either conquered or exacted tribute from the Nubians. Nubia and Egypt had close ties for most of their history since they both relied on the Nile. When the Egyptian pharaohs conquered Nubia during the Middle and New Kingdom periods, they carried over their god Amun. During these times, the Egyptians built numerous temples to Amun and declared that Nubia was Amun's southern residence. This promoted the worship of Amun and legitimized the Egyptians' claim to Nubia. The Egyptians were interested in Nubia because it was abundant in natural resources, such as ivory, ebony, animal skins, and gold.

The close relationship between the two countries led to cultural and religious ties that would endure for centuries. However, as Egypt began declining in power, Nubia used the basis laid by former Egyptian pharaohs as an excuse to invade Egypt. In the 700s BCE, the Kushite king, Piye, was able to annex Karnak and went on to conquer the rest of Egypt. He claimed to be working on behalf of Amun, and he became the first Kushite pharaoh in 744 BCE. Since the Nubians already worshiped Amun, his cult was allowed to continue its duties and enjoyed significant influence over both Egypt and Nubia. When Piye ruled Egypt, he allowed the kings of Lower Egypt to have a measure of power. The Kushite kings had immense respect for the Egyptian culture, and their rule didn't have a negative impact on Egyptian culture as a whole.

Assyria vs. Egypt

For much of Egypt's history, Egyptian kings had purposefully created buffer zones along their borders, which prevented the borders from clashing with powerful enemies who could potentially invade Egypt. However, during the Third Intermediate Period, many of these buffer zones were defeated. They were added to Egypt's territory but also left the state vulnerable to foreign invasion. Around 926 BCE, Pharaoh Shoshenq I conquered Judah. This was considered to be a massive victory, but it also brought Egypt into contact with the Assyrians. When the Kushite king, Piye, died, he was succeeded by his brother, Shabaka. Later, Shebitku, Shabaka's successor, lent support to Judah against the Assyrian king, Sennacherib. This would have been enough to draw Assyria's hostility.

In 671 BCE, Egypt was ruled by Taharqa when the Assyrian king, Esarhaddon, marched against Egypt. He invaded the country and took the royal family hostage. Taharqa was able to escape to Egypt and was succeeded by Tantamani. Tantamani was able to temporarily overthrow Assyrian rule, but he was quickly conquered by Esarhaddon's son, Ashurbanipal, in 666 BCE, who left a puppet king, Necho I, on the throne of Egypt.

Sack of Thebes

While the Kushites maintained a strong hold on Egypt, their influence gradually declined during the Twenty-fifth Dynasty. Tantamani, for the most part, had control of Upper Egypt and Nubia. He still held Thebes, which was an incredibly important foothold. However, in 663 BCE, Ashurbanipal and Tantamani were locked in a war that would determine the outcome of Egypt's future. For a brief period, Tantamani gained the upper hand and was able to conquer Memphis, where he killed the puppet king, Necho I. As a result, Ashurbanipal and Psamtik (Necho I's son) met the Kushite king in battle near Memphis. The Kushites were defeated, and Tantamani retreated to Nubia, which left the ancient city of Thebes unprotected.

Thebes fell to the Assyrian forces and was thoroughly sacked. Most of its riches and inhabitants were carried off to Assyria. It was a resounding catastrophe that left a definite mark on Egyptian history and morale. The sack of Thebes brought a decisive end to the Twenty-fifth Dynasty, as the Kushite kings were never able to regain the land that they had lost. Thebes had been so thoroughly defeated that, six years later, it surrendered to Psamtik's fleet.

Psamtik became king of Egypt and founded the Twenty-sixth Dynasty, which brought an end to the Third Intermediate Period and began the Late Period. The king had Thebes accept his daughter, Nitocris I, as the God's Wife of Amun, which was an incredibly important position in Egypt.

Psamtik was a capable leader who brought peace and unity to Egypt. He commissioned many monuments, restored old buildings, and was a strong military leader. He was succeeded by Necho II, who created an Egyptian navy made up of Greek mercenaries. Necho II was succeeded by Psamtik II around 595 BCE, who proved himself in battle against Kush and famously erased the names of Kushite kings from southern monuments, even going as far as to try and erase his father's name from history. The reasons for his actions are still unknown. He was succeeded by his son, Apries, around 589 BCE. Apries was overthrown in a coup orchestrated by his father's general, Amasis II.

Amasis II

Apries proved to be an unsuccessful military leader. He tried to fight the Babylonians but lost. When he lost his throne, he appealed to the Babylonians for help and was probably killed on the battlefield when he faced Amasis II's army. It is possible that Amasis II was responsible for Psamtik II's victories in Nubia. Psamtik II never did much with his military victories, instead choosing to return to Egypt without firmly establishing his rule. That must have frustrated Amasis II and may have led to his coup.

Amasis II was the strongest pharaoh in centuries and helped return Egypt to some of its former glory. He stimulated the economy and conducted several successful military campaigns. Under his rule, building projects abounded, the economy flourished, and the borders were secure. The art industry received a tremendous boost, which only added to Amasis II's reputation.

While Amasis II was a capable king, he failed Egypt in two fundamental ways. His son, Psamtik III, was wholly unprepared for the challenges of ruling Egypt when he ascended to the throne around 526 BCE. Amasis II may have also been responsible for the Persian invasion. According to the Greek historian Herodotus, the Persian king, Cambyses II, requested to marry one of Amasis's daughters. The Egyptians famously refused to give any of their noblewomen to foreigners, and Amasis wanted to uphold that tradition without making a deadly enemy. In response, he sent one of Apries's daughters to marry Cambyses II. The former princess was so offended by Amasis's actions that she revealed her identity to Cambyses II as soon as she arrived at her destination. This enraged Cambyses II, and according to tradition, he swore revenge on the Egyptians.

Bastet and the Divine Cats

Animals were usually sacred to the Egyptians since they represented various aspects of gods in the Egyptian pantheon. People usually mummified their pets when they died and took great care of them during their life. While most animals were highly regarded, cats were sacred in Egypt. They were the most common pets, and their popularity was directly linked to Bastet.

Statue of the goddess Bastet.

The goddess Bastet was immensely popular, and the Egyptians were terrified of offending her. Bastet was the goddess of women's secrets, fertility, cats, childbirth, and the home. She protected houses, women, and children from disease and harmful spirits. Her role also extended to the afterlife, and she was known for being extremely vengeful. At first, she was associated with the goddess Sekhmet, the goddess of war who destroyed Ra's enemies, since she had inherited some of Sekhmet's more terrifying qualities. Bastet became so influential that people believed she helped correct injustices.

The Egyptians believed that if Bastet was offended, she would unleash devastating plagues on humanity. One way to offend the goddess was by killing a cat. The punishment for killing a cat in ancient Egypt was death. According to Herodotus, if a building was on fire, the cats had to be saved first. And if a household's cat died, they had to shave their eyebrows as a sign of respect to avoid the goddess's wrath.

The Battle of Pelusium

When Cambyses II decided to invade Egypt in 525 BCE, it became clear that he needed to defeat the city of Pelusium to gain access to the rest of the country. The only problem was that Pelusium was highly fortified and would likely only fall after a lengthy battle. Cambyses II was undeterred and mobilized his forces against the city but was quickly driven back. The king was determined to conquer Egypt and came up with a creative plan. The Egyptians' respect and love for cats were well established. As a result, Cambyses had his forces capture various stray animals, mostly cats. His army was then commanded to paint the image of Bastet on their shields. When his army advanced on Pelusium a second time, they drove the animals ahead of them.

As a result, the Egyptians were forced to surrender or risk offending Bastet, which they believed would bring great disaster down upon them. Pelusium fell, and Cambyses II marched through the streets in victory. According to legend, Cambyses threw cats at the Egyptians during this march in order to taunt them. From there, Cambyses II conquered the rest of Egypt.

Persian Rule

It's unlikely that Cambyses II invaded Egypt because of a perceived insult, but Amasis II's actions may have provided him with the excuse he needed to go to war. The Assyrians had proven that the Egyptians weren't equipped to win a war against foreign armies, and the Persians were becoming increasingly powerful and eager to expand their territory. Egypt's riches and cultures were well known in the ancient world, so the nation would have been an irresistible temptation to the Persian king.

Unfortunately for Egypt, Psamtik III was unprepared for the invading Persian forces, and Egypt quickly fell to the Persian army. When Egypt was defeated, Cambyses II took the Egyptian royal family and many nobles to his capital at Susa. Apparently, many nobles and much of the royal family were executed. Psamtik was allowed to live at the Persian court. He was executed shortly after when it was discovered that he was planning a revolt against the Persians. When Psamtik III died, the Third Intermediate Period and the Twenty-sixth Dynasty ended with him.

Accounts vary about Persian rule over Egypt. The Greeks claimed that Cambyses was a tyrannical despot who burned Egyptian temples and showed no respect for the Egyptian culture. However, an Egyptian admiral, Wedjahor-Resne, who was a contemporary of Cambyses II, claimed that the Persian king greatly respected the Egyptians and endeavored to show respect for his new subjects' culture. Unfortunately for the Egyptians, many of them were enslaved by the Persians and forced to serve in Cambyses's army. The Persians managed to maintain a relatively firm hold of Egypt until 331 BCE, when Alexander the Great arrived.

Alexander the Great in Egypt

Alexander the Great was one of the most accomplished military leaders in the world. He conquered many territories and expanded Greek influence farther than it had ever gone before. When he conquered Tyre, he set his sights on Egypt. Many of the towns on the way from Tyre to Egypt quickly submitted to his rule rather than face utter destruction. Unfortunately, Alexander faced trouble in Gaza. The fort was well protected and located on a large hill, which required Alexander to undertake a siege. He was forced to retreat a few times, but his famous determination pushed him to keep fighting until Gaza fell. When the fortress was finally defeated, the women and children became slaves, while the men were executed.

Alexander founding Alexandria

From there, he advanced farther into Egypt and took large portions of territory away from the Persians. The Egyptians eagerly welcomed Alexander into their midst and quickly crowned him king at Memphis since they were desperate to be rid of the Persians. During the Persian rule, many Egyptian temples had been neglected. Alexander won favor with the Egyptians by renovating temples, building monuments, reforming the taxation system, and organizing his military.

In 332 BCE, Alexander sought to legitimize his rule by making large sacrifices to the Egyptian gods and honoring the oracle of Amun-Ra. The Egyptians proclaimed him the son of Amun, and he responded by calling Zeus-Amun his true father. His image was stamped on coins and showed him wearing the horns of Amun, which were meant to symbolize his right to rule. He went on to build the famous city of Alexandria and left a lasting mark on Egyptian history. When he died, he was succeeded by Ptolemy I, who founded the Ptolemaic dynasty.

SECTION TWO:
An Overview of Modern Egypt (332 BCE–2021 CE)

Chapter 5: The Greco-Roman Period (332 BCE–629 CE)

The Greco-Roman period spanned from the time Alexander the Great left Egypt and lasted until the Rashidun conquest of Egypt around 639 CE. This period was marked by great advances in philosophy and science, as well as the Greek and Roman rulers who reigned over Egypt during those years. The culture and religion that marked Egypt's ancient era would mix and form close ties with the Greek and Roman cultures. During this period, Egypt's famous Ptolemaic dynasty rose to power. The Ptolemies were a Macedonian family that ruled over Egypt for centuries while retaining their Greek identity. This was accomplished through intermarriages that kept the Ptolemies strictly Greek.

The last Ptolemaic pharaoh, Cleopatra VII, would form unbreakable ties with Rome and take part in a bloody Roman civil war. Unfortunately, Cleopatra's forces lost, and Egypt became a Roman province. Egypt would serve as Rome's breadbasket until Diocletian split the Roman Empire into two. Egypt became part of the Byzantine Empire. The Greco-Roman period was one of the most influential periods in Egyptian, Greek, and Roman history. During this time, empires rose and fell, Alexandria rose in prominence, and important monuments were built. Some of the most famous figures in history existed during this age and left their mark on history. Egypt left its ancient heritage firmly in the past as it influenced and interacted with the most powerful empires of its time.

Ptolemy I Soter

Ptolemy was a Macedonian nobleman who may have been Alexander the Great's half-brother through Alexander's father, Philip II. Officially, Ptolemy's father was another nobleman named Lagos, and although Ptolemy was older than Alexander, the two became close friends. Ptolemy acted as a historian and recorded many of Alexander's feats while noting his own involvement in various battles. He was also likely at Alexander's side in 332 BCE when Alexander was in Egypt. It was during this time that Ptolemy became one of Alexander's personal bodyguards. This is a clear indication of how highly Alexander esteemed Ptolemy.

Ptolemy I as an Egyptian pharaoh.
https://commons.wikimedia.org/wiki/File:Ring_with_engraved_portrait_of_Ptolemy_VI_Philometor_(3rd%E2%80%932nd_century_BCE)_-_2009.jpg

When Alexander died in 323 BCE, he gave his signet ring to his cavalry leader, Perdiccas, which may have signified Alexander's intention to transfer power to him. Perdiccas decided to keep the empire intact since Alexander's wife, Roxana, was pregnant with a possible heir. However, Alexander's generals, led by Ptolemy, divided the empire amongst themselves, which led to the Wars of the Diadochi (or the Successor Wars). Perdiccas and Ptolemy hated each other, and this hatred culminated in a shocking event—the theft of Alexander the Great's body. Perdiccas sent Alexander's body to be interred in a tomb in Macedonia, but Ptolemy intercepted the body en route and had Alexander buried in a tomb in Alexandria. Perdiccas was disgusted and tried to attack Egypt but failed three times before his men became fed up with him and had him executed.

Ptolemy focused all his attention on ruling Egypt, unlike the other generals who tried to conquer as much territory as they could. He moved Egypt's capital to Alexandria to avoid the power of the priests and managed to stabilize the Egyptian economy. Under Ptolemy's guidance, Alexandria became a primarily Greek city. In order to legitimize his rule, he deified Alexander the Great and declared that he was Alexander's heir. He built a massive museum and library in Alexandria and also started construction on the Lighthouse of Alexandria. Ptolemy I died around 282 BCE and left behind the firmly established Ptolemaic dynasty, which would reign over Egypt for almost three centuries.

Alexandria

Alexandria is a port city on the coast of the Mediterranean Sea in Egypt, and it was founded by Alexander the Great around 331 BCE. The city quickly became popular after it was built and attracted thousands of inhabitants. Its influence grew after it became the capital of Egypt during the Ptolemaic dynasty. The city housed the famous Lighthouse of Alexandria, which became one of the Seven Wonders of the Ancient World. One could also find the Library of Alexandria, which attracted some of the most prominent scholars in the world. Alexander intended Alexandria to connect Greece to Egypt. Although Alexander never returned to Alexandria once he left Egypt, the city accomplished its purpose and became a center of Hellenistic culture.

Lighthouse of Alexandria.
https://commons.wikimedia.org/wiki/File:Philip_Galle_-
Lighthouse_of_Alexandria_(Pharos_of_Alexandria)_-_1572.jpg

Alexandria became home to Greeks, Egyptians, and Jews. The Septuagint, which was a Greek version of the Tanakh (the Hebrew Bible, which includes the Torah, Ketuvim, and Nevi'im), was produced in Alexandria. Ptolemy I had his own vision for Alexandria and wanted to turn it into a prominent and influential community in the Mediterranean. He built the Library of Alexandria and a museum and started construction on the Lighthouse of Alexandria. The library collected thousands of papyrus scrolls filled with knowledge about subjects like history, literature, science, and philosophy. Scholars from all over the ancient world, especially Greece, flocked to the library. The city reflected the glory of the Ptolemaic dynasty, and the ruling family hardly ever left the capital.

Hellenistic Influences on Egypt

It's unsurprising that Egypt was deeply influenced by the Greek language, religion, and culture since its ruling dynasty was proudly Greek. Ptolemy I chose Egypt as his inheritance from Alexander the Great since the country was rich in natural resources and was on good terms with the Greeks. Soon, Egypt was flooded by Greek residents. Ptolemy built a new city in Upper Egypt named Ptolemais to house all the new immigrants. The Ptolemaic dynasty showed great respect for the Egyptian culture but made few attempts to immerse themselves in Egyptian traditions. In fact, the famous Cleopatra VII, the last of the pharaohs, was the only Ptolemaic ruler who learned to speak Egyptian.

The Ptolemies were careful not to upset the established order in Egypt and basically left the Egyptian religion alone. The Egyptian priests were allowed to function as normal and even retained their elite social status. In order to endear themselves to the Egyptians, Ptolemy I returned many religious artifacts that had been stolen by the Persians. He also established the cult of Alexander the Great and the cult of Serapis, a healing god. Serapis's cult never gained popularity and eventually faded away. The Ptolemies introduced many Hellenistic aspects to Egyptian culture and made Greek the official language of the government and economy. For most of the Ptolemaic dynasty, these Egyptian and Greek influences coexisted in harmony.

The Ptolemaic Dynasty

Ptolemy II Philadelphus succeeded his father, Ptolemy I, to the throne around 282 BCE and married Arsinoe I, the daughter of the Thracian King Lysimachus. In return, Lysimachus married Ptolemy II's sister, Arsinoe II. When Lysimachus died, Ptolemy II married Arsinoe II. He fought the Syrian Wars from 260 to 252 BCE, built several trading posts, completed the Pharos (Lighthouse of Alexandria), and established the Ptolemaieia festival. Ptolemy II was known as one of the great pharaohs of Egypt. Unfortunately, the Ptolemaic dynasty would be known for petty jealousy, betrayal, and incest, the latter being something they carried over from the previous Egyptian dynasties.

Ptolemy III succeeded his father around 246 BCE and married Berenice II. When one of their daughters, also named Berenice, died, the Canopus Decree was instituted, which made Berenice a goddess and suggested a new calendar that consisted of 365 days in a year with a leap year every 4 years. However, this calendar wasn't instituted. Ptolemy IV came to the throne around 221 BCE and married his sister, Arsinoe III. He gained some success in the Fourth Syrian War and built the Sema, which was meant to honor the Ptolemies and Alexander the Great. Ptolemy IV and Arsinoe III were the victims of a coup around 205 BCE.

Ptolemy V inherited the throne as a child but faced a series of wars that caused the loss of several Egyptian territories. Ptolemy VI also inherited the throne as a young child and ruled alongside his mother. Unfortunately, his reign was also beset with problems, as he fought outside invaders and his own brother, Ptolemy VIII. Ptolemy VI died in battle around 145 BCE and left the throne to Ptolemy VIII.

Ptolemy VIII was widely hated, and a civil war broke out that lasted from 132 to 124 BCE. Throughout the Ptolemaic dynasty, the royal family and the inhabitants of Alexandria experienced a tumultuous relationship, which led to several rebellions. Ptolemy VIII was succeeded by Ptolemy IX, who was overthrown by his brother for a brief period before he was able to regain the throne.

Meanwhile, Rome was beginning to rise as a formidable power. Several Ptolemaic pharaohs earned distrust from their citizens when they formed close relationships with Rome. Egypt realized that it was only a matter of time before Rome tried to conquer the rich country. The next few pharaohs had relatively little impact. Ptolemy XIII became pharaoh in 51 BCE and married his sister, Cleopatra VII. Ptolemy XIII and his sister Arsinoe fought against Cleopatra and Julius Caesar and were defeated in battle. Arsinoe was taken as prisoner while Ptolemy XIII drowned in battle. Caesar replaced Ptolemy XIII with Ptolemy XIV, who ruled alongside Cleopatra until she allegedly had him poisoned.

Finally, Cleopatra VII took the throne in her own right, becoming the last Egyptian pharaoh.

The Battle of Actium

When Cleopatra took the Egyptian throne in 51 BCE, she began making friends with Rome and her own people. She had a great interest in Egyptian culture and even learned the language. However, when Julius Caesar died in 44 BCE, Rome was gripped by a civil war that ended with the Second Triumvirate, a coalition made up of Julius Caesar's heirs: Octavian, Mark Antony, and Lepidus. The Triumvirate split the empire into manageable portions. Mark Antony chose to rule the eastern part of the empire, which put him into direct contact with Cleopatra. The two began a tempestuous affair.

Battle of Actium
https://commons.wikimedia.org/wiki/File:Castro_Battle_of_Actium.jpg

The relationship between the Triumvirate deteriorated, and soon, Mark Antony and Octavian were locked in a heated feud that culminated in the Battle of Actium in 31 BCE. The two opposing forces used their fleets in the battle, and while Cleopatra supplied Mark Antony with abundant resources, he lost. Mark Antony and Cleopatra were able to escape with some of their ships. A year later, Octavian arrived in Egypt to claim his prize. Mark Antony was killed in battle, and Cleopatra committed suicide. Cleopatra's son by Caesar, Caesarion (the rightful heir to Egypt), was executed by Octavian, who became Caesar Augustus in 27 BCE. Egypt was assimilated into the Roman Empire.

Roman Egypt

During the height of the Roman Empire, the Mediterranean was referred to as the Roman Lake. Egypt became the empire's breadbasket. Crops and food were exported out of Egypt and transported to the rest of the Roman Empire. Egypt's resources were systematically plundered for the good of Rome. For the most part, Rome respected the Egyptian culture, and the Egyptians were allowed to continue as they had under the Ptolemaic dynasty. One of the biggest changes was the fact that Egypt was subject to Roman law, which had precedence over any Egyptian laws. Rome kept control of Egypt through an appointed governor. A flotilla was stationed on the Nile, and three legions ensured Roman control on land.

The Egyptian religion was allowed to remain, but Hellenic citizens received priority and soon made up the elite classes. Major cities had experienced the most influence from the Hellenistic culture, while Egyptian peasants and rural areas still conformed to the old traditions and culture. Under the Roman Empire, the aristocracy was allowed to gain land for themselves and quickly obtained control of massive private estates. Food, spices, and other luxury items from the East were transported along the Nile to Alexandria and then on to the rest of the empire. Soon, Alexandria had a massive Greek and Jewish population, which sometimes led to problems for the Roman emperors. For example, the Jewish population tried to burn down Alexandria's amphitheater during Nero's reign. About fifty thousand people died during the riot, and Rome dispatched two legions to deal with the problem.

At first, Egypt accepted Roman occupation, but by 115 CE, riots had broken out, and it became evident that the Egyptians were tired of Roman rule. For the next few decades, Egypt would continually be a place of riots and rebellions against the Romans until Rome eventually fell.

Vespasian

When Nero died around 68 CE, a series of civil wars broke out as the Romans tried to determine who would be their new leader. Four men tried to make their claim on the Roman throne, which led to the Year of the Four Emperors. Galba, Otho, Vespasian, and Vitellius each tried to become the next emperor of Rome. In time, Vitellius and Vespasian were the only contenders left.

A bust of Vespasian.

Vespasian was from relatively humble origins; his father was a knight and former tax collector. In time, Vespasian joined the Roman Senate and enjoyed a successful military career that led to his praetorship in 39. He made sure to keep on the good side of the next few Roman emperors, including Claudius and Nero. During the power struggle to determine the next emperor of Rome, Vespasian refrained from the fighting since he didn't expect to win against Galba. However, when Galba was murdered, Vespasian emerged as a contender for the throne. Otho was defeated and committed suicide. Vespasian traveled to Alexandria in the hopes of sabotaging Vitellius's supply lines. During that time, Vespasian's allies managed to defeat Vitellius, who was killed in Rome. Vespasian was left as the clear winner and was declared the emperor of Rome while still in Alexandria.

As soon as Vespasian was emperor, he began looking for ways to stabilize the empire after the disastrous rule of Nero and the subsequent civil wars. He increased Rome's revenues (although his financial policies were immensely unpopular and caused discontent in Egypt) and stabilized the military. He died around 79 after a long and successful career.

Diocletian

By 284, the days of remarkable Roman emperors, such as Vespasian and Augustus, were long over. The Roman Empire was a shadow of its former self and faced serious rebellions and unrest. All that changed when Diocletian took the throne. Diocletian was born in the Balkan province around 245. He joined the military and quickly rose to prominence. He served under Emperor Carus as one of the emperor's imperial bodyguards. When Carus died, he left the throne to his son, Numerian, who was likely killed by his father-in-law, Arrius Aper. Diocletian avenged the emperor's death and became the Roman emperor in November 284.

Diocletian realized that Rome had become too large to rule effectively and split the empire in two. He appointed his son-in-law, Maximian, as Caesar of the West Roman Empire while he oversaw the East. Diocletian managed to win great victories in the East against Persia and along the Danube River. He abdicated the throne along with Maximian in 305 and retired to his massive palace in modern-day Croatia. Unfortunately, the Roman Empire was plagued by more problems in the following decades. The Western Roman Empire fell in 476, while the Eastern Roman Empire continued. The Eastern half of the empire is also known as the Byzantine Empire.

The Byzantine Empire

Diocletian was the last Roman emperor who personally visited Egypt. When the Roman Empire was split into two parts, the West ceased having a major effect on Egypt. In 330, Constantinople was formed, which took away some of Alexandria's influence. However, Constantinople still needed grain from Egypt, and Egypt soon became a politically important part of the Eastern Roman Empire. In time, the Byzantine Empire turned into a Christian state. Greco-Roman influences faded as "Oriental" influences took over. However, Alexandria remained an influential city that was dominated by religious violence.

In the 5th century, Egypt was controlled by several important Christian churches. Christianity quickly gained popularity since it appealed to the rich and poor alike. Churches and monasteries provided communal buildings, such as water cisterns, bakeries, workshops, stables, kitchens, and other resources that allowed communities to become prosperous and self-sufficient. However, the churches were dominated by rival patriarchs who fought each other for power. The religion became complicated and political, which may have contributed to the downfall of Christianity during the Arab invasion in the 7th century. While Islam attracted many followers in the region, Christianity remained in Egypt for the next few centuries.

Philosophy in Egypt

For many centuries, the Greeks regarded Egypt as a place of philosophy and knowledge. Many Greek scholars and philosophers were attracted to Egypt, Alexandria in particular, when the Ptolemies took control of the country. According to legend, Pythagoras traveled to Egypt to gain more knowledge since the Egyptians were known for their philosophical pursuits. Pythagoras was accredited with bringing philosophy to the Greeks, at least according to the famous Greek scholar Isocrates. Plato believed the Egyptians invented arithmetic, letters, and numbers. Socrates also held the Egyptians in high regard and claimed that Solon traveled to Egypt in order to refine his own knowledge.

Egypt certainly had one of the oldest political systems in the world, and Aristotle claimed that Egypt was the original land of wisdom. During the Greco-Roman period, Egypt retained its reputation as a land of wisdom, and Alexandria became home to scholars from all over the world. These scholars worked at the Library of Alexandria and contributed to its contents. Unfortunately, the library was neglected during Roman rule and destroyed by a series of fires, which led to the loss of immense knowledge. While Alexandria remained an intellectual center, its influence declined as time passed.

Chapter 6: Medieval Egypt (650–1520 CE)

Ancient Egyptian history is filled with stories of mighty pharaohs who made their empire a glittering world power. Unfortunately, the pharaohs were unable to hold onto their power, which allowed Egypt to be ruled by several foreign dynasties. By the time Alexander the Great reached Egypt, the age of pyramids and powerful autonomous pharaohs was over. Over the next few centuries, Egypt would pass from the Greeks to the Romans before eventually becoming a part of the Byzantine Empire.

However, Egypt was soon lost to the Byzantine Empire when it was conquered by the Sasanid dynasty. In time, Egypt experienced another major upheaval when it was conquered by the Islamic Rashidun Caliphate. This period kickstarted the medieval era, which was marked by foreign Islamic kings who ruled over Egypt. The medieval era was a time of great change, advancement, and discovery for Egypt, but there were also periods of war and devastation.

Sasanian Egypt

For years, Egypt served as a province under the Byzantine Empire; however, the empire met troubled times when Maurice ascended to the throne around 582. Maurice had a difficult reign that was beset by war. At that time, Persia was ruled by the Sasanian dynasty; this empire is also referred to as the Neo-Persian

Empire. Although Maurice was a successful military commander, he pushed his troops too far and was overthrown by Phocas and executed in 602. This event sparked massive unrest within the Byzantine Empire. The Persian shah at the time, Khosrow II, seized this opportunity and began conquering Byzantine lands, including northern Mesopotamia, Palestine, and Syria. In 618, Khosrow II invaded Egypt and conquered Alexandria.

After Alexandria fell, the rest of Egypt was conquered by the Persians, and by 621, Egypt had become a Persian province. The initial invasion of Egypt led to severe damage and losses, but once the Persians were in control, they began rebuilding parts of the country. While Egypt had become part of a different empire, the Sasanians used many of the same administrative policies as the Byzantine Empire. Some Iranian families even settled in the country, which means the two civilizations may have coexisted peacefully.

General Shahrbaraz governed Egypt on behalf of the Persian shah. A few years later, Heraclius, the Byzantine emperor, defeated the Persians, who left Egypt in 629. While the Byzantine Empire was able to regain Egypt, the empire had been weakened by the loss of its key territories and would struggle to hold onto many of its provinces.

The Muslim Conquest of Egypt

The Byzantine Empire managed to hold onto Egypt for another decade before Egypt was invaded again. In 639, the Rashidun Caliphate led a force over the Egyptian border. The army was made up of Roman and Persian soldiers who had converted to Islam. The Rashidun army laid siege to Pelusium, which lasted for about two months. Meanwhile, the invading army had been joined by many Sinai Bedouins, which boosted its numbers. Many Egyptian cities were conquered or surrendered to the invading forces. The Byzantines and Muslims clashed at the Battle of Heliopolis, where the Byzantine army was soundly defeated. In 641, the Rashidun forces set out for Alexandria. The Byzantine forces managed to delay the Muslims' advance, but the invaders soon reached Alexandria.

The Byzantine Empire sent a massive army to defend the city, which led to the siege of Alexandria in 641. Alexandria wasn't an easy city to conquer, and the Byzantine army had installed catapults on the city's walls to protect it from invaders. It was a difficult siege, but the Muslims defeated the Byzantine army, and Alexandria surrendered. When the Muslims marched into Alexandria, they found a magnificent city that boasted palaces, places of entertainment, and massive amounts of wealth. Egypt was very rich, and its loss carried serious consequences for the Byzantine Empire. The Mediterranean had been known as the Roman Lake, but it was now being slowly divided between the Byzantine Empire and the Muslim caliphate. While the Muslims had conquered the Persian Empire, the Byzantines were able to resist invasion due to Constantinople's extensive fortifications.

The Rashidun Caliphate

Prophet Muhammad was the most influential Muslim leader who set the example for Islamic leadership and left behind a large number of Ansar. Their duties included ensuring that the caliphs paid close attention to the Quran and the Sunnah. The Rashidun were the first four leaders (caliphs) of the Muslim community. As caliphs, the Rashidun were responsible for leading prayers at the mosque, delivering sermons, and commanding the army. The Rashidun expanded the borders of the Islamic state to Iraq, Palestine, Iran, Armenia, Syria, and Egypt. They also instituted the Islamic calendar and strengthened the Islamic community through religious studies. During the Rashidun Caliphate, the Islamic state conquered large portions of territory, which eventually became difficult to control. It was clear they would have to implement more practical administrative policies, as theocracy alone wasn't enough to rule the various regions.

Territories of the Rashidun Caliphate.

The first Rashidun caliph was Abu Bakr, who used the title of "Khalifat rasul Allah," which was eventually shortened to *khalifa* and became caliph. Abu Bakr was succeeded by Umar, who created a committee that would be in charge of choosing his successor in 644. The committee chose Uthman ibn Affan to be the next caliph, but his reign was marked by accusations of nepotism since his tribe, the Banu Umayyad, was allowed to gain significant influence. Uthman chose family members to rule conquered territories. Uthman was assassinated in 656 by Egyptian rebels, and the caliphate was offered to Ali ibn Abi Talib.

Ali was assassinated in 661, and his son, Hasan, was appointed as caliph but was challenged by Muawiya, who eventually became caliph instead of Hasan. The Rashidun Caliphate ended with Ali, and the Islamic territories came under the control of the Umayyad Caliphate under Muawiya. Under the Umayyads, the role of caliph became the same as the role of a secular king.

Life in Early Islamic Egypt

When the Muslim forces invaded Egypt, they established a center near Babylon called Fustat, which became the seat of the governor and an administrative center. Soon after the invasion was complete, Egypt was divided into Upper and Lower Egypt again, as this made the territory easier to control. However, Caliph Uthman soon reunited Egypt under one governor who was to reside in Fustat. The governor would be responsible for taking care of

Egypt, and he was allowed to appoint men to control Upper and Lower Egypt.

Artwork from Fustat.

The Muslims had a strong military force that was mostly made up of Arab settlers and soldiers. An elite class made up of men quickly formed and enjoyed significant privileges. Many of the old systems of administration, including taxation, were kept in place, which would have helped the transition of power. Many Egyptians remained Christian and were allowed to practice their religion freely. As long as they provided tribute to the army, they were exempt from military service. At that time, conversions to Islam were still somewhat rare.

The Abbasid Caliphate

The Umayyad dynasty was overthrown by the Abbasid dynasty in 750. During the Umayyad dynasty, non-Arab Muslims, or mawali, were seen as lower class, which caused a lot of friction. When the Abbasids took power, they gave great favor to the mawali and accused the Umayyad caliphs of being immoral and unfit to rule. The Abbasids welcomed Persians to their court and moved their capital from Damascus to Baghdad, which won the approval of their mawali supporters. The Abbasids were descendants of Muhammad's uncle, Abbas ibn Abd al-Muttalib, who won the support of Shia Muslims. (Islam split into two factions, the Sunni and Shia, following the succession crisis after Muhammad's death.) Once the Abbasids began ruling, however, they switched allegiance back to the Sunni Muslims.

The Abbasid dynasty ruled for over three hundred years and accomplished impressive feats, such as strengthening Islamic rule, which then led to the Golden Age of Islam. This period is known as a time of great scientific, economic, and cultural advancements in Islamic culture. During the Abbasid dynasty, the office of vizier and elected local emirs (title of a high office within the Muslim community) gave certain men incredible influence. In time, caliphs became ceremonial positions while viziers exerted greater power. This led to the decline of the Abbasid Caliphate. During the 860s, Egypt founded the Tulunid Emirate, which was led by Ahmad ibn Tulun. This emirate ruled separately from the caliphate. The Tulunids managed to control much of Egypt, Palestine, and the Hijaz (a region in western Saudi Arabia).

In 909, the Shia Ubayd Allah al-Mahdi Billah declared himself the caliph, which began a new caliphate in North Africa. This new caliphate was ruled by the Fatimid dynasty, who were the descendants of one of Muhammad's daughters.

The Fatimid Caliphate

The Fatimid dynasty rejected the Abbasid dynasty as usurpers since they were controlled by Sunni Muslims who wanted to take control of the entire Islamic caliphate. However, the Fatimids were only able to secure North Africa and parts of the Middle East. While other caliphs had been happy to recognize the Abbasids and only wanted to control specific regions, the Fatimids were determined to create an entirely new caliphate. The Fatimids set themselves up along the coast of Tunisia, where they tried to conquer Egypt. It took them several decades, but they finally achieved their goal in 969. The Fatimids managed to conquer the Nile valley. From there, they took Sinai, Palestine, and southern

Syria. The Fatimids based their empire in Egypt and never wavered in their goal to become the only Islamic caliphate.

At its peak, the Fatimid dynasty controlled Sicily, North Africa, parts of the Red Sea coast, Palestine, Syria, Yemen, Mecca, and Medina. The control of the holy cities was extremely important since it added incredible religious prestige to a Muslim ruler's reign. During the Fatimid rule, the overthrow of the Abbasid Caliphate was perhaps the most important mission, and the Shia rulers sent missionaries and agents into Abbasid territories to gain support and converts. By 1057, the Fatimids had expanded into the east and nearly managed to take control of Baghdad. However, the Fatimids ultimately failed in their ultimate mission since the Sunni branch of Islam was reluctant to adopt Shia doctrines. By the 12th century, the Crusades had begun, which forced the Sunni and Shia to fight the invading Christians.

Egypt during the Fatimid Caliphate

When the Fatimids conquered Egypt, they built the city of Cairo, which was supposed to be the royal residence of the Fatimid caliph. Fustat remained the administrative capital of Egypt until 1169. Egypt thrived under the Fatimid rule since the dynasty developed trade routes and boosted the economy. Soon, Egypt's trading routes ran along the Mediterranean Sea and the Indian Ocean and went as far as China. The Fatimids practiced religious tolerance, allowing Christians and Jews to live peacefully in Egypt. They also placed a high emphasis on ability over nepotism, which meant that anyone could rise quickly within the government if they had the skills.

The Fatimids kept a massive army of Mamluks (slaves), which allowed the Mamluks to become an elite class of knights and warriors. Some Mamluks became sultans and were allowed to hold positions of power. Besides the economy, the Fatimid caliphs also encouraged intellectual pursuits and built sophisticated libraries. They promoted freedom of thought, which allowed scholars to express their thoughts and views without fear of persecution. Once again, Egypt became a center of knowledge, philosophy, and literature. Scholars came from all over the world to benefit from this exchange of knowledge and praised Egypt's great libraries. The Fatimid caliphs were patrons of many scholars and appointed these scholars to prominent positions within their court. Unfortunately, the Fatimid dynasty declined during the 11th century, which allowed Saladin to invade Egypt in 1171.

Saladin was the founder of the Ayyubid dynasty, which led to the return of Fatimid lands to the Abbasid Caliphate.

The Black Death in Egypt

Before we dig into Saladin and the political situation in Egypt, let us take a look at an important event that occurred during the medieval age. The Black Death was a pandemic of bubonic plague that took place from 1346 to 1353 and caused up to seventy-five million to two hundred million deaths in Eurasia and North Africa. It's likely that the Black Death first started in Central Asia, but the first evidence of the pandemic was traced to Crimea in 1347. From there, the plague was carried by fleas that infested rats on trading vessels, which allowed the plague to be transported throughout the known world. It spread through the Mediterranean Basin to Africa, West Asia, and Europe. Once people caught the plague, it spread quickly, which caused the plague to spread to areas that could not be reached by trading vessels. Experts have theorized that the Black Death caused the world's population to go from around 475 million to around 350 to 375 million.

The pandemic caused the death of millions of people, which had a lasting effect on many civilizations. Since many areas experienced serious depopulation, the plague caused social, religious, and economic changes. The Black Death reached Alexandria around 1347 when an infected merchant ship carrying slaves arrived from Constantinople. By the next year, the plague had reached Cairo, which was the largest city in the Mediterranean Basin, as well as the cultural center of the Islamic community. According to some estimates, the plague decimated about 40 percent of Egypt's population. Before the plague, Cairo had about 600,000 inhabitants, and the Black Death killed about a third of the city's population. While the city had a functioning hospital, the severity of the plague and the sheer number of infected people overwhelmed the city's resources. The Nile was reportedly clogged with dead bodies because grave diggers and practitioners of funeral rites couldn't keep up with the demand.

The devastating effects of the Black Death differed according to geographical locations. Crowded urban centers were the most affected areas, but that doesn't mean rural towns were exempt from the tragedy.

The Mamluk Sultanate

Mamluks were slave soldiers who formed an elite fighting class in Egypt and later in the Ottoman Empire. They first served the Abbasid caliphs and were usually Turkic non-Muslims who had been captured in regions north of the Black Sea, now modern-day Russia. These soldiers converted to Islam and were tasked with protecting and serving caliphs, although they eventually became extremely powerful, especially in Egypt. Mamluks were trained as cavalry soldiers and had a code of conduct called the *furusiyya*, which encouraged values such as courage and generosity. Each Mamluk went through extensive training, which ensured that Mamluk forces were always ready to fight.

When Saladin conquered much of the Middle East, he founded the powerful Ayyubid dynasty. When he died, his heirs fought over control of his vast empire. Each of his heirs employed large retinues of Mamluk forces in the hopes of taking the empire for themselves. Saladin's brother, Al-Adil, finally managed to secure the whole empire after defeating his brothers and nephews and adding their Mamluk retinues to his own. The Ayyubids continued this practice until they were completely surrounded by the Mamluks, who eventually became an essential part of the Ayyubid court.

In 1250, Egyptian Sultan Turanshah died, causing his wife, Shajar al-Durr, to take power with Mamluk support. However, she needed a male counterpart, so she married a Mamluk commander named Aybak during the Seventh Crusade. Aybak was later assassinated, and a Mamluk named Qutuz took power and formed the Mamluk Sultanate, which would rule Egypt until around 1517 when it was defeated by the Ottoman Empire.

The Ottoman-Mamluk War

In 1453, Constantinople fell to the Ottoman Empire, which would bring the Ottomans into contact with the Mamluks. The two powers struggled for a monopoly on the highly lucrative spice trade. The Ottomans conquered many regions in the Middle East, including the Islamic holy cities, and they had their eyes on Egypt.

The Mamluks responded by drafting people from rural areas to join their army, but this led to a shortage of food and necessary supplies since there weren't enough people to keep up the work on the farms. This shortage led to a famine that severely weakened Egypt. The Ottomans and Mamluks eventually went to war in 1516, and while both armies had around the same numbers, the Ottomans had a clear advantage. Only a small portion of the Mamluk army was trained soldiers, and they fought with outdated weapons such as bows and arrows. The Ottomans had a battle-hardened army equipped with modern weapons such as the arquebus. The Mamluks were incredibly proud and chose to rely on traditional methods, which led to their downfall. The Ottomans won the war in 1517 and took control of Egypt. Despite their defeat, the Mamluks were allowed to continue as a slave-soldier class but never regained the power and status they enjoyed during the Mamluk Sultanate.

The Ottomans placed a governor in Egypt, who was then protected by a highly trained force of Ottoman soldiers. Thanks to their victory in Egypt, the Ottomans were able to launch attacks on other African kingdoms, expanding their borders further. Thanks to their military victories, the Ottomans had control of the Islamic holy cities, which made the Ottoman rulers the caliphs over the entire Muslim world, including Egypt. They would hold onto that distinction until the 20th century.

Chapter 7: Early Modern Egypt (1520–1914 CE)

Egypt's medieval history was filled with wars, deadly plagues, and ever-shifting governments that had a powerful effect on the country and its people. During that time, the national religion changed several times, as the Egyptians went from a traditional pagan religion to Christianity and then to Islam. Besides affecting the Egyptian populace, these changing religions also had an effect on legal, economic, and administrative policies. The medieval period started with the Sasanid invasion and ended with the Ottoman invasion, which made Egypt a part of the Ottoman Empire. This change in government led to the beginning of Egypt's early modern period, which would last until the First World War.

While the early modern period was several centuries shorter than the medieval period, it was no less exciting. During the early modern period, Egypt had to adjust to life under the rule of the Ottomans, which contributed to the decline of Egypt's economy and culture. Egypt would also survive a terrible famine, weak and powerful rulers, a French invasion, the arrival of the British, and economic turmoil as foreign forces meddled in Egyptian affairs. All these events helped to shape Egyptian culture as the country left behind the medieval era and began its journey to modernity.

The Ottoman Empire

When the Ottomans took over Egypt, the country once again became a province. The Ottomans ruled from Constantinople and used Egypt as a granary and a source of income, which they obtained through taxation. Unfortunately, Egypt had begun to decline under the rule of the Mamluks, and the Ottoman invasion did little to help Egypt's economic position. As a result of the economic decline, Egypt's culture took a hit and began a steady decline. However, the Ottomans weren't solely responsible for these changes, as the Ottomans instituted several policies to ensure that they benefited from Egypt's prosperity. However, Egypt's elite class often didn't work with the government, which would have impacted the Ottomans' attempts to revive the economy.

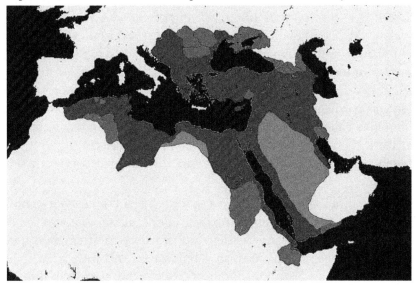

Map of the Ottoman Empire at its peak.
Dodobondo, CC BY-SA 4.0 https://creativecommons.org/licenses/by-sa/4.0 via Wikimedia Commons; https://commons.wikimedia.org/wiki/File:Ottoman-Empire-peak-1590-map.jpg

The Ottomans were quick to establish their authority in Egypt, and in 1525, Suleiman the Magnificent appointed a grand vizier, Ibrahim Pasha, who was responsible for ruling Egypt on behalf of his monarch. Ibrahim appointed a viceroy and a council of advisors who would be supported by a sizeable army. The Ottomans also separated Egypt into four manageable provinces, which would be assigned to inspectors who would oversee administration and taxation. The Egyptian government was controlled by officials from Constantinople, but in time, the Mamluks were able to obtain positions within the government.

Once the Ottomans established their authority in Egypt, they set their sights on expanding their borders farther south. Egypt was the perfect base for their new invasions, and soon, the Ottomans were able to control Nubia. They also fought the Portuguese for control of the Red Sea. They established a colony at Mitsiwa (modern-day Eritrea) and conquered Yemen and Aden. The Ottoman Empire was primarily Muslim, and they used their religion as the basis of many functions of government.

The Mamluk Elite

The Mamluks had long been an important class in Egypt. At first, they were simply a slave-warrior class, but in time, they developed into one of the most important classes in Egyptian society. While they lost much of their power after losing the Ottoman-Mamluk War, they were still allowed to exist in Egyptian society under the Ottoman Empire. In time, the Ottomans appointed Mamluks to act as inspectors or *kashifs* of specific Egyptian provinces. The Egyptian army also had a large number of Mamluks called the Circassian Mamluks. The Mamluks were able to work their way into higher offices within the government, and eventually, the Mamluks were part of the viceroy's advisory council.

Over time, the Mamluks were once again able to establish themselves as a powerful political and military power. The Mamluks retained many of their old practices to strengthen their ranks. The elite Mamluks would buy slaves and then train them according to the Mamluk traditions. Once the slave was trained, they were incorporated into the Mamluk household before being granted their freedom. By the 17th century, elite Mamluks served as beys. A bey was usually the governor of a province (or an equally important position). Beys were given salaries by the Ottoman Empire. While the Mamluks still paid tribute to the Ottomans and were overseen by the viceroy, they were essentially the most powerful class in Egypt. By the 18th century, the title of shaykh al-balad was created, which meant chief of the city. This title was given to the strongest bey. Eventually, two emirs, Ali Bey and Abu al-Dahab, were able to establish independent power. In 1786, the

Ottomans tried to conquer the Mamluks but were forced to withdraw their army a year later. The Mamluks set up a coalition of two rulers (Murad Bey and Ibrahim Bey), which ruled Egypt until 1798.

Egyptian Culture during the Ottoman Empire

Egypt experienced a culture boom during the rule of the Mamluks and the Fatimid dynasty. Important individuals of those ruling powers made a habit of supporting scholars. This resulted in a surge of historians who documented events and left behind diligent records of the time periods in which they lived. However, during the Ottoman Empire, the Ottomans didn't place as much emphasis on education, knowledge, and culture. The Mamluk period, in particular, produced a high number of important historians, while only one significant Egyptian historian emerged during the reign of the Ottomans.

Egypt had been the home of international scholars and had been an intellectual center, but under the Ottoman Empire, the country lost that influence and prestige. The decline of Egyptian culture during this period is obvious in the lack of noteworthy public buildings that were constructed by the Ottomans. The Byzantine Basilica became a popular blueprint for mosques. And few advances were made in Egyptian architecture since architects were commissioned to recreate replicas or imitate building practices from Constantinople. During the Ottoman Empire, Egypt remained a primarily Muslim country, but Christians and Jews were permitted to practice their religion as long as they paid tribute to the Ottomans. However, this treatment varied throughout the empire's history.

The Famine of 1784

For most of its history, Egypt relied on the Nile for water and irrigation. The Nile was the source of life, and its regular flooding and water cycles fertilized the soil and allowed farmers to harvest a massive amount of food. Unfortunately, this dependence also meant that if the Nile didn't flood or if it was affected by a drought, the entire country suffered. In 1783, the Nile didn't rise like it was supposed to, which meant that many farms didn't have enough water for their fields and crops. There was also a lack of seeds, which meant that farmers fell behind with their work. The same conditions persisted the next year, which plunged Egypt into a severe famine. Experts estimate that the famine caused the population of Egypt to drop by one-sixth. It was the worst disaster to affect Egypt since the Black Death a few centuries earlier.

Since the famine occurred while the Ottoman Empire was ruling Egypt, it is seen as one of the ways the Ottomans failed Egypt since so many Egyptians died. A study conducted in recent years by Rutgers and funded by the National Science Foundation and the National Aeronautics and Space Administration (NASA) showed that an eruption of an Icelandic volcano may have been responsible for the Nile's low flow during 1783. Since the Egyptian economy relied heavily on the Nile, the change in the Nile's flow had disastrous consequences for the economy.

The French Invasion

In the 17th and 18th centuries, France periodically investigated the possibility of occupying Egypt. However, when Napoleon Bonaparte sailed for Egypt in 1798, he was thinking specifically of using Egypt to strike a blow against Britain. If he managed to accomplish his goal, he would be able to curb Britain's trade routes and be in a better position to negotiate a peace treaty with the British. The French were also looking into the possibility of helping Egypt return to its ancient glory, which would have positive consequences for France since they would benefit greatly from Egypt's potential wealth. When Napoleon's forces set off for Egypt, they were joined by scientists who were tasked with creating a report on Egypt's condition and resources.

The first challenge the fleet faced was the British Mediterranean fleet, which was commanded by Horatio Nelson. Since France and Britain were at war, if the French fleet was caught, it would have to survive a naval battle, which would weaken its chances of occupying Egypt. Napoleon was able to navigate his fleet to Egyptian shores without attracting the attention of the British navy and landed at Aboukir Bay on July 1st. The next day, the French took Alexandria. Napoleon issued a proclamation in Arabic, assuring the Egyptians that he planned to overthrow the Mamluks. He also promised that he had no problems with Islam or the Ottomans. When Napoleon addressed his men, he promised to give them land in Egypt but warned them not to disrespect the Muslims since they would be living among them. The Egyptians were skeptical of Napoleon's promises, and the French invasion would soon meet serious challenges.

Napoleon in Egypt

As soon as Napoleon conquered Alexandria, he mobilized his army and marched toward Cairo. However, the Mamluks weren't about to give up that easily, and Murad Bey led an army against Napoleon at Shubra Khit on July 13th. Napoleon won the battle, and the armies met again at the Battle of the Pyramids on July 21st. The French were attacked by the Mamluks, who controlled an army of about six thousand men. Napoleon defeated the Mamluks and took Cairo on July 25th. Murad Bey was forced to flee to Upper Egypt while Ibrahim Bey retreated to Syria.

Napoleon in Egypt.
https://commons.wikimedia.org/wiki/File:Napoleon_in_Egypt_by_Jean-Leon_Gerome,_French,_1867-1868,_oil_on_wood_panel_-_Princeton_University_Art_Museum_-_DSC07051.jpg

While Napoleon experienced great victories on land, the British navy was close to Egypt and would arrive at the end of the month. Napoleon didn't waste any time in Cairo and appointed a series of councils to advise him as he took control of the Egyptian government. For the first time in centuries, Egypt was once again introduced to the West; it had been sheltered by the Mamluks and Ottomans, who mostly focused on the East. The French succeeded in opening Egypt up to Europe. They also managed to weaken the Mamluk ruling force, which would never return to its former glory.

During the occupation, French scholars uncovered the Rosetta Stone, which bore trilingual carvings and helped scholars decipher hieroglyphs. It was an astounding discovery that would form the basis of Egyptology and expose Egypt's ancient culture to the modern world.

The early part of Napoleon's Egyptian campaign was successful, which may have bolstered French morale. However, the French and British would soon meet in a climactic naval battle that would turn the tide against Napoleon and cause him to return to France the next year.

The Battle of the Nile

When the British discovered that Napoleon planned to occupy Egypt, they sent Horatio Nelson to scout Napoleon's operations at Toulon. However, when Nelson arrived, he found the port was empty and that Napoleon had already left. Nelson correctly guessed what Napoleon wanted to do and headed to Alexandria, which was also empty. The British navy had arrived too early. Nelson sailed for Sicily. When he returned to Egypt in August, he found the French fleet at Aboukir Bay. The French fleet was commanded by Admiral François-Paul Brueys d'Aigailliers.

Battle of the Nile
https://commons.wikimedia.org/wiki/File:Loutherbourg - battle of the nile.jpg

Nelson seized his opportunity and commanded the British forces to attack the French fleet at once. During the night, Napoleon suffered a head wound, and the French flagship, *L'Orient*, was destroyed by the British. Brueys was onboard at the time and died along with most of the sailors aboard. The French fleet was almost completely destroyed; only a handful of ships were able to escape. It was a devastating blow to Napoleon's army, and it was the beginning of the end of the French occupation.

It soon became apparent that the Egyptians were dissatisfied with French rule, as Napoleon had to deal with an uprising in Cairo in October 1798. The Ottoman sultan, Selim III, declared war on France in September. In August 1799, Napoleon left Egypt and returned to France, leaving Jean-Baptiste Kléber in charge. The French would be forced to surrender in 1801 when British forces landed at Aboukir. On top of this, the Ottomans advanced into Egypt from Syria, and the British-Indian army landed on the Red Sea coast.

Muhammad Ali of Egypt

Once the French left Egypt, the Ottomans were determined to recover Egypt. The British forces left Egypt in 1803, but the

Ottomans still had to fight the remaining Mamluk factions that wanted to reassert their power. As a result, the Ottomans relied on an Albanian fighting force, which helped the Ottomans take back Egypt and appoint a viceroy who would protect Ottoman interests. However, the Albanians had their own plans and rebelled against the Ottomans. Their leader became the new viceroy, but he was quickly assassinated, which led to the appointment of his successor, Muhammad Ali, who overthrew the Mamluks and Ottomans.

Muhammad Ali was appointed as viceroy by the Ottoman sultan in an effort to end revolts that erupted in Cairo in 1805. The new viceroy proved to be a competent military leader who won several important battles. In 1807, the British tried to occupy Egypt in an effort to gain a strategic position over Napoleon's army. However, Muhammad Ali defeated their expedition, and the British were forced to retreat. Since the Ottoman Empire was facing serious difficulties, he was allowed to separate himself from the empire, declare himself Egypt's leader, and conquer vast amounts of lands that had previously been controlled by the Ottomans. Afterward, he expanded Egypt's territories to central Arabia and northern Sudan, which allowed him to take advantage of a lucrative slave trade route. Unfortunately, Muhammad Ali's Arabian Empire fell apart during his lifetime, but he continued ruling over Egypt.

As Egypt's leader, he modernized the Egyptian Army, boosted the economy, encouraged education, and founded several educational institutions. He sent several Egyptians to French universities, which separated Egypt from the Ottoman culture. Muhammad Ali also introduced vaccinations for children, forced labor, and military conscriptions. He turned Egypt into a coercive state. The Egyptians weren't happy under Muhammad Ali's rule, and there were several peasant revolts, all of which were quickly subdued. In 1848, Muhammad Ali had become senile, and his son, Ibrahim, took control of Egypt. Ibrahim ruled for a few months before his death and was succeeded by his son, Abbās I. Muhammad Ali died in 1849.

Muhammad Ali
https://commons.wikimedia.org/wiki/File:ModernEgypt,_Muhammad_Ali_by_Auguste_Couder,_BAP_17996.jpg

The Khedivate of Egypt

When the French were expelled from Egypt and Muhammad Ali founded his dynasty, Egypt became the Khedivate of Egypt. It was an autonomous state that was allowed to act independently but had to pay tribute to the Ottoman Empire. While Muhammad Ali managed to rule Egypt effectively for several decades, his successors struggled to do the same. In 1863, Ismail took the throne, and he was determined to modernize Egypt. Unfortunately, his lofty goals and extravagance led to bankruptcy, which resulted in European interference in Egypt's economy and development. Ismail managed to receive the title of khedive, which essentially made him an independent sovereign from the Ottoman Empire, but this privilege meant he had to pay more tribute to the Ottomans.

Ismail was brought increasingly under European control, and for some years, Egypt was ruled jointly by the French and British. In 1879, Ismail was forced out of office, and his son, Tewfik, was proclaimed khedive. However, a few years later, an officer named Ahmed 'Urabi caught wind of discontent among the army and lower classes. He quickly created a revolt against the Europeans and Turks. The government was unable to stop 'Urabi, and he quickly rose within the government and became a cabinet member. This wasn't enough for him, and soon, widespread revolts broke out.

In 1882, the British and French took their fleets to Alexandria to suppress the serious rebellion and protect European interests, but the French retreated. The British stayed, suppressing the revolt and installing their troops in Egypt. It was meant to be a temporary measure, but the British would remain in Egypt until 1956. 'Urabi was defeated and forced into exile, and the khedive was allowed to rule again. At first, the British government didn't establish formal political control in Egypt since they knew it would cause trouble with the Ottomans and other European nations. However, the British claimed to be protecting their interests in Egypt, which required their military presence in the country.

While the British never established their formal political presence in Egypt, they still had significant power in Egypt. For example, when Tewfik and his government placed 'Urabi and his conspirators on trial, the rebels were originally sentenced to death. However, the British interfered and commuted the rebels' sentences to exile. Tewfik formed his own cabinet, with Riaz Pasha acting as a leading member. However, after the British interference, Riaz quit, and the khedive worked with the British ambassador in Istanbul to reorganize the Egyptian government. During his time as khedive, Tewfik posed little resistance to British interference. However, when he died, he was succeeded by his son, Abbās II, in 1892. He wasn't as complacent as his father and would pose serious problems for the British.

Chapter 8: Late Modern Egypt (1890–2013 CE)

Once the British occupied Egypt, they began interfering with Egyptian politics, as they had invested heavily into the Egyptian economy and wanted to ensure that their investment was being protected. Unfortunately, their interference often didn't line up with Egypt's best interests, which led to conflict and enmity. While many of Muhammad Ali's successors worked with the British, that cooperation ended under the rule of Abbās II. Almost as soon as the British were finished dealing with Abbās II, another threat loomed on the horizon. When Britain declared war on the Ottoman Empire during World War I, Egypt became a base of operations, and it would suffer greatly during the war years.

Soon after the First World War, Egypt emerged as an independent kingdom before transforming into a republic. Finally free from foreign leadership, Egypt's government went through several transformations as new political groups sprang up and vied for dominance. Among these were the Wafd and the Muslim Brotherhood, which would both have a serious impact on modern Egyptian politics. In recent years, Egypt has also endured tumultuous events that shaped its government, people, and culture. This new period in Egyptian history may not have the prestige of ancient Egypt, but it is still fascinating.

Abbās II

When Abbās II inherited the office of khedive from his father in 1892, there was growing resentment about British influence in Egypt. Unlike his father, Abbās wasn't willing to submit to British rule and almost immediately showed that he didn't appreciate British interference in his government. This won him the support of Egyptian nationalists, and Abbās appointed a prime minister who shared his views. Abbās also provided support for the *Al-Mu'ayyad*, which was an anti-British newspaper. After his loud criticism of the British, Lord Cromer, the British consul general in Egypt, decided that the khedive's influence was growing too strong.

However, in 1906, Egyptian nationalists declared they wanted a constitutional government, but Abbās denied their petition. The next year, the National Party was established, led by Mustafā Kāmil. By that time, Lord Cromer had been replaced by Lord Kitchener as consul general, and he took more serious steps to curb Abbās's independence. He also struck a blow to the National Party by exiling or imprisoning all its leaders.

Court of Shah Abbās II.
Credit: Sorosh Tavakoli from Stockholm, Sverige, CC BY 2.0
https://creativecommons.org/licenses/by/2.0 via Wikimedia Commons;
https://commons.wikimedia.org/wiki/File:Shah_Abbas_II.jpg

Abbās wasn't about to give up. He bided his time. His chance presented itself when World War I broke out, as the British were preparing to enter the fray. Abbās urged his supporters, the Egyptians and the Sudanese, to fight against the British occupation.

Abbās's plan was to join the Central Powers (the coalition of the German Empire, the Ottoman Empire, and Austria-Hungary, which was at war with France, Britain, and Russia). However, Abbās's appeal failed, and he was deposed in 1914. He was replaced by his uncle, Husayn Kāmil, who became the first sultan of the British protectorate. Abbās II spent the rest of his life in exile.

World War I

In November 1914, Britain declared war on the Ottoman Empire. Since the khedive of Egypt was allied with the Ottomans, he was deposed, and a British protectorate was formed. While Egypt had no formal part in the war, it became a British base camp, and over a million Egyptians were drafted. According to sources from the time, the Egyptians suffered greatly in the war because they weren't given appropriate supplies, such as tents, food, and medical resources. Worse still, the forced conscription led to serious economic consequences that caused a recession and poverty in Egypt. During the war, the soldiers were treated worse than animals, and many of them died from foreign diseases and wounds.

The Egyptians were unaccustomed to conditions in France and died from cholera or the cold. When the soldiers returned, they were rewarded with little compensation, and disabled Egyptians weren't supported. They also brought foreign diseases, such as cholera, with them. The Egyptian medical system wasn't equipped for the onslaught of victims.

Due to its strategic position, Britain stationed troops in Egypt and made several fortifications in Egyptian cities, such as a giant cannon in Alexandria. Residents were forced to stay at home during certain hours due to raids. Public buildings were turned into hospitals, while British, Indian, and Australian troops were sent to Egypt during their breaks. In order to support the war efforts, the Egyptians were forced to pay tribute to the British, which added to Egypt's financial strain. If the Egyptians failed to pay the levies, they would be placed under martial law. The British also ended Ottoman rule in Egypt, and when the Ottoman Empire fell, its lands were divided between Britain and France.

While the whole world was impacted by World War I, Britain took advantage of Egypt by forcing its citizens into the army and using its resources for its own gain. All of this led to widespread revolution in Egypt in 1919 and Egypt's eventual independence.

The Wafd

As World War I raged on, Egyptians became increasingly unhappy with British rule. As soon as the war ended, Egypt tried to claim complete independence from Britain. During this time, a delegation of notable Egyptians created the Wafd Party, which was a nationalist liberal political party. The Wafd Party was led by Saad Zaghloul, who was an immensely popular and charismatic leader. For the next few years, the Wafd would be intimately involved in Egyptian politics, but it was only allowed to become a formal party in 1924.

Picture of the Wafd Party
https://commons.wikimedia.org/wiki/File:Blue_Shirts_(Wafd_party).jpg

The party was strictly organized according to a hierarchy, with the executive council at the top. They also had organizers who worked in cities and villages to create support for their cause. The Wafd was mostly made up of urban Egyptians who belonged to the upper and middle classes, but they quickly endeared themselves to most Egyptians who longed for freedom from the British. While Saad Zaghloul served as the party's president, there were also a number of prominent women among their ranks. Zaghloul's wife, Safiya, became an important voice in the struggle for women's rights, along with Huda Sha'arawi. Unfortunately, the Wafd faced serious challenges from the British and the Egyptian monarchy, which both sought to undercut the Wafd's influence.

Saad Zaghloul

Saad Zaghloul was born to a peasant family in the Nile River delta. His family made enough money to send him to the Al-Azhar University in Cairo, and he later attended the Egyptian School of Law. In and later married Safiya, the daughter of the Egyptian prime minister, Mustafa Pasha Fahmi. Safiya, like her husband, was active in politics and became an influential revolutionary and feminist. In 1906, Zaghloul became the head of the Ministry of Education. Around this time, Egyptian nationalism was on the rise, and Zaghloul helped create Hizb al-Umma, the People's Party.

Saad Zaghloul
https://commons.wikimedia.org/wiki/File:ModernEgypt,_Saad_Zaghloul,_BAP_14781.jpg

During Zaghloul's time in the government, he worked with British occupiers, which didn't win him any favors with the nationalists. However, by 1913, he had been elected to the Legislative Assembly and began criticizing the government and British involvement. When Egypt became a British protectorate, Egyptians suffered due to conscription, martial law, and inflation. It was becoming clear that the British were planning to turn Egypt into a colony, and the Egyptians were livid. During World War One, Zaghloul was busy forming various activist groups throughout the country.

On November 13th, 1918, Zaghloul led the Wafd to call upon the British high commissioner (the British representative in Egypt), Sir Reginald Wingate. They declared their intention to lead the Egyptians and demanded that the protectorate be replaced with a treaty of alliance. The Wafd wanted to negotiate this treaty directly with the British government, but their requests were denied. This led to widespread revolts in Egypt, known as the 1919 Revolution. In 1919, the leaders of the Wafd were arrested and exiled, which only infuriated the Egyptian populace further.

Wingate was immediately replaced with General Edmund Allenby, who released the Wafd leaders. Zaghloul then represented Egypt at the Peace Conference in Paris, and while his attempts were unsuccessful, he became a national hero. During the next few years, Zaghloul became increasingly popular. The British allowed a new constitution in 1923 (Egypt was allowed to become a constitutional monarchy), and in 1924, the Wafd won the general elections, making Zaghloul the new prime minister of Egypt. Zaghloul was immensely popular, but this popularity was only partly due to his charisma. His humble background endeared him to the Egyptian populace, and he became the catalyst of a movement that would outlive him.

The Egyptian Kingdom

After the 1919 Revolution, Britain realized its protectorate was failing and that new measures were needed. In 1922, the Unilateral Declaration of Egyptian Independence was negotiated, and the Kingdom of Egypt was established. However, this independence was only nominal, as the British were allowed to have some involvement in Egyptian politics, and British troops remained in

Egypt. The kingdom was led by King Fuad I and later by his son, Farouk I.

During Zaghloul's later years, he agreed to form a coalition government with Lord Lloyd, the British high commissioner. When Zaghloul died in 1927, Mustafā al-Nahhās became the president of the Wafd. In 1936, he signed the Anglo-Egyptian Treaty, which allowed the British to keep their troops along the Suez Canal. The treaty also allowed the British to keep control of Sudan. Since radical fascism was on the rise in the 1930s, the Wafd created the Blue Shirts, a militant youth group.

The Effects of World War II

Egypt was forced to support Britain during World War II, but few Egyptians expected Britain to win. During the war, Italy aligned itself with Nazi Germany and declared war on Britain and France in June 1940. Egypt remained neutral, but due to the Anglo-Egyptian Treaty of 1936, the British were allowed to occupy the Suez Canal if it was threatened. It wasn't long before Italy began launching raids on Egypt from the Italian colony of Libya. The Italians tried to reach the Suez Canal but were stopped by the British before they could attain their objective.

In 1942, Germany nearly invaded Egypt, which caused Britain to interfere in the Egyptian government. In the 4 February Incident, King Farouk was forced to make al-Nahhās his prime minister. While this may have seemed like a victory for the Wafd, as they had succeeded in winning the elections in March 1942, it became clear that the Wafd weren't the champions of Egyptian nationalism anymore since Nahhās cooperated with the British.

World War II completely destabilized Egypt. As the Wafd declined, other political parties fought for dominance and called for a revision of the 1936 treaty. Egyptians wanted the British to withdraw their troops from the Suez Canal and end British control of Sudan. Extremists gained popularity, and groups like the Muslim Brotherhood committed violent activities and supported unrest. All of this led to a revolution that began in 1952. The revolution, which was led by Gamal Abdel Nasser, included a military coup that brought a sudden end to Egypt's constitutional monarchy. The revolution led to a time of profound political and social changes in Egypt. On June 18th, 1953, Egypt became a republic, with Mohamed Naguib as its first president.

The Muslim Brotherhood

The Muslim Brotherhood is Egypt's oldest political Islamic group, and it isn't allowed to operate as a political party in some countries. The group was founded in 1928 in Egypt by Hassan al-Banna. The group was created because its founder dreamed of forming a system of Islamic rule that would be founded firmly on Islamic laws and principles. Hassan al-Banna thought he could achieve this dream by offering various social services to the people. Eventually, the Muslim Brotherhood set its sights on reforming all existing governments in the Arab world.

During its history, the Muslim Brotherhood has been accused of committing acts of violence and terrorism. At first, the Muslim Brotherhood focused on preaching Islam, setting up hospitals, boosting the economy, and teaching the illiterate. Since it was founded during a time when there was widespread unrest due to British occupation, it was only a matter of time before the Muslim Brotherhood entered the political arena.

The Muslim Brotherhood cooperated with the Free Officers (which was a group of revolutionary nationalist officers in the Egyptian Armed Forces) at first, but when there were differences of opinions between the groups, they stopped working together. In the 1950s, there was an assassination attempt on Gamal Abdel Nasser. This led to the imprisonment of Sayyid Qutb, who was a leading member of the Muslim Brotherhood. While in prison, he advocated the benefits of an armed struggle against the Egyptian regime. Eventually, he was executed, but his writings were still used by Islamist groups to advocate armed struggles. The Muslim Brotherhood agreed to abandon violence in the 1970s, and in 1995, they adopted democracy. Over time, the Muslim Brotherhood spread to other Arab countries and influenced various Islamic groups.

The Nasser Regime

Gamal Abdel Nasser was born in 1918 and participated in anti-British protests during his youth. After studying law for a few months, he entered the Royal Military Academy and graduated in 1938 as a second lieutenant. During World War II, he helped form a secret organization called the Free Officers. In 1952, the

Free Officers, led by Nasser, formed a coup that deposed King Farouk. Mohamed Naguib became the Egyptian prime minister in 1953, but Nasser removed Naguib from power in 1954 and became the new prime minister instead.

Nasser proved to be a popular and effective leader. In 1956, his new constitution and presidency were confirmed by the Egyptian voters. Nasser then made an arms agreement with the USSR, which caused the British to refuse to pay for Nasser's High Dam project that would be built across the Nile in Aswan, Egypt.

In response, Nasser nationalized the Suez Canal, which was technically owned by France and England. In October 1956, Israel, France, and Britain attacked Egypt. The foreign forces were able to occupy the Suez Canal but were pressured to retreat by the United Nations and Soviets. In 1957, the Suez Canal was completely under Egyptian control. In 1970, the Aswan High Dam was completed, which provided a massive boost to the Egyptian economy. Nasser was highly respected throughout the world, and his independent policies made him a beloved leader among the Egyptians. Two months after the completion of the Aswan High Dam, Nasser died of a heart attack and was succeeded by Anwar el-Sadat. Nasser's regime ended 2,300 years of foreign rule and introduced a new era in Egyptian history.

Anwar Sadat

Anwar el-Sadat was born in 1918 and graduated from the Cairo Military Academy in 1938. During World War II, he was arrested by the British for plotting to overthrow them. He managed to escape in 1950 and joined the Free Officers, helping Nasser to overthrow the monarchy. During Nasser's regime, Sadat held several positions in the government until he eventually became Nasser's vice president. When Nasser died, he became the president of Egypt in September 1970.

Anwar Sadat

While Sadat upheld some of Nasser's policies at first, he quickly began setting himself apart from Nasser's legacy. He instituted a program of economic reforms that involved attracting foreign investment. His efforts weren't very successful; they led to inflation, the unequal distribution of wealth, and food riots in 1977. He famously ended Egypt's partnership with the Soviets. In 1973, he entered the Arab-Israeli War and retook some territories in Israel. However, Sadat soon began working toward peace in the Middle East and made a historic visit to Israel. Sadat also began negotiating for peace with Israel's prime minister, Menachem Begin, which resulted in the Camp David Accords, a preliminary peace treaty between the two countries. This action also earned Sadat and Begin a Nobel Peace Prize in 1978. In 1979, Sadat succeeded in obtaining a treaty of peace between Israel and Egypt.

Unfortunately, not everyone supported the peace treaty, which led to opposition within Sadat's government. The economy was also worsening, which caused public unrest. In September 1981, Sadat fought back by imprisoning 1,500 of his opponents from every walk of life. The next month, he was assassinated by the

Egyptian Islamic Jihad, a militant Islamist group. Sadat was succeeded by Hosni Mubarak in 1981, who would serve as president for three decades.

The Egyptian Crisis

On January 25th, 2011, Egyptian youths felt compelled to protest against Hosni Mubarak's regime in Cairo. Crowds gathered in Tahrir Square to protest rising poverty and unemployment. The protests lasted for eighteen days and quickly became a revolution. Egypt descended into violence, repression, and a political deficit. The aim of the protests was to overthrow Hosni Mubarak. While Mubarak was removed from office during the revolution, things quickly got worse when political parties fought against the Muslim Brotherhood for dominance. Hundreds of protestors were killed during the revolution, which only added to the frustration and unrest.

In June 2012, Mohamed Morsi won Egypt's democratic elections and became prime minister. However, the unrest in Egypt was far from over. Morsi's presidency was marked by diplomatic, economic, and security challenges, as well as energy shortages. In 2013, Abdel Fattah al-Sisi led a coup that overthrew Morsi, allowing him to become the president of Egypt.

SECTION THREE: Egyptian Society Through the Ages

Chapter 9: Society and Its Structure

Egypt underwent many changes during its long history. The region developed from separate scattered tribes into a highly organized empire with an intricate religious system. During ancient Egypt, society had a pyramid-like structure, with the pharaoh and gods at the top and slaves forming the wide base of Egyptian society. When the Egyptians came under foreign rule, they were subjected to the traditions, cultures, and social structures of various other countries. As the spread of Christianity became prevalent, Egyptian society underwent more changes, as the pagan priestly classes were replaced by monks.

While Coptic Orthodox Christians remained in Egypt, the vast majority of people eventually adopted Islam, which once again changed the traditional social structure. Over the years, Egyptian society adapted and formed its own unique identity that stood apart from other Islamic kingdoms, especially when the Mamluks took over. These changes affected everything from laws to clothing.

Ancient Egyptian Society

The most important value of ancient Egyptian society was ma'at, which signified harmony and balance. If ma'at wasn't preserved, it was believed that society would collapse into chaos. One way to preserve ma'at was by maintaining the social balance, which is why the intermediate periods were seen as periods of lawlessness and chaos. The social order broke down during Egypt's various intermediate periods, which caused scholars and historians to describe these ages as dark times. The ancient Egyptian social hierarchy was shaped like a pyramid with the king at the top. After the king came his vizier and courtiers, followed by the scribes and priests. Next came the nomarchs (or regional governors). After the nomarchs came the generals, then artists and supervisors of worksites. At the bottom were the peasants and slaves.

Pyramid of Egyptian society.
Reptail82, CC BY-SA 4.0 https://creativecommons.org/licenses/by-sa/4.0 via Wikimedia Commons; https://commons.wikimedia.org/wiki/File:Govt12e.gif

In ancient Egypt, the gods reigned supreme, and the people believed that the gods had created them and placed them in a perfect home. They believed that the gods appointed a ruler whose primary responsibility was representing the gods' will to the people and preserving the all-important ma'at. If the pharaoh was able to fulfill their duties, then everything would work as it should. Since the social order was so intricately tied to religion, social mobility wasn't an option. People couldn't easily climb ranks or switch to a different class since this would upset the natural order of things.

Since the pharaoh had so many duties, the position of vizier was created to help them. The vizier took care of many of the practical duties of administration, such as delegating duties, overseeing the governors and military, tax collection, and checking on the ruler's building projects. The peasant farmers made up the vast majority of the population, although the slave class was an integral part of Egyptian society. Slaves were usually criminals, people who couldn't pay their debts, or prisoners of war.

Ancient Egyptian Law

Tradition was extremely important in Egyptian culture, and the ancient Egyptians promoted strict obedience to the natural order of things, including the legal system. The Egyptians had developed their own legal system as early as the Predynastic period, which stretched from around 6000 to 3150 BCE. As Egypt developed, so did its laws. Once again, ma'at came heavily into play, as most of the Egyptian legal system revolved around preserving ma'at. The Egyptians believed that people needed help to stay on the path set out by the gods. If someone disobeyed those laws, they were punished severely, as everyone understood that keeping to the laws was within everyone's best interests. Unfortunately, this meant that the Egyptians often believed that people were guilty unless it could be proven otherwise. If a person was accused of committing a crime, they would likely be punished, although there were isolated cases of leniency.

Although no official law codes have been found in Egypt, it's clear that the Egyptians followed a legal system because legal precedents already existed by the time of the Early Dynastic period (3150-2613 BCE). It seems that laws were enforced by police officers who were tasked with keeping the peace. If a criminal was caught, they would face the judicial system. The ancient Egyptians believed that their laws were handed down from the gods at the moment of creation, which made the king the head of the judicial system. The vizier usually had a say in judicial matters but could be overruled by the king. Viziers typically appointed magistrates and could be prevailed upon to get involved in local courts, but these instances were rare. Nomarchs would also be responsible for ensuring that justice was dispensed within their districts. There is some evidence that priests acted as judges in certain cases, as the people believed they could consult with the gods to receive an accurate judgment.

Adultery was a serious offense, and both husbands and wives were allowed to take their spouses to court if their infidelities were exposed. Families were extremely important to maintain ma'at and social balance. A woman guilty of infidelity could be divorced, have her nose amputated, or be burned to death. While a man could receive up to one thousand blows, he wouldn't face the death penalty. The judicial system relied heavily on the testimonies of witnesses, which meant that false witnesses were given incredibly harsh sentences. However, in most cases, public disgrace was a terrible enough prospect that most people tended to obey the laws. Ancient Egyptians relied heavily on their communities, so public humiliation or ostracization would have been a terrible fate for any family.

Daily Life in Ancient Egypt

Everyone had their designated place in ancient Egypt, and people were generally proud of their work. They believed they were fulfilling their roles within the natural order and were contributing to keeping the balance of things intact. It is believed that ancient artisans and workmen volunteered their time and skills to a king's building project. For years, it was believed that the pyramids were completed with slave labor, and while slaves certainly helped build the monuments, the king's public projects were a source of national pride, which drew free men to offer their services too.

Family formed the basis of Egyptian society, and tomb offerings were made to the deceased. If a family didn't have time to present the offerings themselves, they could hire priests to make offerings on their behalf.

The ancient Egyptians were extremely clean and took time to groom themselves. Farmers wove flax into fine linen. Peasants and working men wore long garments tied with a sash at the waist, as well as short kilts. Rich men wore knee-length shirts and kilts with jewelry and makeup. Many Egyptians went barefoot, but many also wore papyrus sandals. Working-class women wore long wrap-around dresses, while wealthy women were able to wear elaborate adornments with their dresses. Jewelry usually consisted of beads, armlets, bracelets, necklaces, and earrings.

Daily Life in Ptolemaic Egypt

By the time the Ptolemies ruled Egypt, the country had already been influenced by the Hellenistic culture and religion. The pyramid-like structure of society had broken down, with most of the important positions in the government being given to Greeks or Greek descendants. The Ptolemies kept the Egyptian religion, but the country was becoming increasingly diverse. The Egyptians were allowed to follow their own traditions and laws, but the Greeks were governed according to Greek laws, which meant that life in Egypt differed according to a person's lineage.

When Alexander the Great conquered Egypt, he made it a part of his ethnically diverse empire. This meant that Egypt was opened up to different cultures, with many people moving into Egypt and bringing their cultures with them. Cities like Alexandria became cosmopolitan melting pots of cultures, religions, and intellectual theories. While the Egyptian religion was allowed to continue, the Greeks brought new practices of worship and soon blended the Egyptian and Greek religions together.

The Ptolemies owned most of the land in Egypt, and farmers were subjected to government control, which allowed the Ptolemies to grow richer. Although taxes rose and oversight increased, the government sponsored irrigation projects that helped to boost the economy. Egypt participated in trade with many foreign countries, and port cities were given access to exotic luxury goods. Since the Greeks prized education, wealthy women were educated and allowed to participate in certain religious rites. Unfortunately, Egypt's fertility and grain production made it an irresistible prize to the Roman Empire, and soon, Egyptian society changed again.

Roman Influences on Egyptian Society

While the Ptolemies kept themselves apart from the Egyptians, they still remained in Egypt during their rule. However, when Egypt became a Roman state, the Roman emperor allied himself with the pharaohs but ruled from Rome. The first Roman emperor, Augustus, appointed a governor who controlled the region and reported back to the emperor. Egypt became the home to Roman legions until Augustus was sure the Egyptians wouldn't rebel. The Romans changed the laws in Egypt so that they conformed to Roman laws, and business was conducted according to Roman procedures. The local administration also changed to the Roman system and dictated that landowners were responsible for carrying out public services and had to take care of their lands.

Once again, special privileges were reserved for Greek and Roman citizens. As Rome's breadbasket, Egypt had to supply Rome with grain, and its natural resources were used for the good of the Roman Empire. However, it would seem that the Egyptians also had an impact on the Romans, as Roman architecture bore resemblances of Egyptian styles. The Egyptians were also exposed to new ideas, as Alexandria attracted many notable scholars. Meanwhile, daily life in rural areas stayed mostly the same, although the wealthy were expected to contribute to society, and everyone was governed according to Roman laws.

Byzantine Social Structure

When the Roman Empire was split into two distinct sections, Egypt fell under the Byzantine Empire, which soon developed its own identity that distinguished it from the Western Roman Empire. Byzantine society was controlled by the royal family and the wealthy elite. However, unlike in ancient Egypt, social mobility was much more frequent, as people could advance due to wars, imperial favor, land ownership, or intermarriage. Ordinary people likely adopted their parents' profession, but ambitious individuals could realistically hope to advance their social standing.

The Byzantine Empire was also astonishingly diverse, and its cities became incredibly cosmopolitan. Alexandria was allowed to gain influence again and was the gateway for merchants, refugees, mercenaries, pilgrims, and travelers. Byzantine society was still somewhat stratified and consisted of two main classes: the privileged (*honestiores*) and the humble (*humiliores*), which basically meant the rich and everyone else. Slaves had their own social class, but this class was lower than all the others. This social divide meant there was a definite difference in standards of living. The rich had more than enough to survive and still live lavishly, while the poor struggled to make a living. However, the wealthy class didn't depend on blood or descendancy anymore since dynasties changed quickly. A family could fall out of favor just as quickly as it had risen.

Christian Society

During the Byzantine era, Christianity was widely accepted, and the majority of the population converted to it. The clergy formed their own class and played a very important part in society. The Eastern Church was headed by the patriarch of Constantinople. However, the Byzantine emperors also had a measure of control over the church. The emperor was allowed to appoint or remove patriarchs as he saw fit. Beneath the patriarch were local bishops, who took care of smaller regions and reported back to Constantinople.

Stained glass in a Coptic church in Egypt.
someone10x, CC BY 2.0 https://creativecommons.org/licenses/by/2.0 via Wikimedia Commons; https://commons.wikimedia.org/wiki/File:Coptic_church_in_Egypt_(9198216449).jpg

Priests were allowed to marry, but once they became a bishop, they were required to separate from their wives in order to concentrate on their appointment. The wife would then have to retreat to a monastery. Women were allowed to become nuns and dedicate their lives to Christ. Nuns were required to take care of the poor and sickly. Monasteries were communal buildings that often served the needs of the community.

Islamic Society

As Egypt became an increasingly Islamic society, the rules and customs of the country changed once again. During the Arabic caliphates, regions were required to report back to the capital of the empire, and Arabs enjoyed a privileged position in the social hierarchy. However, in time, the caliphates' power dwindled, and smaller regions broke away under opposing caliphates. In Egypt, a person's status depended on their social class, gender, legal status, religion, and ethnicity. While other religions were allowed to coexist among Muslims, at least for the most part, the treatment of non-Muslims varied greatly. Non-Muslims were required to submit to Islamic law and pay a special tax called the jizya, which allowed them to become a part of a protected class called the dhimmi. Unfortunately, the dhimmi didn't enjoy the same social and legal privileges as Muslims.

During the Umayyad Caliphate, non-Arabs were known as mawali and didn't enjoy the same privileges as Arabs. In time, Persians and other non-Arabs were incorporated into the Abbasid state, which allowed the mawali to advance socially. Islamic society was dominated by Islamic laws and traditions, but this also depended on whether a person was a part of the Sunni or Shia branch of Islam. Women were usually allowed to participate in agriculture and develop artisanal skills but were more often relegated to roles that involved homemaking, food preparation, midwifery, and medicine. However, there were different rules that women had to live by according to their religion or socio-economic status. Women were allowed to retain financial and legal independence, which was unusual in other medieval societies. Women were also allowed to invest money, manage their wealth, trade, get divorced, or be included in inheritance (although they often inherited less than their male relatives).

Most cultures dictated that a family would be led by a patriarch. However, some societies, such as the Mamluk society, allowed people more freedom, and women had more independence. During this time, Egyptian society was divided into the urban elite, merchants, landowners, ordinary people (including farmers and artisans), and slaves. When the Mamluks took over, they became the dominant social class.

Ottoman Social Structure

The Ottoman Empire was incredibly large and comprised of different cultures, which means that its social structure had to be complex to accommodate the diversity. Muslim Ottomans generally held more influence than Christians and Jews. The Ottomans also used the millet system, which meant that people of each faith were judged according to their laws. This meant there were different laws for Jews, Christians, and Muslims. Non-Muslims were forced to pay higher taxes, and Christians paid a blood tax (their firstborn sons were taken away, converted to Islam, and forced to serve in the Ottoman army).

The highest social positions were held by people within the sultan's government, which included the sultan's household, the army, bureaucrats, scribes, judges, lawyers, and teachers. The Turks made up the most of this class and were able to rise within the government more easily than others. Meanwhile, the vast majority of the population were laborers, which included farmers and artisans. Conversion wasn't widely promoted; Muslims paid lower taxes, and this would have caused disaster for the Ottoman Empire if everyone had become Muslim.

In Egypt, Cairo became just another provincial city, robbing it of the influence that the Mamluks had lavished on it during their reign. However, the Mamluks continued to be a powerful social class. Unfortunately for Egypt, the Ottomans forced the Europeans to change their trading routes, which meant Egypt became isolated from the rest of the world. Its culture and society remained virtually unchanged for decades.

Life during the British Occupation

When the French invaded Egypt, they interrupted a period of prolonged stagnation of Egyptian culture. They once again opened Egypt to the rest of the world, but that didn't always help the

Egyptians. They were forced to live through several violent wars, as well as British interference in their politics. British and French soldiers were stationed in Egypt, while European diplomats and officials moved to Egypt, where they received special treatment.

As a result of European interference, the Egyptian government and economy were destabilized, which led to disastrous consequences for ordinary Egyptians. While foreigners were given special privileges, Egyptians received aid and support from European countries, such as Britain and France, which allowed the Europeans to meddle in Egyptian affairs under the guise of protecting their financial interests. During the 20th century, Egypt had grown tired of European interference, and fierce nationalism swept the nation. This led to riots, uprisings, and revolutions, which further destabilized the country and society. During the British occupation, Egyptians faced martial law, higher taxes, inflation, and forced military conscription. In time, Egypt was able to win its independence, and Egyptian society was allowed to develop naturally.

Chapter 10: The Nile and Its Key Role

The Nile is the longest river in Africa and flows through several countries directly into the Mediterranean Sea. It is the main source of water for Egypt, Sudan, and South Sudan, which makes it a vitally important river that also supports the economies of those countries.

Historically, the Nile River was thought to be the world's longest river, but researchers discovered that the Amazon River is slightly longer. The Nile is comprised of two major tributaries: the White Nile and the Blue Nile. The White Nile flows from Lake Victoria in Uganda, while the Blue Nile begins in Ethiopia. The northern part of the river flows through the Sudanese River directly into Egypt, where it forms a large delta, where Cairo was built. From there, it flows into the Mediterranean Sea, where Alexandria was built.

Thanks to its annual flooding, the plains surrounding the Nile are incredibly fertile, which allowed several civilizations to make their homes on its banks. The river was vitally important to the ancient Egyptians, and that importance is reflected in their religion. For thousands of years, the Nile played a massive role in Egypt's economy and daily life. Later, the search for the source of the Nile would be an enduring mystery that plagued scientists and explorers. Due to its impact on its surroundings, the Nile has a fascinating story to tell.

Foundation of the Egyptian Civilization

Thousands of years ago, North Africa had a much different climate. The region used to experience much more rainfall. However, in time, the lush wetlands dried up and turned into deserts, which forced ancient civilizations to relocate to wetter areas. Thankfully, many of them didn't have to move too far, as the Nile flowed directly through the desert and created fertile plains that were perfect for farming. When the first inhabitants arrived on the banks of the Nile, they discovered that there was plenty of food. They also realized that there was a period of six months when the river rose, then receded, leaving behind a layer of silt. This silt was perfect for farming, and soon, several cultures lived on the banks of the Nile and raised crops.

Once those early cultures discovered irrigation, farming became a regular practice and the basis of many cultures. The Nile provided a regular source of food, and people grew crops such as wheat, cotton, and beans. Since people no longer needed to move around to find food, they were able to establish permanent settlements that eventually turned into cities, which then gave rise to the Egyptian kingdoms. However, the Nile wasn't always regular, which led people to believe that the gods had something to do with the annual flooding. The ancient Egyptians believed that the Nile was a gift from the gods, and much of their culture was structured around the Nile. For instance, their calendar was centered around the Nile, as their year began with the first month of flooding. In an effort to please the gods and ensure regular flooding, the Egyptians developed an intricate religious structure that involved offerings and festivals.

Besides farming, the Nile also allowed the Egyptians to develop skills like boat-making, which later led to them using the Nile as a source of transportation and trade.

Geography

The Nile is about 4,160 miles (around 6,700 kilometers) long and flows northward from east-central Africa to the Mediterranean. It's comprised of tributaries that are fed by smaller rivers, and the flow depends on the arrival of the rainy season. The Blue Nile, one of the most important tributaries, begins from Lake Tana in

Ethiopia, where it flows for about 870 miles (about 1,400 kilometers) until it meets up with the White Nile in Khartoum, Sudan. Ethiopia's rainy season usually takes place in the summer, which leads to strong flowing waters that cause erosion and carry highly fertile silt. However, during the dry season, the flow is extremely slow, and in some places, the river dries up completely.

Parts of the Nile Basin can be found in a number of African countries, namely Tanzania, Rwanda, Burundi, the Democratic Republic of the Congo, Uganda, Kenya, South Sudan, Ethiopia, Sudan, and Egypt. The ancient Egyptians used the Nile to make sense of the world around them and divided their region into two important areas. The first part was Kemet, the fertile land of the Nile Valley and surrounding oases. The second part was the Deshret, which was desert lands that didn't have enough resources to sustain people and was, therefore, linked to death and disorder.

Flora and Fauna

Since the Nile runs through such a long stretch of land, there are different regions, and each has a unique environment. The land surrounding the Nile in Egypt was carefully cultivated over thousands of years and provided regular crops of wheat, flax, cotton, papyrus, and barley. These staple crops provided enough grain to feed the Egyptians and allow them to trade with other countries. The Egyptians were also able to grow lentils, peas, watermelons, leeks, and spices, such as cumin and coriander.

The Nile housed many different species of animals. If Egyptians didn't want to be farmers, they could rely on the Nile to provide enough fish to make a living. Fishermen could catch Nile perch, bolti, catfish, tigerfish, or the elephant snout fish. The Nile crocodile, soft-shelled turtle, and hippopotamus were also regular sights for ancient Egyptians. The Nile is home to monitor lizards and around thirty species of snakes, including the infamous asp that may have played a part in Cleopatra's suicide. In less watered areas, flora and fauna are scarcer, and the desert areas around the Nile have fewer forms of life. Some areas have thinly foliaged trees with some grass and herbs.

Irrigation and Farming

Every year, the rains allowed the Nile's water to surge toward Egypt. As it flowed, it carried rich, nutritious soil from the Horn of

Africa that was so dark it often looked black. Once the water arrived, the Egyptian farmers were able to begin their farming season. Historians believe the Egyptians were among the earliest farmers who learned to irrigate their lands, although they did so through a process of trial and error. When the Nile flooded, it would cover the land with water, which would destroy homes and fields. While the flooding brought life-giving nutrients, the Egyptians soon realized they would need to find a way to control it. This led ancient Egyptians to dig channels and basins, which would have been a lengthy process.

As the ancient Egyptians developed irrigation, they formed a system called basin irrigation. The farmers would dig networks of land to create basins. From there, they built channels that would funnel the Nile's waters into the basins, where the water would stay and sink into the soil. Once the water evaporated, the land would be ready for planting.

In order to keep track of the Nile's water level, the ancient Egyptians used nilometers, which were basic columns with markings. Nilometers could help Egyptians determine if they were facing unusual flooding. Both too much and too little water would be disastrous. In the 1950s, Gamal Abdel Nasser began the Aswan High Dam building project, which was completed in the 1970s. The Aswan Dam increased the amount of hydroelectric power that could be generated from the Nile and regulated the Nile's flooding. This led to better agricultural practices that benefited Egypt's farmers and economy.

Transportation and Trade

Besides developing agriculture and irrigation, the ancient Egyptians also discovered that they could use the Nile for transportation. In time, Egyptians were able to create wooden boats with sails and oars that could travel great distances. Smaller boats were made of papyrus reeds that had wooden frames. These smaller boats were for small-scale traveling or fishing. As early as the Old Kingdom, Egyptians transported cattle, fish, bread, wood, and vegetables, which were taken to different parts of the kingdom or other kingdoms for trade. Boats quickly became an integral part of Egyptian culture. Kings and important officials were usually buried with their boats, which were perfectly built and could have been used on the Nile.

Ancient mosaic of the Nile.

Since Egypt had access to rich agricultural resources, the Egyptians were able to trade their goods with other countries. Not only did this make the kingdom richer, but it also led to peaceful diplomatic ties with their neighbors. Thanks to the Nile, goods could be quickly transported through Egypt. Egypt also occupied an advantageous geographical position that connected it to international trade routes. The empire was connected to Mediterranean trade routes thanks to Alexandria, as well as trade routes with the East because of its position on the Red Sea. Trade was an invaluable part of the Egyptian economy, and Egypt's trade routes developed quickly due to the Nile's extensive waters.

Economy

Agriculture was a massive part of Egypt's economy. Due to Egypt's year-round warm weather and the Nile's regular flooding, Egyptians could sometimes produce as many as three harvests in a year. They produced much more food than they needed, while neighboring Middle Eastern countries often faced droughts and famine, which meant that they sorely needed grain and crops that Egypt could provide. The ancient Egyptians had access to flax, papyrus, stone, and gold, which could be used to make cloth, buildings, jewelry, and paper. As artisans developed their crafts, they were able to create beautiful artworks, such as icons and carvings, which could also be traded for considerable amounts of money. Besides crops, the Nile provided enough water and grazing lands for animals such as cattle and sheep. Oxen were used to plow fields and allowed farmers even quicker yields. Besides labor, animals also produced meat and milk.

Papyrus was another crucial part of Egypt's economy. The plant grew abundantly on the banks of the Nile and could be used to make boats, baskets, and paper. The Egyptians were the first culture to discover how to make paper, and it quickly became Egypt's main export, which caused the Egyptians to conceal the paper-making process so that they could control the paper trade. Egypt also produced massive amounts of gold, wood, iron, silver, and spices. This led to the development of superior weapons and metalwork. Egyptian royalty made sure to benefit by taxing harvests and property. Taxes could be paid with grain, animals, or labor, while merchants had to pay additional taxes. This enriched the pharaoh and the government, allowing them to build public buildings and support the country during times of crisis. Pharaohs were also responsible for opening new avenues of trade, which would have boosted the economy further.

Nilus

The Greeks were fascinated by Egypt and thought that it was a mysterious land filled with wisdom. Eventually, the two cultures merged and were heavily influenced by each other when Alexander the Great conquered Egypt. The Greeks knew that the Nile was the source of life in Egypt, and like the Egyptians, they attributed its abundance to the gods. However, the Greeks didn't share the same beliefs as the Egyptians and developed their own Nile god called Nilus. In fact, the modern word "Nile" comes from the Greek word "Nelios" (another way to spell Nilus), which means river. The ancient Egyptians called the Nile "Ar," which means black. It's as if the Egyptians named the river after the dark sand that was responsible for their nutritious crops.

Nilus was a minor Greek god who didn't have much of an impact on Greek mythology. According to the Greeks, Nilus was the son of the Titans Oceanus and Tethys. Oceanus was the son of

Gaea and Chaos, and he married his sister. Together, the Titans had many children called the Oceanids and Potamoi, who were the gods and goddesses of the seas, rivers, and springs. According to Greek mythology, the Titans had so many children that they overproduced and caused floods. In response, the Titans got divorced to prevent flooding the whole Earth with water. Nilus had several children of his own, including Memphis, Europa, and Thebe, among others.

Hapi and Khnum

The Nile was closely associated with ancient Egyptian religion, and most gods and goddesses were involved with the Nile in one way or another. However, according to the ancient Egyptians, there were two main gods who were responsible for the Nile's gifts: Hapi and Khnum. Khnum was the god of fertility, and he was usually involved with procreation and water. He was depicted as a man with a ram's head and often had long, twisting horns. The ancient Egyptians believed that Khnum created humans from clay. This would have resonated with the ancient Egyptians since vast amounts of clay could be found along the banks of the river. The god had several cults, including one at Herwer (his cult's main center). During the New Kingdom, he was associated with the island of Elephantine and thought to be the lord of the First Cataract of the Nile River. He was often associated with the goddesses Satis and Anuket.

Hapi was believed to be the personification of the annual flooding of the Nile. He was also associated with fertility, and he wielded an immense amount of influence in ancient Egypt. Hapi was a somewhat androgynous figure with a large body, a massive belly, and drooping breasts, which would have represented the god's amazing fertility. The god was also depicted as wearing a false beard and a loincloth, which were the garments often worn by workers. Hapi was sometimes depicted as a hippopotamus. While Hapi was closely associated with the Nile, he wasn't considered the god of the Nile but rather the god of the Nile's flooding. He was usually portrayed as a caring father, and his priests carried out rituals that were supposed to ensure the steady flow of the Nile. Hapi's priests also took care of the official nilometer, which they monitored carefully.

The Nile and Egyptian Religion

Besides Khnum and Hapi, the ancient Egyptian religion was intimately connected to the Nile. In fact, the principle of ma'at, which governed Egyptian religion and daily life, may have been influenced by the river. The Nile rose consistently in the middle of July and then fell sometime in September, which may have impressed the importance of harmony and balance to the Egyptians. If the Nile failed to rise or fall on time, it would have disastrous consequences for the Egyptians. Therefore, the Egyptians became keenly aware of what could happen if the world's forces were out of balance, and they were greatly concerned about the order of things staying in balance.

The Egyptians believed that the gods were responsible for the rise and fall of the Nile and that the gods had gifted the Nile to their people. Most of the gods in Egyptian mythology had something to do with the Nile. Sometimes, the gods were directly involved in the Nile's processes or were influenced by the Nile in some way. For example, in the myth of Seth and Osiris, Seth got rid of his brother's body by throwing him into the Nile. In some myths, either Osiris or Isis was responsible for helping the Egyptians discover agriculture and irrigation. The Nile was known as the "Father of Life" and was an extension of Hapi, who was responsible for giving life to the land. It was also known as the "Mother of All Men" since the goddess Ma'at (the godly manifestation of the concepts of harmony and truth) was closely associated with the Nile.

Search for the Source of the Nile

When Europeans began exploring Africa, they quickly discovered the importance and sheer magnitude of the Nile River. This left them with a burning question: what was the source of the Nile? In 1856, an expedition was organized by the Royal Geographical Society. John Hanning Speke and Captain Richard Burton were both accomplished explorers who joined the search. In 1858, they discovered Lake Tanganyika, but Burton was forced to turn back due to illness. Speke continued onward and discovered Lake Victoria, which he correctly claimed was the source of the Nile. Burton didn't agree and thought the source of the Nile was Lake Tanganyika. The two men would continue to argue about the matter until Speke's death in 1864.

While Lake Victoria is considered to be the source of the Nile, it was discovered that the lake is fed by various tributaries, which made it difficult to locate the "true" source of the Nile. In 2006, explorers claimed that they found the remotest part of the Nile in the Nyungwe Forest near Lake Kivu.

Herodotus, the ancient Greek historian, once wrote that Egypt was the gift of the Nile. It's clear that if it weren't for the Nile, the ancient Egyptians might not have made their permanent home in the Nile Valley. The face of history would have been very different. As scholars delve deeper into the impact of the Nile River on Egypt's history, it becomes clear that if there was no Nile, there would have been no Egypt, or at least not the Egypt that we've come to know.

Chapter 11: The Development of Religion

Religion has always played an important role in Egyptian culture. From its earliest history, an intricate system of worship developed around a pantheon of gods who represented everything from balance to chaos. The ancient Egyptians used religion to relate to the world around them and accredited the gods with everything, both good and bad. They believed that if they kept to the natural harmony by adhering to the strict social hierarchy, contributing to society, and worshiping the gods acceptably, then disasters could be avoided. Whenever disaster struck, the Egyptians believed that it was because the natural balance had been lost.

As Egypt came under foreign rule, its new leaders brought their religions with them. Most foreign empires allowed Egyptians to continue worshiping their traditional religion and had little impact on the Egyptian belief system. When the Greeks took over Egypt, they brought elements of their own religion with them, which led to the formation of new cults. However, when monotheism spread throughout the region, the ancient polytheistic religion began to decline in popularity. Christianity swept through the region, and the new converts rejected the old religion entirely. For years, the Orthodox Church ruled over Egypt, but it eventually gave way to the spread of Islam, which remains Egypt's national religion today.

Ancient Egyptian Religion

The ancient Egyptians believed that all life was sacred and that nature was controlled by the deities. Their pantheon included both major and minor gods, as well as some humans who had been deified before or after their deaths. In order to avoid disaster, the Egyptians believed they were responsible for angering or appeasing the gods, which meant that religion was involved in every aspect of life, especially in the government. The pharaoh was the head of the religion and the bridge between humans and the gods. As a result, the ancient Egyptians spent enormous amounts of money on rituals, temples, and offerings. While alive, the pharaoh was seen as the son of Ra, a representation of the god Horus. Once he died, the pharaoh was deified and became associated with Ra and Osiris.

The ancient Egyptians also believed in *heka* (magic), which could influence their lives or cause things to happen. Ma'at was also a vital part of the religion, and people believed that ma'at could be renewed. The annual flooding of the Nile was believed to renew ma'at in the universe since it echoed the creation of the universe. Sacred rituals and ceremonies were an important part of Egyptian life, and there were even ceremonies involving names and births. Gods could rise and fall over time, as their cults could gain or lose popularity. In some cases, older gods were replaced by new gods, who then took on the powers or significance of the old god they had replaced.

Egyptian Pantheon

Religion played such an important part in ancient Egyptian culture that the Egyptians worshiped over two thousand gods and goddesses. However, only a few of those gods played major roles in daily life and Egyptian mythology. Some gods became extremely important and became state deities, while others merely represented certain regions or played a specific role in mythology. For example, Seshat was the goddess of specific measurements and written words. Each god had their own name and specific personality. They were highly individualistic and represented by different clothing, objects, or animals. Some gods changed over time to adopt new personalities or took on a different meaning. For example, the goddess Neith was a war goddess who eventually became a nurturing mother goddess who settled the gods' disputes.

Statue of Horus, Isis, and Osiris.
Metropolitan Museum of Art, CC0, via Wikimedia Commons;
https://commons.wikimedia.org/wiki/File:Isis,_Osiris_and_Horus_triad_MET_23.6.11_001.jpg

Some of the most important gods were Isis, Osiris, Horus, Amun, Ra, Hathor, Neith, Sekhmet, Bastet, Thoth, Anubis, Seth, and Ptah. Isis, Osiris, and Horus were frequently depicted in carvings, and their myth dictated the basis of pharaonic authority and the Egyptian afterlife. Hathor was a goddess strongly associated with entertainment; she was the goddess of dancing, drunkenness, and music. She was also the reflection of the Nile River and was originally known as Sekhmet, a destructive goddess who was also associated with Bastet.

Amun or Amun-Ra was another fascinating Egyptian god. At first, he was a minor god, but by the New Kingdom, he was almost exclusively worshiped throughout Egypt and became known as the most powerful of the gods. His priesthood was extremely influential. Specific royal women were appointed as the God's Wife of Amun, which was such a powerful position that it made her almost as powerful as the pharaoh. Sometimes, the Egyptians adopted other gods, such as Anat, the goddess of fertility, sexuality, and war. Anat was originally worshiped in Syria and Canaan but eventually was worshiped in Egypt and became Seth's consort.

The Afterlife

Death was an important part of Egyptian life, as the Egyptians believed their souls lived on after death. This belief caused the Egyptians to build elaborate tombs, craft grave goods (items that were taken with the deceased to the next life), and give offerings to the dead. According to ancient Egyptian mythology, all humans possessed ka, or life essence, which left the body after death. In order to survive in the afterlife, the ka had to consume the life essence of food offerings left by family members. Funeral rites were conducted to release a person's personality so that it could rejoin their ka. Mummification was also an important part of religion, as it was believed that a person's body needed to be kept intact in order to be transported to the afterlife.

Judgment of the dead before Osiris.
https://commons.wikimedia.org/wiki/File:The_judgement_of_the_dead_in_the_presence_of_Osiris.jpg

Once a person's heart was weighed on the scales in front of Osiris, they were either allowed to pass into the afterlife or be devoured by the devourer of souls, Ammit. If a person passed into the afterlife, they were met by a divine ferryman who carried them across Lily Lake into the Field of Reeds. The Field of Reeds was the Egyptian paradise, where everything was like it was on Earth except for sickness, death, and disappointment. However, a person had to pass Osiris's judgment by living a good life in order to enter the Field of Reeds. A lesser goddess known as Amentet met the dead souls as they arrived in the afterlife and provided them with food and drink. Hathor also played a role in the afterlife, as she guided the dead to paradise.

The Cults of Alexander and Serapis

When Ptolemy I began ruling Egypt, he realized that one way to unite the Greeks and Egyptians was through religion. As a result, he created the cults of Alexander and Serapis. The cult of Alexander worshiped the recently deceased Alexander the Great, who was seen as a mighty conqueror and hero. The Egyptians were immensely fond of Alexander, which made it easier for his cult to gain popularity. Ptolemy I constructed a magnificent tomb for Alexander the Great and appointed a priest to perform religious rites at the tomb. This priest became the most important priest in Egypt, and Alexander's tomb became an influential pilgrimage site. Eventually, the Ptolemies associated themselves with the cult, and deceased Ptolemies became gods as well. This enhanced their prestige and firmly established their position over the Egyptians.

Meanwhile, Serapis was a blend of Egyptian and Greek gods, namely Osiris, Apis, and Zeus. This selection was meant to represent the diverse population of Egypt. Serapis had similar powers to Osiris and Apis, which gave him certain transformative abilities, and he had the same authority as Zeus, who was seen as the king of the Greek gods. The cult of Serapis wasn't very popular in Egypt, but it soon spread to Rome and Greece.

Judaism in Egypt

Some of the earliest evidence of Judaism in Egypt can be dated back to around 650 BCE. Around 597 BCE, a large number of Judeans took refuge in Egypt when their governor was assassinated. During the Ptolemaic era, a large number of Jews immigrated to

Egypt and settled in Alexandria. By the 3rd century, Jews were living in a number of Egyptian cities and villages and were allowed to exist peacefully in Egypt as they opened businesses and took part in trade. The Ptolemies assigned the Jews a section of the city, as they eventually made up a large number of Alexandria's population. This allowed the Jews to keep their religious practices free from pagan influences. In Alexandria, Jews enjoyed political freedom and lived alongside other religious groups.

In Hellenistic Alexandria, the Jewish community was able to translate the Old Testament into Greek, which came to be known as the Septuagint. However, when Christianity gained popularity in Alexandria during the Byzantine era, the Jews were expelled from the city around 415 CE by Saint Cyril. According to contemporary historians, the Jews were forced to leave the city after a series of controversies and an alleged Jewish-led massacre. During the medieval period, Jews were allowed to live alongside Christians and Muslims, although there were several periods of persecution.

The Spread of Christianity

Christianity began to spread in Egypt in the 1st century CE and quickly became a popular religion, as it appealed to people from all walks of life. It caused the rapid decline of the traditional pagan religion, which had been around for about three thousand years. By the 4th century, Christianity was the most prominent religion in Egypt, and by the 5th century, the Coptic Church had been established. Traditionally, the spread of Christianity in Egypt has been accredited to Saint Mark, but he may have been helped by the missionary Apollos. The Coptic Church had a definite impact on Egyptian culture and art. While Egypt had been conquered by other foreign powers, those empires didn't have much of an impact on Egyptian culture, but Christianity was embraced by the Egyptians, changing many aspects of Egyptian life.

Egypt also played a massive role in the worldwide spread of Christianity. Egypt had a diverse population and received visitors from all over the world due to its intellectual community. The bishops of Egypt played a leading role in developing Christian doctrine, and soon, the religion was influenced by Egyptian beliefs and practices. Monasteries replaced temples and priesthoods as the focal point of daily Egyptian life. However, Christians weren't always left in peace. The Romans allowed conquered lands to keep their religions as long as they recognized the Roman emperor as one of their gods, which the Christians refused to do. This often put them at odds with the Roman Empire, as their refusal to worship the Roman emperor was seen as an act of defiance. During the early years of Christianity, most of the known world was more familiar with polytheism, which made it hard for others to understand the concept of exclusive devotion to one supreme ruler.

Diocletian's Persecution of Christians

Diocletian was the Roman emperor who ruled from 286 to 305 CE. He hoped to reach a compromise with the Christians and declared that he was the son of Jupiter (the king of the Roman gods) and that he was Jupiter's apostle on Earth. This story was likely concocted in an effort to align himself with Christian beliefs, especially with regard to the significance of God's son, Jesus Christ. However, the Christians refused to accept Diocletian's new status and rejected his compromise. While Diocletian was an adept ruler, he was egotistical and took this refusal as an insult. As a result, Diocletian began persecuting Christians throughout the Roman Empire.

The Egyptian Church called this age of persecution the Age of Martyrs due to the number of Christians who were brutally martyred and killed. Thousands were tortured by Roman legions before being murdered, and churches were destroyed, looted, and burned to the ground. Diocletian expected these new acts to force Christianity into extinction. Instead, the persecution only strengthened the zeal of the Christians, and larger numbers began converting to the religion. The early Christians were forced into Roman temples, where they were supposed to worship the statues of Roman gods.

Despite the threat of severe punishment, Christians clung to their beliefs. At first, this surprised Diocletian, but eventually, their defiance enraged him, which led to more atrocities. It was a bloody and violent time for the Romans, but eventually, support for the persecution waned. When Diocletian retired in 305 CE, his persecution ended too. Christians were allowed worship in peace, as Diocletian was the last Roman emperor to severely persecute the

Christians. In 306 CE, Constantine became emperor of the Byzantine Empire, and he converted to Christianity. Eventually, Christianity became the Byzantine national religion.

The Spread of Islam

Following the death of Prophet Muhammad, the caliphates were created. They quickly began conquering territories and took the message of their religion with them, which caused Islam to spread to the newly acquired territories. As soon as areas converted, the army was joined by new recruits who were zealous to support the cause. Islam was able to spread quickly because its army kept growing, and eventually, the Islamic Empire grew to hold a significant amount of territory. The most significant time of expansion took place during the Rashidun Caliphate in around 632 CE. During the Rashidun Caliphate, Egypt was conquered and brought under the caliphate's authority, which ruled over Egypt for hundreds of years.

The Rashidun Caliphate based its rule on Islamic principles and brought Muslim economics and trading with them. They were responsible for starting the Islamic Golden Age and introducing a new era of gunpowder warfare. By the 7th century, many Egyptians had converted to Islam, replacing Christianity as the state religion. The Islamic world was diverse and led to the creation of centers of culture and science. Trade also boomed, as the Muslim world traded resources and developed diplomatic relationships based on their religion. Several dynasties rose to dominance, but the massive ruling caliphate was soon replaced by smaller, regional caliphates, such as the Fatimid Caliphate in Egypt. This change had massive consequences for Egypt, as the former ruling caliphs belonged to the Sunni branch of Islam, while the Fatimids belonged to the Shia branch of Islam.

Islam during the Fatimid Caliphate

The Shia and Sunni branches of Islam share many similarities; for instance, they all accept the importance of the Quran, they both draw from the Hadith, and they accept the five pillars of Islam. However, their main differences center around the question of religious authority, and their split occurred shortly after the death of Prophet Muhammad. When the prophet died, there were serious questions about who would be his successor. Some preferred his cousin, Ali, and they later formed the Shia branch of Islam. Meanwhile, the Sunni followed the prophet's closest friend, Abu Bakr. The Sunni base their worship on the example of Prophet Muhammad, while the Shia focus on Muhammad's successors in the form of imams (religious instructors), who are thought to be divinely appointed.

The Fatimids were firmly Shia Muslims and were determined to bring an end to the Abbasid Caliphate, as they hoped to become the rulers of the Muslim world. This would allow them to impose their belief system on other Muslims and finally settle the matter of Prophet Muhammad's succession. Despite this goal, the Fatimids are known for being remarkably tolerant toward all religions. They allowed Christians, Jews, and Sunni Muslims to advance within the government and valued certain women's rights. The Fatimids used Egypt as their base and promoted religious scholarship and Egypt's economy. Their rule was a time of cultural enlightenment and advancement in Egypt. However, many of their policies were reversed by Saladin when he conquered the region.

Modern Egyptian Religion

The Egyptian state religion is still Islam, and the country remains firmly embedded in the Muslim world. The population is primarily made up of Sunni Muslims who follow the Maliki school of thought. However, the state is also comprised of Shia Muslims, Christians, and Jews, who together make up about 10 percent of the population. Egypt remains a diverse country with a wide array of Islamic views. There are sporadic reports of religious intolerance, but this is true in most countries.

Chapter 12: Language, Art, and Architecture

As soon as the Egyptian civilization developed, its culture grew along with its population. The ancients found ways to make sense of the world around them, which influenced everything from their beliefs to their architecture. Ancient Egyptian culture was so strong that we still see echoes of it thousands of years later. By taking a look at the fascinating art, architecture, and literature left behind by the ancient Egyptians, we can gain a unique perspective on their lives. Thousands of artifacts were left behind in sealed tombs, which provide scholars with ample evidence of what the Egyptian culture looked like before it was influenced by foreign conquerors.

When powerful empires invaded and took over Egypt, they left their mark on Egyptian culture. While some foreign rulers allowed the Egyptian culture to stagnate, others took a keen interest in the land of pharaohs and made valuable contributions to Egypt's language and art.

Hieroglyphics

The first evidence of hieroglyphic script can be traced back to around 3100 BCE, just as Egypt developed its unique pyramid-like social structure. While the script uses pictures, the pictures don't always mean what they represent. Rather, hieroglyphs depict certain sounds in the ancient Egyptian language, just as the characters in modern alphabets represent sounds. Hieroglyphs were first used in royal tombs to leave a record of the king's life and deeds. In time, other Egyptians began using hieroglyphs, but hieroglyphs remained the primary script for royal tombs and monuments. While hieroglyphs are intimately associated with Egyptian culture, most Egyptians didn't use hieroglyphs or understand what they meant. Since hieroglyphs were difficult to create, the Egyptians developed hieratic writing, which was a type of cursive script. Later, demotic writing was developed for ordinary documents.

Egyptian hieroglyphs.

Hosni bin Park, CC BY-SA 4.0 https://creativecommons.org/licenses/by-sa/4.0 via Wikimedia Commons; https://commons.wikimedia.org/wiki/File:Egyptian_hieroglyphics.jpg

In ancient Egypt, hieroglyphs weren't common among the lower classes, which meant that only priests were able to read them. Ordinary people were taught demotic instead. In time, hieroglyphs died out as the pharaohs were replaced by foreign rulers. The Ptolemies made Greek the official court language, and in 384 CE, the Roman emperor outlawed the Egyptian pagan religion, which caused hieroglyphs to die out. The Rosetta Stone eventually allowed historians to decipher hieroglyphics, but it's still a tricky endeavor. The Egyptian verbal system was never fully written out, and hieroglyphics contain many quirks, which makes them difficult to translate. The translation of hieroglyphs can also be subjective, which has led to a lot of confusion in the scholarly community.

Ancient Egyptian Tombs

The Egyptians were extremely concerned about preserving their bodies after death and ensuring they had a successful transition from the living world to the afterlife. As a result, the first kings of Egypt began building elaborate tombs, which were filled with everything they felt they needed in the afterlife. The first of these tombs were called mastabas. These tombs usually had inscriptions with the king's name. The mastabas were cut into rocky outcrops and featured sunbaked bricks and wooden boards. It's possible that when a king died, a large number of servants were sacrificed so they could serve the king in his afterlife. This practice is evidenced by a large number of graves containing women and dwarves that have been found around the mastabas. The royal tombs were also filled with jars, furniture, and various offerings that were buried with the king so that he could maintain his luxurious lifestyle in the afterlife.

Eventually, royal tombs and monuments became more elaborate, which led to the construction of large pyramids. However, grave robbing became prevalent, which was a serious concern for the royal family. If their tombs were plundered, they would be stranded in the afterlife without all their riches. As a result, the royals of the New Kingdom chose a new remote location for their tombs, which became known as the Valley of the Kings.

The Pyramids of Giza

The Egyptian rulers had good reason to worry about their afterlife. They believed they would be gods and rulers in the next life, which meant they had to prepare their tombs with everything they would need to be good leaders. As a result, the construction of royal tombs was a matter of national importance. Pharaoh Khufu was the first king to build his pyramid at Giza, beginning the project around 2550 BCE. The pyramid is a magnificent building made up of about 2.3 million stone blocks and stands at about 481 feet (147 meters). Khufu's pyramid is the biggest as well. Khafre, Khufu's successor, followed his father's example and built his pyramid at Giza too. He may also have been responsible for the Sphinx, which watches over the grand complex. Finally, the last pyramid at Giza was built by Menkaure around 2490 BCE. While Menkaure's pyramid isn't as big as the others, it has an intricate mortuary complex.

The Pyramids of Giza
Walkerssk, CC0, via Wikimedia Commons;
https://commons.wikimedia.org/wiki/File:Pyramids_in_Giza_-_Egypt.jpg

The pyramids were meant to be more than just tombs and were built on a massive complex that featured temples and palaces. Since the pyramids were a matter of national importance, ordinary Egyptians contributed to the projects. Historians have found evidence of a temporary city that showed the workers of the pyramids were generally happy and well-fed. It also seems that skilled workers volunteered to be part of the pharaohs' projects.

The Temple at Saqqara

The temple complex at Saqqara may be one of Egypt's most famous and important archaeological sites. Saqqara is south of Cairo and is marked by the Step Pyramid, which was built by Djoser during the Old Kingdom. The Step Pyramid is also the oldest known stone building complex in history. There are several other important pyramids and tombs at the site, which is about five miles long. Historians have found thousands of artifacts at the site, which give them an invaluable glimpse into ancient Egyptian life. The necropolis has also revealed "mega-tombs," which contained hundreds of coffins, mummies, and mummified cats. Burial goods, such as portrait masks, gems, and artworks, have also been uncovered at Saqqara.

The site has a large number of underground caverns, which were used for burials but have been looted as time passed. Saqqara first attracted scholarly attention around 1850 when it was discovered by Auguste Mariette, a French Egyptologist. According to his report, the site had been looted, as he found mummy wrappings lying in the sand. He was the first to note the significance of the sphinx-lined street that led to the Serapeum, an important temple at Saqqara. The temple was also the burial place of the Apis cult's bulls, which represented the gods Osiris and Ptah. For three thousand years, Saqqara served as the site of important non-royal burials and religious ceremonies. It became a UNESCO World Heritage Site in 1979.

The Great Sphinx in Gaza

The Great Sphinx is one of Egypt's most famous and recognizable monuments. Sphinxes were mythological creatures with the body of a lion and the head of a human. The Great Sphinx was cut from limestone and stands at about 66 feet (20 meters) high and is 240 feet (73 meters) long. The face of the Sphinx seems to represent Pharaoh Khafre, but its nose was broken off sometime between the 3rd and 10th century CE. Despite the mystery of what happened to its nose, the Great Sphinx is known as the oldest monumental sculpture in Egypt and is certainly a unique piece of architecture that has endured for thousands of years.

The Great Sphinx.
Hamerani, CC BY-SA 4.0 https://creativecommons.org/licenses/by-sa/4.0 *via Wikimedia Commons;* https://commons.wikimedia.org/wiki/File:Great_Sphinx_of_Giza_(2).jpg

The construction of the Great Sphinx has been a source of fascination and mystery for hundreds of years. It appears that the Sphinx was made from the same stones that were used to build the pyramids and may have originated from the same quarry. Some historians have suggested that the head was carved first out of a large rock that had already been shaped by the wind. The Sphinx's body was made out of the same stones that were used to build the temple that stands in front of it. Strangely, the temple was never completed, and there's no evidence that there was ever a sphinx cult in Egypt. It's possible that Khafre built the Great Sphinx in order to protect the Saqqara complex, which was an important site in ancient Egypt.

Fortresses

Egypt was an extremely fertile and profitable region, which meant that it attracted the attention of neighboring countries that would have seen the value of invading the country and adding its riches to their own nation. As a result, the pharaohs of Egypt had to be constantly on guard. In order to keep their nation safe, the pharaohs built fortresses, border posts, and walls to protect areas that were vulnerable to attack. Most pharaohs concentrated on defending the territories they already had, which means that for most of Egypt's history, it didn't have a standing army. The ancient Egyptians spent a lot of time and effort building and maintaining border fortresses that kept them safe from the threat of invasion.

One of the most important fortresses was built between the Second and First Cataracts of the Nile and was called Buhen. It served as an Egyptian outpost as early as around 2770 BCE and became an important fortress during the New Kingdom. The complex was made up of massive outer walls, interior temples, and bastions, which were common features of ancient Egyptian fortresses. Buhen was made out of rocks and bricks and was built along the river and a rocky slope. In order to prevent invaders from scaling it, a steep ditch was carved into the rock. Hatshepsut built a temple in the southern part of Buhen, and later pharaohs either renovated the site or added their own shrines.

Ramesses II, or Ramesses the Great, was also known for building extensively, and he built a number of fortresses along Egypt's northwestern coast.

New Kingdom Temples and Tombs

The New Kingdom was known as Egypt's golden age. As Egypt gained more influence and wealth due to its foreign conquests, the pharaohs were able to build on a much larger and grander scale than ever before. Hatshepsut, in particular, was known for building incredible structures that were unlike anything that had been built in Egypt before. The Temple of Hatshepsut was the queen's mortuary temple and features a stunning colonnaded structure that predates the Parthenon. It was built into a cliff face and houses a series of terraces that were once filled with cultivated gardens.

Ramesses II was another great builder. He constructed the Tomb of Nefertari in the Valley of the Kings, as well as the Ramesseum. The Tomb of Nefertari features stunning wall paintings, and the Ramesseum features enormous carvings that depict highlights from the king's reign.

Luxor Temple.

Important New Kingdom temples include the Luxor Temple. This complex was built near the ancient city of Thebes and featured six massive temples. The temples contain many examples of illusionism and symbolism, which were prevalent in ancient Egyptian architecture. For example, two obelisks were built to emphasize a pathway and give the illusion that they're the same height even though they aren't. The temples at Karnak are another important ancient site. They were used to worship the god Amun, whose priesthood wielded incredible influence in Egypt. The complex is now the biggest ancient religious site in the world and a popular museum.

Copts

The Copts are Egypt's largest indigenous Christian community and have existed in Egypt ever since the original spread of Christianity. The Coptic Orthodox Church remains the largest Christian church in Egypt. Before the spread of Islam, Egyptians spoke a form of language called Coptic. However, Muslim Egyptians eventually stopped using Coptic, and it came to identify the Christian minority. The Coptic dialect family descended from the ancient Egyptian language and emerged around the 3rd century CE. It quickly became the most popular language in Egypt, as it spread throughout the country along with Christianity. The language bore many Greek influences and was written using the Coptic alphabet, which was a mixture of the Greek and demotic scripts.

Some of the oldest Coptic scripts predate the Christian era and are written in Old Coptic. However, most Coptic literature features texts that were written by members of the Coptic Church, who later became saints. Shenoute was a saint known for popularizing and improving Coptic through his homilies, sermons, and treatises, which make up a large portion of early Coptic literature. For several centuries, Christianity was Egypt's main religion, and it had a massive influence on Egyptian art and led to distinct buildings and artworks.

Coptic Art and Architecture

When Roman Emperor Theodosius outlawed pagan religions, Christianity became the national Egyptian religion. Egypt was forever changed. The Coptic Christians often transformed existing ancient temples, tombs, and shrines into monasteries, churches, and martyrs' shrines. Christians from all over the Byzantine Empire visited the significant holy sites associated with the saints, and the Bible was translated into Coptic, which led to the development of original Egyptian Christian literature. Coptic churches were lavishly decorated with colorful murals, natural motifs, and inscriptions of Bible extracts, psalms, and monastic accounts. Gravestones were often decorated with crosses, doves, and foliage patterns.

Saint Mark's Coptic Orthodox Cathedral, Egypt.

Floral and faunal motifs became popular themes in Coptic architecture, as they often represented paradise. Pottery also bore similar markings and featured inscriptions from the Bible. The Copts built great cathedrals, such as Saint Mark's Coptic Orthodox Cathedral. Monasteries also became popular, and many ancient monasteries, such as the Monastery of Saint Anthony, still exist in Egypt. Some Coptic cathedrals shared similar floor plans and architectural elements with earlier temples. For example, some churches had a hidden inner sanctuary, which was a common feature in Egyptian temples. However, Coptic churches were eventually influenced by Byzantine architecture. As the centuries progressed, Coptic buildings began to show evidence of Islamic influence.

Arabic

When the Rashidun Caliphate arrived in Egypt in the 7th century, Coptic was the national Egyptian language, although Greek was still used for administrative matters. While Coptic and

Greek were widely used, they were still relatively new languages. Greek had been introduced as a state language by the Ptolemies but was mainly used by statesmen and foreign merchants. Christianity gained traction in Egypt around the 4th and 5th centuries, which caused a massive shift from classical Greek practices and religion. By 451 CE, there was a massive divide between the Egyptian and Greek churches, which put an even greater distance between the Egyptians and Greeks. While Coptic was the main literary language in Egypt, it was still a relatively new language since it was a unique blend of Greek and ancient Egyptian.

Coptic remained popular in Egypt even under Arabic rule, as it was the sole language of the church. For the first century or so of Arabic rule, Arabic was still reserved for Arab immigrants, government officials, and the ruling elite. Eventually, a large number of Arabs moved to Egypt, and the Islamic rulers were forced to defeat a Coptic peasant revolt. In time, many Egyptians converted to Islam, and the Copts were forced to pay excessive tax rates. By the 8th and 9th centuries, most Egyptians were speaking Arabic, and it became the primary language in the country. In modern times, the national language of Egypt is Modern Standard Arabic, which is a standardized literary version of Arabic. It was developed during the 19th and 20th centuries and conformed to a written standard.

Islamic Art and Architecture

During early Islamic rule in Egypt, Cairo became the center of administration and religion. As a result, it became home to some of the most magnificent examples of Islamic architecture in the world. Islamic art is intricately tied to the religion and usually represents the principle of divine unity. Calligraphy is extremely popular, as it is used to write out portions of the Quran. Mosques are probably the first thing that comes to people's minds when they think of Islamic architecture. Over time, Egypt's architecture began bearing Ayyubid, Fatimid, Mamluk, Ottoman, and other modern styles, which reflected the styles of each ruling class and their periods.

The Mosque of Ibn Tulun.

One of the most stunning examples of Islamic architecture in Cairo is the Mosque of Ibn Tulun. Ibn Tulun set up a ruling dynasty in Egypt after he was sent there to serve as a governor in Fustat. The mosque was built to resemble the great mosque in Samarra, Iraq, which was Ibn Tulun's childhood home. It also featured elements of Spanish architecture. Egypt is also home to the ancient Mosque of Amr ibn al-As, which was built just a few years after the death of Prophet Muhammad and shortly after the Islamic conquest of Egypt. The Mosque of Amr ibn al-As was the oldest mosque in Africa; it has been rebuilt several times over the centuries.

Besides mosques, madrasas and minarets came to dominate the Egyptian skyline. In fact, Cairo has so many minarets that the city is known as "the City of a Thousand Minarets."

SECTION FOUR: Key Figures in Egyptian History

Chapter 13:
Tutankhamun and his Cursed Tomb (1341–1327 BC)

King Tutankhamun is one of the most famous Egyptian rulers of all time. Unlike many of his predecessors, he isn't famous for his mighty military conquests or prosperous reign; rather, he is widely recognized because of his tomb. When Tutankhamun was still a young boy, he inherited a country that had been plunged into chaos because of his father's fanaticism. The boy king worked with experienced advisors to correct the nation's course. However, those advisors had their own agendas, which would soon become evident when Tutankhamun died. In keeping with the traditions of Egyptian monarchs, Tutankhamun was mummified and placed in a tomb full of riches. Unfortunately, he was placed in a makeshift tomb that was a far cry from the tombs of his predecessors.

Tutankhamun was forgotten by history, as he was replaced by his vizier, Ay, and later by General Horemheb. It wasn't until a British Egyptologist named Howard Carter uncovered the king's tomb in 1922 that Tutankhamun's story was revealed to the world. His tomb was filled with incredible archaeological discoveries, but it soon became the center of rumors and controversy as a supposed curse ripped through Howard Carter's team. Over the next few decades, Tutankhamun's story would fascinate the world as his tomb revealed the secrets of ancient Egyptian politics. Experts have also worked to find the truth behind the fatal "curse."

Tutankhamun's Parents

Akhenaten was a pharaoh during the Eighteenth Dynasty of the New Kingdom. He was the son of the great king Amenhotep III and his wife, Tiye. At first, Akhenaten was known as Amenhotep IV, but he later changed his name to Akhenaten in order to show honor to the god Aten. He was also the husband of the legendary queen Nefertiti, who was known for her capabilities as a ruler and her beauty. During the last years of Amenhotep III's reign, his son ruled as co-regent in order to learn the intricacies of ruling Egypt.

Akhenaten and his family worshiping Aten

Romagy, CC BY-SA 4.0 https://creativecommons.org/licenses/by-sa/4.0 *via Wikimedia Commons;* https://commons.wikimedia.org/wiki/File:Akhenaten_and_the_his_family_worshipping_the_Aten.jpg

However, soon after Akhenaten converted to monotheism, he lost interest in ruling and became obsessed with Aten's religious cult. This meant that his advisors and main wife, Nefertiti, had to pick up the slack and were forced to rule on his behalf. There is some evidence that he occasionally participated in state affairs, but for the most part, he neglected Egypt. Akhenaten was known as a family man and may have had seven or eight children by different wives. Records show that toward the end of his reign, Akhenaten was ruling with a co-regent, possibly his wife Nefertiti or his daughter, Meritaten.

There was some dispute about Tutankhamun's mother, as some thought that Nefertiti was his mother while others believed that his mother was Meketaten, the daughter of Akhenaten and Nefertiti. However, all those claims were proved false when three female mummies were discovered in Amenhotep II's tomb. DNA testing showed that one of the mummies, nicknamed "the Younger Lady," was Akhenaten's sister and Tutankhamun's mother. In 2013, an Egyptologist named Marc Gabolde challenged that theory. He claimed that further DNA testing proved that the Younger Lady was Nefertiti's daughter. In time, historians may find Nefertiti's body and prove that she was Tutankhamun's true mother.

Early Life

As with most monarchies, the Egyptians were very careful when it came to the line of succession. Toward the end of Akhenaten's life, it seems that his duties had been assumed by either one or two co-regents. Not much is known about these co-regents, and their names only appear on a few monuments in Akhetaten that have been dated to the very end of Akhenaten's reign. The inscription refers to Smenkhkare, who shared the coronation name Ankhkheperure with an individual called Neferneferuaten. In ancient Egypt, coronation names were unique to one ruler and weren't shared. This has led many to believe that Smenkhkare may have really been Neferneferuaten (Nefertiti's full name). It's clear that a co-regent was appointed during the last years of Akhenaten's reign. The co-regent ruled for a short period after Akhenaten's death since Tutankhamun was only a child at the time.

Carving of Tutankhamun

Harry Burton (1879-1940), Public domain, via Wikimedia Commons;
https://commons.wikimedia.org/wiki/File:Tutankhamun_tomb_photographs_4_326.jpg

Some historians believe that Smenkhkare may have been Akhenaten's oldest daughter, Meritaten. It isn't clear if she was elevated to this position through marriage to her father or if she was simply given the position. Still, some suggest that Smenkhkare may have been Meritaten's husband. A few scholars have theorized that Smenkhkare could have been one of Akhenaten's sons and that Smenkhkare and Tutankhamun were brothers. The evidence of co-regents suggests that attempts were made to hold the throne until Tutankhamun was old enough to rule. Since not much is known about Smenkhkare, it isn't known how the co-regent's rule ended, but shortly after Akhenaten's death, nine-year-old

Tutankhamun became king.

Reign

Tutankhamun inherited the throne around 1333 BCE and promptly married his sister, Ankhesenamun, who was probably his oldest surviving sister. He took on the coronation name of Nebkheperure. Due to his age, he ruled alongside two advisors, Ay and Horemheb. Ay was an accomplished courtier who had long held close ties to the royal family, while Horemheb was a capable military man who had proven himself on the field of battle. Tutankhamun had been named Tutankhaten at birth, but after three years of ruling, he named himself Tutankhamun and moved the royal capital from Akhetaten back to Memphis. It was a decisive move that separated his reign from his father's. Tutankhamun restored the old gods and began restoring the cult of Amun.

During his reign, he also built a temple in Thebes, a palace at Karnak, and added the Colonnade of the Temple of Luxor. Unfortunately, the temple and Karnak were destroyed sometime after his reign. Tutankhamun and Ankhesenamun had two daughters, but the children were stillborn and may have died as a result of complications caused by incest. While Tutankhamun only ruled for about nine years, it's clear that he put a lot of effort into reversing his father's religious policies.

Death

Since Tutankhamun became more famous after his tomb was found, it's only natural that people would be fascinated by the cause of his death. Historians don't agree about what may have killed the king, which has led to the development of several theories. It has been discovered that Tutankhamun was relatively tall but suffered from a terrible bone disease that resulted in a club foot. He probably wasn't a strong child and may have been sickly. Surprisingly, scholars found a hole in the back of his skull, which led many to believe that the young king had been assassinated. This theory was overturned recently when it was revealed that the hole was likely made during the mummification process.

Tests have shown that the king's left leg was broken and infected. The king had multiple malaria infections, all of which could have killed him. CT scans revealed that the young king had a curved spine, a long head, and a cleft palate. His upper vertebrae were fused, which may have made the king's life difficult. Some scholars have theorized that Tutankhamun was involved in a chariot crash that left his legs and pelvis broken. He then contracted an infection that poisoned his blood and killed him.

Unfortunately, experts are unable to tell which of Tutankhamun's bones were broken during his life and what damage was caused by Howard Carter's team. Tutankhamun was buried with several necklaces and rings, which were all removed by Carter's team. The removal process damaged the fragile mummy, which has made identifying his cause of death extremely difficult. It's possible that scholars may never discover what killed the young king, but they certainly won't stop trying to find out.

The Race to Bury King Tutankhamun

While it's not clear why Tutankhamun died, it is clear that he died suddenly and without warning. The line of succession was hazy, and it seems that Horemheb may have been Tutankhamun's accepted successor since he may have had the title of "Crown Prince." Historians theorize that Horemheb had been appointed as Tutankhamun's heir in case the king died without one. As soon as Tutankhamun died, the Egyptian court was plunged into turmoil. Horemheb was in Asia with the Egyptian army and turned back to Egypt as soon as he heard the news, but he would only be able to return after a few months. Ay was still at court and set his sights on becoming king. In order to do that, he would have to be the one to bury the young pharaoh. Ay also had to deal with an unexpected challenge.

Tutankhamun burial chamber.

Tutankhamun's widow, Ankhesenamun, quickly established herself as a contender for the throne, as she may have petitioned the Hittite king to allow her to marry his son. Hittite records indicate that the Hittites received an urgent letter from an Egyptian queen named Nibkhururiya. She begged the Hittite king to send her one of his sons so that she could marry him. The Hittites sent an emissary who returned with another urgent plea and several assurances. If Ankhesenamun truly intended to become queen of Egypt in her own right, her plan would have been abominable to the Egyptians, as it would have been a breach of ma'at to have a foreign king on the throne. The Hittite prince never arrived in Egypt, and it's possible that he was murdered by Ay. There is also evidence that Nefertiti may have been the queen who begged the Hittites for a husband.

While the royal family and courtiers squabbled for dominance, the matter of Tutankhamun's tomb had to be solved. Since the king died before his official tomb was completed, a private tomb was found in the Valley of the Kings and quickly converted. It would appear as though some of Tutankhamun's burial gifts were rushed, and his mummification process may also have been sped up since his skull was likely damaged shortly after his death. In time, the location of Tutankhamun's tomb was lost, and workmen's huts were built over the entrance.

Successors

According to ancient records, it appears that Ay served Akhenaten in Akhetaten as one of his courtiers. Ay likely began his civil service in the military and eventually became the master of the horse and troop leader. Sometime during his career, he became an exceptionally close friend to the royal family. His wife, Tey, also became one of Nefertiti's nurses. It has been suggested that Ay and Tey were Nefertiti's parents, although that claim would be difficult to prove. As soon as Akhenaten died, Ay became one of Tutankhamun's closest advisors and may have led the young king to reverse many of Akhenaten's policies.

Soon after Tutankhamun died, Ay became the king of Egypt, doing so around 1323 BCE. He may have taken the young king's tomb and mortuary temple for himself, as his tomb was much more luxurious than Tutankhamun's. Scholars have found several artifacts bearing the names of Ay and Ankhesenamun, which have led some to believe that Ay married Tutankhamun's widow, but there isn't much evidence to support that fact. While Ay won the throne, he died around 1319 BCE, leaving the throne to Horemheb.

Once Horemheb became king, he continued restoring the temples and cults of the old gods but also began erasing the names of his predecessors, namely, Ay, Tutankhamun, and Akhenaten. He carved his names over their monuments and combined the records of their reigns with his own reign. It's surprising that Horemheb chose to erase his predecessors from history since he was married to Mutnodjmet, who was likely related to the royal family. His marriage and relationship with Tutankhamun suggest that he was close to the royal family. Horemheb would be the last king of the Eighteenth Dynasty and was succeeded by his vizier, Ramesses I.

Howard Carter

Howard Carter was born on May 9th, 1874, in Swaffham, Norfolk, England. He was one of eleven children and showed great artistic talent, which prompted one of the family's neighbors, Lady Amherst, to arrange for Carter to go to Egypt. When he was seventeen years old, he participated in an archaeological survey of Egypt. While working on the survey, he proved his talent by adeptly copying tomb decorations. He later became the inspector general of the Egyptian antiquities department. In 1902, he helped discover the tombs of Hatshepsut and Thutmose IV. Carter kept a diary during his life, which provides an in-depth view of the excavations he oversaw and his discoveries.

During Carter's time as the inspector general, he oversaw numerous excavations and restorations in the Valley of the Kings. In 1904, he was transferred to Lower Egypt, where he was allowed to lead his own excavations. However, he resigned a year later after Egyptian site guards were involved in an altercation with French tourists. He chose to support the Egyptian guards and refused to apologize to the French. In 1907, he was tasked with supervising more excavations in the Valley of the Kings after he was sought out by the 5th Earl of Carnarvon.

Discovery of Tutankhamun's Tomb

Carter and Lord Carnarvon worked together for several seasons but were forced to take a break during World War I. As soon as they were able, they began excavations in the Valley of the Kings. The men soon found several pieces of evidence bearing Tutankhamun's name, which caused Carter to believe they were close to finding the king's tomb. Unfortunately, after years of searching, Carter only found ancient workmen's huts and a few calcite jars. Lord Carnarvon began to lose interest in Carter's theories, but Carter managed to convince the earl to support him for one more season.

Howard Carter examines Tutankhamun's sarcophagus.
https://commons.wikimedia.org/wiki/File:Tuts_Tomb_Opened.JPG

Carter's final season began on November 1st, 1922. He decided to excavate the workmen's huts, and by the time they were done exposing them, they found a step had been carved into the ground. The workers soon revealed a staircase that ended in a covered entrance that bore the seals of the royal necropolis. Later, Carnarvon arrived in Luxor, and the team was able to begin excavations on the tomb. It quickly became apparent that the tomb had been robbed twice after Tutankhamun had been buried, but the tomb had been resealed, which led the team to believe there was still something left. According to Carter's diary, he made a small hole in the tomb's entrance and conducted a few tests to make sure the air in the tomb was safe. Once he determined that it was, he peered into the hole and saw that the tomb was full of "wonderful things."

Contents of the Tomb

Tutankhamun's tomb was much smaller than those of other pharaohs, but due to its small size and obscure location, it was protected from grave robbers. While the entrance hall was plundered soon after his death, the tomb's inner chambers remained untouched. Carter's team found about 5,000 artifacts in the tomb, which included clothes, 130 walking sticks, chariots, furniture, and artwork. There were so many artifacts in the tomb that it took Carter and his team about a decade to fully document their findings.

Tutankhamun tomb photographs.
https://commons.wikimedia.org/wiki/File:Tutankhamun_tomb_photographs_2_026.jpg

One of the most astounding finds was the king's sarcophagus, which was made up of three coffins that all fit into each other. King Tut's coffin was made out of solid gold and still held his body. He was buried with golden statues and jewelry. While the treasures were astounding and certainly valuable, the archaeologists were extremely excited by the discovery of Tutankhamun's mummy. The tomb also contained an unusual dagger with a blade likely made from a meteorite. The objects of the tomb provided a rare glimpse into the lives of the pharaohs and allowed historians a closer glimpse into ancient Egyptian metalworking processes. Tutankhamun's grave goods also revealed the rushed nature of his burial since many of the items were originally meant for other recipients, namely Smenkhkare and Neferneferuaten.

Tutankhamun's Curse

Carter's discovery was impressive because most archaeologists believed that all the tombs in the Valley of the Kings had been completely plundered by grave robbers. When his discovery was announced, the news swept the world, and it became a sensational story. Tourists and reporters streamed to the tomb, and every time something was taken from the tomb, hundreds of cameras went off. During the initial months of the excavation, the tomb was the site of a media circus. As the news spread throughout the world, rumors of a curse were also reported.

Tourists and reporters outside Tutankhamun's tomb.
https://commons.wikimedia.org/wiki/File:Tourists_outside_Tutankhamun%27s_tomb,_February_1923.jpg

Several magazines and newspapers reported that "the most dire punishment follows any rash intruder into a sealed tomb." Shortly afterward, Lord Carnarvon died in Cairo, and the city experienced a blackout. This spurred more rumors, and Arthur Conan Doyle joined the fray by telling the press that an evil spirit had been created by the ancient Egyptian priests in order to protect the king. In the following years, the story was perpetuated when several notable people connected to the tomb's discovery died due to mysterious or violent causes. In 1923, Prince Ali Kamel Fahmy Bey was shot by his wife. In 1924, Sir Lee Stack (the governor-general of Sudan) was assassinated in Cairo. In 1928, Arthur Mace, a member of the excavation team, died of arsenic poisoning. In

1929, Richard Bethell, Carter's secretary, was smothered in his bed. And in 1939, Howard Carter died from Hodgkin's disease. While the rumors of a curse became synonymous with Tutankhamun's tomb, no mention of a curse was ever found in the tomb, and many people who were involved with the excavation lived long and happy lives.

Chapter 14: Hatshepsut and Cleopatra: Women in Power

Ancient Egypt was ruled by many powerful individuals who changed the course of history. Two of those rulers were women who came to rule Egypt in their own right by using tricky political situations to their advantage. Hatshepsut and Cleopatra weren't the first women to rule Egypt, but they were able to hold onto the throne for many years and left a lasting influence. Although their reigns were unusual for the time period, they were both successful rulers who managed to endear themselves to their subjects. The success of their reigns can be attributed to their skill, ingenuity, and creative problem-solving.

Hatshepsut was the legitimate heir to the throne and proved her capabilities by ruling on behalf of her ineffectual husband. She was eventually able to rule in her own right and came up with a creative way to maintain the Egyptian principle of harmony and balance, which required both a male and female ruler on the throne. Cleopatra, on the other hand, had to outsmart her family and navigate her way through a deadly political situation to secure the throne. Unfortunately, both women had their reputations tarnished, and their legacy had been obscured by time, rumors, and vindictive successors and scholars.

Hatshepsut's Rise to Power

Hatshepsut was born around 1504 BCE to Thutmose I and his wife, Ahmose. It seems that Hatshepsut was extremely proud of her father and even reburied him in her own grand tomb. She also claimed that he named her as his successor before he passed, but this was unlikely since female pharaohs were unheard of at the time. Thutmose I was a capable king who expanded Egypt's borders. He was famous for his military campaigns and allegedly sailed home to Thebes after a successful Nubian campaign with the naked body of a Nubian chief hanging from his ship.

Traditionally, the throne was passed from the pharaoh to his son. Usually, the honor went to the pharaoh's son by his queen, but if the queen didn't have a son, then the son of a secondary wife (a concubine in the harem) would be chosen. Ahmose seems to have provided Thutmose I with two sons, but they both died early. As a result, Thutmose I's heir was Thutmose II, his son by one of his secondary wives, Mutnofret. In order to strengthen Thutmose II's lineage, he married Hatshepsut when she was only twelve years old. Sculptures depicting her as Thutmose II's wife show her standing behind her husband.

However, Thutmose II was weak and couldn't live up to his father's legacy. As the queen of Egypt, Hatshepsut was elevated to the position of God's Wife of Amun. During her marriage, Hatshepsut gave birth to Neferure, a daughter and Hatshepsut's only known child.

As the God's Wife of Amun, Hatshepsut played a role in policy-making and presided over Amun's festivals. Although not much is known about her exact responsibilities, it is likely that she would have played an important role in Egyptian society and been worshiped as a divine being. She would also have been required to sing and dance for Amun at all his festivals in order to get him to take part in them. Her role as the God's Wife of Amun would have exposed her to the inner workings of the government.

Thutmose II died around 1479 BCE, and the throne was passed to Thutmose III, the son of one of Thutmose II's secondary wives. Hatshepsut was appointed as the prince's co-regent and was only supposed to rule until he was old enough to take the throne. This was a common practice in Egypt, as widowed queens would usually rule on behalf of their younger male relatives until they were old enough to rule alone. Although Hatshepsut was definitely ruling the kingdom, Thutmose III was recognized as the king of Egypt.

All that changed in the seventh year of her regency. She declared herself the pharaoh of Egypt and took on all the pharaoh's titles. While she still used feminine grammatical terms when she inscribed her titles, she began depicting herself with the male pharaonic beard. Thutmose III was displaced. He was depicted in carvings with Hatshepsut but was usually smaller than her or placed directly behind her. It was clear who was truly ruling the kingdom.

Reign

Hatshepsut realized that she would have to be creative in order to strengthen her rule since she had no precedent to follow. One of her first acts was to marry her daughter, Neferure, to Thutmose III and make Neferure the God's Wife of Amun. Her actions ensured that even if she was somehow deposed, she would still be one of the most powerful people in all of Egypt. She also claimed that the god Amun had visited Ahmose one night and tricked the queen into believing he was Thutmose I. When the god revealed himself to the queen, she was overcome, and they conceived Hatshepsut. She also claimed that Thutmose I had appointed her as his co-regent and that her reign had been prophesied by an oracle some eighty years earlier.

Hatshepsut statues, portrayed on the right with the pharaonic beard.

Hatshepsut's efforts succeeded, and she was the first woman to rule Egypt in her own right. Sobekneferu likely ruled before Hatshepsut, but it is hard to know in what capacity due to the lack of information. Hatshepsut launched various military campaigns and began numerous construction projects. She also relied heavily on one of her advisors, Senenmut. The courtier attained astonishing influence during Hatshepsut's reign and was placed in charge of all her construction projects. He was also tasked with taking care of Neferure. Hatshepsut proved to be a capable leader who brought prosperity to the country. She fostered new trade routes and was even able to launch her own expedition to the neighboring Kingdom of Punt. According to records, she returned with boats loaded with ivory, myrrh trees, exotic animals, and gold. She considered the expedition to be her greatest achievement and had the event carved into the walls of her mortuary temple. It was such a success that her popularity and influence were greatly increased.

Hatshepsut's Building Projects

Hatshepsut put a lot of effort into legitimizing her reign, and one of the ways she strengthened her position was by building extensively. Her projects provided many jobs for the common people, and they were incredibly beautiful. The fact that she was able to complete so many projects shows that she was responsible for all of Egypt's resources, as she wouldn't have been able to complete any of them without access to significant wealth. It also attests to the fact that the country must have been at peace during her reign since she wouldn't have been able to divert that many resources if she had been preoccupied with defending her orders or invading other countries.

Temple of Hatshepsut.

She was able to expand the temple at Karnak and build her grand mortuary temple at Deir el-Bahari. Scholars have noted that her temples were elegantly constructed. Hatshepsut's mortuary temple featured courtyards of trees, pools, and a terrace. One of the terraces was lined with columns that led to another impressive terrace. Her burial chamber was at the back of the building and carved into the mountain itself. The temple was decorated with inscriptions, statues, and reliefs. Hatshepsut was one of the first to build in the Valley of the Kings, and her temple inspired future pharaohs to also build their temples in the valley. Hatshepsut was a great patron of the arts. She commissioned so many pieces that almost every museum featuring ancient Egyptian art has a piece that was commissioned by her.

For most of Hatshepsut's reign, Thutmose III served as a general in the Egyptian army. Around 1457 BCE, Thutmose III went on a campaign to suppress a rebellion in Kadesh, which became known as the Battle of Megiddo. When he returned, he became king, and Hatshepsut disappeared from the ancient records. Hatshepsut had likely died by that point. However,

Thutmose III changed his regnal date to begin after the death of his father and took credit for all of Hatshepsut's accomplishments.

Cleopatra's Early Life

Cleopatra was born in 69 BCE and was named Cleopatra VII Philopator. Sometime during her youth, she became her father's co-regent. Cleopatra's father was Ptolemy XII Auletes, and her mother may have been Cleopatra V Tryphaena. In 51 BCE, Ptolemy XII died (likely of natural causes) and left eighteen-year-old Cleopatra the throne. Tradition dictated that she had to rule with a male counterpart, and she was married to her brother, Ptolemy XIII. However, she soon dropped his name from the official records and ruled in her own right.

Cleopatra proved to be a competent leader and a gifted polyglot. She was able to converse naturally in Egyptian, Greek, and several other languages. This allowed her to develop close relationships with diplomats. She was known for being charismatic. Plutarch reported that she personally worked with diplomats from "barbarian nations" without needing a translator. However, she soon caused friction with her own councilors since she often made decisions without consulting them. In 48 BCE, she was betrayed by her advisors when they led a coup against her and installed her brother on the throne. Cleopatra and her sister, Arsinoe, were forced to flee to safety.

Julius Caesar

Around this time, Pompey the Great (a Roman politician) was fighting against Julius Caesar. Pompey had spent a lot of time in Egypt and believed the Ptolemies were on his side. When he lost the Battle of Pharsalus, he fled to Egypt, hoping to gain sanctuary and support. As soon as he arrived in Alexandria, he was murdered on the shore, apparently as Ptolemy XIII watched. It's possible that Ptolemy XIII's chief advisor, Pothinus, advised the young king to murder Pompey, as it was believed that Julius's victory over Pompey was a sign of divine favor. Unfortunately for Ptolemy XIII, Julius Caesar was deeply offended by Pompey's murder. When he arrived in Alexandria, he declared martial law and made himself the interim ruler of Egypt, forcing Ptolemy XIII to flee to Pelusium.

Cleopatra welcoming Caesar.
https://commons.wikimedia.org/wiki/File:Cleopatra_welcoming_Caesar.jpg

When Cleopatra heard about the situation, she knew she had to gain favor with Julius Caesar. According to legend, Cleopatra rolled herself into an expensive rug and was carried into the palace. Julius Caesar was immediately smitten by the young woman, and the two became lovers. When Ptolemy XIII returned to his palace the next day, he found that Cleopatra had won over Caesar. As a result, war broke out between the Roman legions and the Egyptian army. During that time, Cleopatra and Caesar were forced to hide in the palace until Roman reinforcements arrived. The war took place in Alexandria, and the city was greatly damaged. More Roman soldiers arrived six months later, and their victory seemed inevitable. While Cleopatra likely felt secure in her position alongside Julius Caesar, she was about to be betrayed again, this time by the sister she had taken with her into exile.

Arsinoe

Sometime before the Roman victory, Arsinoe escaped from the palace and joined Ptolemy XIII. She was then proclaimed as the queen of Egypt in place of her older sister. This would have been a massive blow to Caesar's and Cleopatra's cause, as Ptolemy XII's will read that his successors would be his son and daughter, who ruled side by side. Arsinoe managed to turn the tide against the Romans and even trapped Caesar in a section of the city by blocking off certain streets. Afterward, her forces poured seawater into the Roman cisterns, which would have contaminated their freshwater supplies. Caesar attempted to launch an attack on the Lighthouse of Alexandria in an effort to gain the upper hand. Arsinoe's forces managed to trap him there, but he stripped off his armor and jumped into the harbor.

At one point during the war, Arsinoe was betrayed by her troops and given as a prisoner to Julius Caesar in exchange for Ptolemy XIII (who had been captured sometime during the fighting). Soon after, the Romans won the war, and Ptolemy XIII drowned in the Nile during a battle. In 46 BCE, Arsinoe was a part of Julius Caesar's victory parade in Rome. According to Roman tradition, she was supposed to be executed after the procession, but she won sympathy from the Romans, and Julius Caesar was forced to spare her life. Instead of allowing her to return to Egypt, where she would pose a threat to Cleopatra's rule, she was sent to the Temple of Artemis at Ephesus, which was a famous sanctuary for political prisoners. Arsinoe was murdered in 41 BCE when Mark Antony commissioned assassins to kill her. She was dragged out of the Temple of Artemis and strangled on the steps, which caused a massive scandal in Rome. The temple sanctuary was supposed to be sacred, and the murder was seen as an obscene violation of Roman law.

Reign

After Julius Caesar won the war in Alexandria, he restored Cleopatra to the throne. She was joined by her younger brother, Ptolemy XIV, who was thirteen years old at the time. He chose to stay in Egypt along with Cleopatra, and the two of them toured extensively throughout Egypt as Cleopatra established her authority. In 47 BCE, Cleopatra gave birth to Caesar's son,

Ptolemy Caesar (Caesarion), who became Cleopatra's heir. At this point, she began aligning her image with that of the mother goddess, Isis. Sometime around 45 BCE, Cleopatra traveled to Rome with Julius Caesar and remained there until Caesar was murdered in 44 BCE.

While Cleopatra was becoming popular in Egypt, she didn't gain much influence in Rome. Caesar had openly continued his relationship with Cleopatra despite being married to Calpurnia. He even publicly acknowledged that Caesarion was his son. The Romans had strict laws against bigamy, and Caesar's actions were highly unpopular. As a result, the Romans criticized Cleopatra harshly, and she gained few Roman allies. Sometime after Cleopatra returned to Egypt, Ptolemy XIV died (it's rumored that he was poisoned by Cleopatra), and Caesarion became Cleopatra's co-regent. At this point, she began representing herself as Isis and her son as Horus.

Mark Antony

After Julius Caesar was assassinated, Rome was plunged into a time of political chaos as the government tried to find a successor. Eventually, Mark Antony and Octavian emerged as Caesar's successors and became joint rulers of Rome. Mark Antony controlled the eastern part of the empire, while Octavian controlled the west. In 41 BCE, Antony summoned Cleopatra to Tarsus and planned to charge her with giving aid to Roman rebels. Cleopatra purposefully arrived late, and when she finally sailed into Tarsus, she presented herself as the goddess Aphrodite. She reportedly arrived in a gilded barge with purple sails and sat under a canopy made of golden cloth. Mark Antony was smitten with Cleopatra, and the two entered into a relationship that would last for ten years. During those years, Cleopatra gave birth to twins: Alexander Helios and Cleopatra Selene II. Mark Antony even divorced his wife, Octavia, and married Cleopatra.

Cleopatra sailing into Tarsus.
https://commons.wikimedia.org/wiki/File:Alma-tadema-antony-cleopatra.jpeg

Unfortunately, Mark Antony's relationship with Octavian eventually declined, and Rome was plunged into war. Mark Antony had lost support in Rome due to his flagrant disregard for Roman tradition. It certainly didn't help Mark Antony's case that he publicly humiliated Octavian's sister when he divorced her in favor of Cleopatra. Mark Antony and Cleopatra lost the Battle of Actium in 31 CE. A year later, they were forced to contend with the Roman army, which was set on invading Egypt. According to legend, Mark Antony stabbed himself after hearing that Cleopatra had been killed. Octavian reportedly allowed Mark Antony to be returned to Cleopatra, where he died in her arms. She committed suicide soon after, and Octavian would eventually become the sole Roman emperor. Unfortunately, Cleopatra's grand claims for Caesarion led to his execution, but her twins were allowed to continue living.

Chapter 15: Saladin: The First Sultan of Egypt

Saladin was the first sultan of both Egypt and Syria. His efforts founded the Ayyubid dynasty, and he was instrumental in unifying the medieval Muslim states, although his campaigns against other Muslim leaders earned him many enemies. During his peak, he ruled over Syria, Egypt, parts of Mesopotamia, western Arabia, Yemen, parts of North Africa, and Nubia.

Early Life

Saladin was born in Tikrit, Iraq, around 1137 CE. He was named Yusuf Ibn Ayyub and was part of a powerful military family. His father, Ayyub, and uncle, Shirkuh, served under the governor of northern Syria, Imad al-Din Zangi. Saladin's lineage would have exposed him to influential figures and given him the skills that he would later employ in his military campaigns. He grew up in Damascus and quickly proved his worth. Saladin gained a reputation for being an expert horseman and polo player. As a young man, he rose quickly through the military ranks and served under his uncle when they were sent on a military expedition to Egypt.

Shirkuh served under Zangi's son, Nur al-Din. In 1169, Shirkuh died, and Saladin was chosen to take his uncle's place. At that point, Saladin was appointed as a vizier to the Fatimid Caliphate. Two years later, the last Fatimid caliph died, and Saladin immediately proclaimed himself the governor of Egypt. The rulers of the Fatimid dynasty had been Shia Muslims, but Saladin was a Sunni Muslim. He immediately began curbing Shia influence. During his time as the Egyptian governor, he strengthened Egypt, and it became a powerful Sunni base. As vizier, Saladin began reforming the social and economic conditions in the kingdom. He eliminated taxes that were contrary to Islamic law and began building a powerful navy. Saladin still ruled in Nur al-Din's name; at the time, Nur al-Din was the governor of Aleppo and Edessa. However, Saladin began putting family members in positions of power within his government and pushed back against Nur al-Din's rule. Finally, Saladin's chance came in 1174 when Nur al-Din died. His successors immediately began fighting for dominance. The chaos provided Saladin with an opportunity to announce that he was the sultan of Egypt.

Sultan of Egypt

As soon as Saladin was in control of Egypt, he set his sights on a larger goal. He organized his state according to Islamic law and began removing Shiite influence in Egypt. This boosted his reputation and influence in the Muslim world, especially when he declared that he was the protector of the Sunni Orthodoxy. Saladin decided that he wanted to form a Muslim coalition, which would prove to be an extremely difficult task. The Muslim world was made up of highly independent states with their own rulers. Some of those states were made up of Shia Muslims, which meant that Saladin had to overcome regional and religious differences.

Sometime in 1174, he uncovered a plot to put the Fatimids back in power, and he dealt with the traitors in a swift and brutal manner. He also built several mosques and madrasahs in order to expand Sunni influence within Egypt. His popularity among the Sunni Muslims grew, and he appointed Sunni Muslims to positions within the government and courts. Saladin allowed Egyptians to hold power within his government, which gave him insight into the traditions of the Egyptian populace. He was famously tolerant of other religions and allowed Coptic Christians and Jews to continue practicing their beliefs. During Saladin's reign, the Egyptian economy continued to flourish as it had during the Fatimid Caliphate.

Muslim Coalition

In 1174, Saladin managed to capture Damascus, which was an impressive feat. From there, he went on to conquer Aleppo, Mosul, and Yemen. He soon came to control the Red Sea region, which brought him one step closer to his ultimate goal. However, Saladin didn't simply rely on military methods to gain new territories. He was an adept diplomat who fostered strong relationships with other leaders, which gave him many allies. In order to establish the legitimacy of his rule, he married Nur al-Din's widow since she was the daughter of a previous ruler of Damascus. Saladin also won widespread respect in the Muslim world by taking the lead in the efforts to protect Islam against the invading Christians.

While Saladin proclaimed to be a protector of Islam, he had no problem fighting Muslim enemies. The caliph of Baghdad recognized most of Saladin's authority, but Aleppo remained beyond his reach. It was ruled by Nur al-Din's son, who proved to be a dangerous enemy. Saladin survived numerous attempts on his life. The Assassins, or the Nizari Ismailis, was a dangerous Muslim sect that held a number of forts in Persia and Syria. They were known for choosing prominent leaders and then sending small teams of highly skilled assassins to kill them. Saladin didn't take kindly to these attempts and promptly pillaged an Assassin castle in Masyaf, Syria. He finally managed to capture Aleppo in 1183 after using the Egyptian fleet. By 1186, Saladin was in control of Syria, Palestine, and northern Mesopotamia, which allowed him to unify most of the Muslim world.

Holy War against Christianity

Saladin built up an impressive reputation and proclaimed that he was the only one who could win the war against the Crusaders. Throughout his reign, he met the Franks (what the Crusaders from Europe were called back then) in battle on a number of occasions. In 1177, he lost a battle to the Franks but managed to secure a small victory in 1179 at Marj Ayyun, where he was able to take hold of an important fortress on the Jordan River.

While Saladin set about unifying the Muslim world, he also sought to prove that he could expel the Franks from Muslim lands. However, he had to focus on strengthening his own lands first, as he couldn't successfully win the war if he was constantly checking his borders. This meant he had to be content with small battles until he could be certain that his own borders were secure. The Muslim coalition that he dreamed of was within his grasp, but it was also clear the coalition was somewhat fragile and would fall apart if he wasn't careful.

By 1187, Saladin could finally focus all his attention on the holy war. In May 1187, a force led by Saladin's son, al-Afdal, attacked Kerak Castle, which was held by the Franks. Meanwhile, Saladin gathered an army made up of troops from Aleppo, Jazira, Syria, and Egypt. The Franks were forced to mobilize their own forces, and the two armies met at Hattin.

Battle of Hattin

On July 3rd, 1187, Saladin's forces began the battle when his mounted archers repeatedly fired on the Franks, after which they would retreat and begin firing again. The Franks were forced to advance under near-constant attack. Saladin's army was made up of about twenty thousand men. The Franks were led by Guy of Lusignan, King of Jerusalem. (The Kingdom of Jerusalem was the Frankish kingdom of Palestine. It was established in 1099 after the First Crusade.) The Franks had 15,000 troops and 1,300 knights. Saladin held the clear advantage with his larger army, but he also had a steady stream of supplies thanks to his camel trains. The Franks, on the other hand, were quickly running out of water.

Saladin and Guy of Lusignan
https://commons.wikimedia.org/wiki/File:Saladin_and_Guy.jpg

Saladin realized the Franks were dealing with thirst and ordered his men to set fire to the dry bush around the battlefield, which would have made the Franks unbearably thirsty. The Franks were desperate and had managed to assemble their biggest army ever, but they were quickly overcome by Saladin's forces. The Franks' formation fell apart, which allowed the Muslim forces to break through their lines and defeat the army. After the battle, Saladin famously offered his new captive, Guy of Lusignan, an iced sherbet. Saladin ransomed some nobles but executed hated nobles who had attacked or pillaged Muslim communities. He also executed some of the Knights Hospitaller and Knights Templar since they were extremely dangerous due to their fanaticism. The captives who couldn't be ransomed were sold as slaves.

In September 1187, Saladin finally managed to capture Jerusalem. The victory was extremely important, as Jerusalem was the symbolic prize for both religions. He either ransomed or sold the Western Christians into slavery. The Eastern Christians were allowed to remain, but most of their churches were turned into mosques. Saladin's victory at Hattin and Jerusalem turned him into a hero in the Muslim world. He successfully captured several other cities held by the Franks. Eventually, the Franks only held Tyre.

Third Crusade

The Crusaders suffered massive losses during Saladin's rule, and he made it clear that he intended to rid the Middle East of the Franks altogether. When Saladin captured Jerusalem, Pope Gregory II persuaded some of the most powerful kings in Europe to wage a holy war. Saladin was prepared for them; he also wanted to engage in a holy war, as this would finally bring an end to the Crusaders' presence. Three European kings responded to the pope's call, and soon, Richard I of England, Philip II of France, and Frederick I Barbarossa of the Holy Roman Empire and Germany were on their way to the Middle East.

Meanwhile, Guy of Lusignan began a siege on Acre in August 1189. When Philip and Richard's army arrived, the battle turned in favor of the Crusaders. They managed to capture the city in 1191, along with a large portion of Saladin's navy. From there, the Crusaders made their way to Jerusalem. In September 1191, the Crusaders and Muslims met at Arsuf and engaged in a large battle.

The Crusaders won, and Saladin's reputation was greatly damaged due to his successive losses. Other Muslim leaders criticized Saladin's reluctance to attack Tyre when he had the chance, but Saladin's strategy had always been to attack an enemy where they were weak and wear them down. While the Crusaders marched toward Jerusalem, the Muslim army launched small-scale attacks and slowly wore down the Christian army. By the time the Crusaders arrived at Jerusalem, they were in no position to recapture the city. In 1192, Saladin agreed to a truce with Richard the Lionheart, which brought an end to the Third Crusade.

Reputation

During his lifetime, Saladin employed a number of talented biographers who helped boost his reputation as a generous, just, noble, and chivalrous leader. Saladin was also known for enjoying gardening and poetry. He was hailed as a hero in the Muslim world for his victories against the Crusaders. Saladin carefully cultivated his reputation as the ideal Muslim ruler who lived according to Islamic law and ruled fairly over conquered states. It must be noted that Saladin was famously tolerant of other religions and allowed Christians and Jews to live peacefully in his empire. He also chose not to massacre Christian populations when he recaptured the Franks' territory. Most Sunni historians gave Saladin enormous amounts of praise, and his reputation as a competent military leader and pious man would endure long after his death.

Christian writers were also positive in their descriptions of the Muslim conqueror. They portrayed him as a reasonable and generous man who allowed many Christians to go free. Medieval European societies placed a lot of emphasis on the value of chivalry and courtesy. Saladin was known for these qualities, which painted him as a worthy adversary to the Crusaders.

Death

The end of the Third Crusade and the departure of the Crusaders meant that Saladin had successfully won the holy war, which had been one of his most important goals. He had also managed to unify the Muslim states into a mighty empire. However, he died on March 4th, 1193, just a few months after his truce with Richard the Lionheart. He was around fifty-five years old. He likely died from fatigue or exhaustion caused by his extensive military campaigns. Unfortunately, his Muslim coalition wouldn't survive long after his death. Once Saladin died, his three sons took control of a portion of his empire, namely Egypt, Aleppo, and Damascus. The rest of the empire was divided among other family members and high-ranking officials.

The Ayyubid dynasty continued to rule over Egypt and Syria but was overthrown by the Mamluks between 1250 and 1260. Saladin's reputation endured in Islamic and Christian literature, and he was upheld as an example of chivalry in Europe. The fact that his good reputation was maintained even after his empire disintegrated is a testament to the power he held during his lifetime.

Chapter 16:
Mubarak and Morsi

Ancient Egyptian politics is usually a source of intense study and fascination, and rightly so because ancient Egypt was a remarkable empire. Modern Egyptian history is also worth observing since the country plays an important role in the worldwide economy. Two of the most important politicians in modern Egyptian history are Hosni Mubarak and Mohamed Morsi. Both of these men were highly influential politicians who left a definite mark on their country. They were both presidents during the 21st century and were often at the center of political controversy. Coincidentally, both were involved in a revolution that ended with their removal from the government.

Mubarak ruled for decades and was a seasoned politician before Egypt erupted into protests that called for his resignation. Morsi was an engineer who won Egypt's first democratic election but was removed from his position after a few months and forced to stand trial. People remain divided on their legacies, especially since Morsi died while being held in a detention center. There are a lot of theories and interesting stories about the men, which makes looking into their lives a worthwhile endeavor.

Hosni Mubarak: Early Life

Hosni Mubarak was born in Kafr El-Meselha, Monufia governate, Egypt, in May 1928 and joined the Egyptian military academy during his youth. He graduated in 1949 and received advanced flight and bomber training from the Soviet Union. Mubarak eventually earned a degree in aviation sciences and served in the Spitfire fighter squadron for two years. During his time in the Egyptian Air Force, he held several positions of power before becoming the director of the air academy. He was appointed as the chief commander of the air force and the deputy minister of defense in 1972 by President Anwar Sadat.

Mubarak played an important part in the war with Israel in 1973. At the beginning of the war, the Egyptian Air Force surprised the Israeli troops on the east bank of the Suez Canal. The attack was extremely successful, as the Egyptian pilots hit the vast majority of their targets. As a result of his military successes, Mubarak became very popular and was promoted to air chief marshal. The Egyptian Air Force played an important role in the war, and they proved to be a morale booster for Egyptian ground troops.

General Hosni Mubarak
https://commons.wikimedia.org/wiki/File:General_Hosni_Mubarak.jpg

In 1975, Sadat appointed Mubarak as his vice president.

Vice Presidency

As the vice president of Egypt, Mubarak played an important role in government consultations concerning the results of the war with Israel. He went on a mission to Riyadh and Damascus to discuss the disengagement agreement between Egypt and Israel. The aim of the mission was to persuade the Syrian and Saudi Arabian governments to accept the agreement. During this time, Mubarak fostered a friendship with Saudi Arabian Crown Prince Fahd. He also managed to make powerful friends with various other Arab leaders.

Sadat often sent Mubarak to consult with foreign leaders, so he was a regular part of sensitive government meetings. He played an important role in the negotiations of Middle Eastern policies. Mubarak was chosen to serve as a mediator during the dispute between Algeria, Morocco, and Mauritania over the fate of Western Sahara. Sadat made good use of Mubarak during his vice presidency, and it's clear that Mubarak used this time to make important allies.

President of Egypt

Anwar Sadat was assassinated on October 6th, 1981, during the anniversary celebrations of the Yom Kippur War. Mubarak was injured during the assassination but was still able to become the next president of Egypt. Due to Sadat's choice to negotiate a peace treaty with Israel, Egypt's membership was suspended from the Arab League since it didn't agree with Sadat's plan. When Mubarak became president, he entered into negotiations with King Fahd of Saudi Arabia. Egypt and Saudi Arabia were both powerful forces in the Arab world; Egypt was very populous, while Saudi Arabia was extremely rich. In 1982, Saudi Arabia presented an Egyptian peace plan that dictated Israel should resolve the Israeli-Palestinian conflict by ensuring the formation of a Palestinian state. In return, Israel would be at peace with the Arab world. During Mubarak's presidency, he fostered good relationships with the other Arab countries and the United States. He also reaffirmed the peace treaty with Israel as per the Camp David Accords, but he didn't have the same close relationship with Israel as his predecessor.

George W. Bush and Hosni Mubarak.

In 1987, Mubarak was elected to a second term. Mubarak supported the Saudi plan to invite the US military coalition to recover Kuwait during the Persian Gulf crisis and the ensuing war. By 1993, Mubarak was facing political unrest from opposing political parties that wanted to usher in new democratic electoral reforms in Egypt. The unrest led to guerilla warfare. Mubarak condemned the actions of the Islamic fundamentalists after an attack at Luxor in 1997 that killed sixty tourists. For most of his presidency, he was a vocal supporter of peace in the Middle East.

Mubarak faced assassination attempts in 1995 and 1999, with the second attempt leaving him slightly wounded. In 1999, he was reelected as president since he ran unopposed. In 2005, Egypt's first multi-candidate presidential election took place, although it was plagued by reports of inconsistencies and low voter turnout. Unsurprisingly, Mubarak was reelected to another term.

Revolution and Overthrow

In 2011, Egypt was gripped by widespread protests against Mubarak's presidency, which was beset by rising poverty and allegations of corruption and repressive policing tactics. The protestors called for Mubarak's resignation, and the police clashed violently with the protestors. Millions of Egyptians protested against Mubarak, calling for his immediate resignation. During the revolution, 846 people were killed, and over 6,000 were injured. On January 28th, Mubarak gave a speech announcing he had no intention of resigning; however, he intended to introduce political change by dissolving his cabinet. He also promised to instigate other political and social changes, but his promises did little to stop the protestors. In order to gain the protestors' trust, Mubarak appointed the first vice president of his presidency, Omar Suleiman. He then announced he wouldn't take part in the Egyptian presidential elections in September 2011.

Egyptian protests (January 25th, 2011).
Adam Makary, CC BY-SA 2.0 https://creativecommons.org/licenses/by-sa/2.0 via Wikimedia Commons; https://commons.wikimedia.org/wiki/File:Egyptian_Revolution_protests_(25_January_20 11)_-_03_-_Flickr_-_Al_Jazeera_English.jpg

On February 10th, 2011, Mubarak gave Suleiman some of his duties, but instead of resigning immediately as the protestors wanted, he declared he would remain as president until the end of his term. He also claimed that he would reform the electoral system. The next day, he left for his house in the Sinai Peninsula. On that same day, Suleiman addressed the nation and told the people that Mubarak had stepped down and left the Supreme

Council of the Armed Forces in control of the government. The announcement led to celebrations in Tahrir Square and other urban centers.

Death

After Mubarak was forced from his position, the government began cracking down on former officials and business leaders accused of corruption or abuse of power. Soon, there were calls to investigate the former president, as the Mubarak family had been accused of stealing money from the state and hiding it in foreign accounts. Mubarak's sons, Alaa and Gamal, were investigated. Mubarak denied the serious accusations that he and his family were facing. On April 12th, he reportedly suffered a massive heart attack that caused him to be held in a hospital in Sharm el-Sheikh. It was determined that the former president was too weak to be transferred to a prison.

In May, it was announced that Mubarak would stand trial for abuses of power and ordering the killing of protestors during the revolution. Mubarak attended his trial in a hospital bed and denied all the charges. In January 2012, it was announced that the prosecutors intended to seek the death penalty for the former president. In June of that year, the court declared that Mubarak had been complicit in the deaths of the protestors. He was sentenced to life in prison. He was acquitted of the corruption charges, but in January 2013, the court announced that Mubarak had to be retried for corruption and the killings of the protestors. Later in the year, he was transferred to a military hospital in Cairo. In 2014, Mubarak received a three-year sentence for embezzling public funds, while his sons received a four-year sentence. However, the court later dismissed the charges that Mubarak was responsible for the deaths of the protestors. In January 2020, Mubarak was admitted to the hospital for surgery but died in February at the age of ninety-one.

Mohamed Morsi: Early Life

Mohamed Morsi was born in the Al-Sharqiyyah governate in Egypt on August 8th, 1951. He came from a humble background; his father was a farmer, and his mother was a housewife. In the 1960s, he began studying at Cairo University and received a bachelor's in engineering with high honors. In 1976, he completed his military service in the Egyptian Army, where he served in the chemical warfare unit. Once he finished his military service, he returned to Cairo University, where he earned a master's in metallurgical engineering in 1978. He also earned a scholarship that allowed him to complete his studies in the United States, where he received a PhD in materials science from the University of Sothern California. When he returned to Egypt, he became a professor at Zagazig University.

Mohamed Morsi.

Morsi became a member of parliament in 2000. He was a member of the Guidance Office of the Muslim Brotherhood and served as an independent candidate in parliament, as the Muslim Brotherhood was banned from running for government. In 2011, the Muslim Brotherhood founded the Freedom and Justice Party, and Morsi became the first president of it. He condemned the two-state solution of the Israel-Palestine conflict, condemned the 9/11 attacks, and criticized the United States for invading Afghanistan and Iraq after the attacks. His views were supported by many Egyptians, but he was harshly criticized by his enemies. Morsi was arrested during the protests in January 2011 but managed to escape prison.

President of Egypt

After Mubarak resigned, the Freedom and Justice Party was allowed to run for election. In April 2012, Morsi became the party's candidate. He was the party's second choice, but his predecessor, Khairat al-Shater, was disqualified. Morsi won the election; however, the interim military government made a constitutional declaration in June that essentially took away most of the president's authority. The Supreme Constitutional Court also dissolved the People's Assembly, which was led by the Muslim Brotherhood. Regardless, Morsi was sworn into office on June 30th.

As president, Morsi reversed the interim military government's constitutional declaration, and several members of the council retired at the same time. In November 2012, Morsi helped negotiate a ceasefire between Israel and Hamas (a Palestinian Sunni-Islamic fundamentalist militant and nationalist organization) in the Gaza Strip, which earned him international praise. However, he later issued a decree that stipulated his authority wouldn't be subject to any judicial oversight until a permanent constitution was established. The decree took away the court's ability to monitor the Constituent Assembly, which was responsible for coming up with a new constitution. This move led to widespread protests, with the Egyptians claiming that Morsi was making himself a dictator.

In the midst of the protests, Morsi took back some of his decrees, although he kept the decree that prevented the removal of the Constituent Assembly. The Constituent Assembly had created a draft constitution, which was made by Muslims without input from Christian or secular members. In December, Morsi declared martial law, which allowed the military to arrest anyone whom they deemed as a threat, and the draft constitution was approved by voters. Morsi faced overwhelming opposition during his term, and many of his opponents weren't open to negotiations, which forced the president to take drastic measures.

Overthrow and Trial

Morsi's presidency was plagued by worsening political situations, a decline in public services, and a weakening economy. These failures drew harsh criticism, and by June 30th, 2013, anti-Morsi protests were taking place throughout the country. The protests grew steadily out of control, and soon, there were calls for his removal. In July, the head of the Egyptian Armed Forces, General Abdel Fattah al-Sisi, decided to take decisive action. He announced that unless Morsi was able to placate the protestors, the military would be forced to step in and prevent the country from descending into anarchy.

Morsi's situation was becoming more precarious by the day. Morsi offered to negotiate with the protestors but declared that he wouldn't resign from his post. He rejected the military's ultimatum and declared that he would find his own way to reconcile the nation.

Anti-Morsi protests in Tahrir Square.
Y. Weeks/VOA, Public domain, via Wikimedia Commons;
https://commons.wikimedia.org/wiki/File:Thousands_of_people_gather_in_Tahrir_Squar
e_to_protest_Egyptian_President_Mohamed_Morsi_-_30-Nov-2012.jpg

Two days later, the military removed Morsi from his post and suspended the constitution. Morsi and many of his Muslim Brotherhood colleagues were put in prison. Morsi's supporters erupted into protests over his removal, especially since Morsi's supporters were being repressed. In July and August, the military clashed violently with the protestors. More than one thousand protestors were killed, with most of the deaths taking place at Rabaa al-Adawiya Square. In September, the Muslim Brotherhood was outlawed again. Al-Sisi then left the military and became the Egyptian president in 2014.

Morsi was forced to stand trial for inciting Muslim Brotherhood supporters to kill protesters during an anti-Morsi protest and for colluding with foreign groups, such as Hamas and Iran's Revolutionary Guards. During his trial, Morsi declared that the allegations were false and that he was still the rightful president of Egypt. The proceedings were widely denounced and criticized.

Death

In April 2015, Morsi was found guilty of inciting violence against anti-Morsi protestors and sentenced to twenty years in prison. He was also charged with conspiring to commit acts of terrorism in Egypt and was sentenced to life in prison. On top of this, he was sentenced to death for committing violence during a mass prison break in January 2011. In 2016, an Egyptian court ordered a retrial and overturned the death sentence. While the new trial began, Morsi was kept in jail. Unfortunately, the conditions were deplorable, and he wasn't allowed access to adequate medical attention. The prison conditions led to Morsi's poor health, and on June 17th, 2019, he collapsed in court and died.

In response, the United Nations called for an independent inquiry into Morsi's death. Mosques all around the world gave special prayers for the former Egyptian leader. Many foreign governments denounced the coup and blamed the Egyptian government for Morsi's death. The Muslim Brotherhood claimed that Morsi wasn't allowed to receive regular visits from allies or family members and that Morsi wasn't provided with necessary medicine. Apparently, the details of his health had been kept secret.

The Freedom and Justice Party held the Egyptian government responsible for Morsi's "deliberate and slow death." They claimed that Morsi was placed in solitary confinement, fed disgusting food, and not given basic human rights. His allies also called for an independent international investigation into Morsi, saying the results should be made available to the public. Mohamed Morsi was buried by his family in Al-Wafaa Wa al-Amal cemetery in Cairo. So far, this independent investigation has not happened, but it might still happen in the future.

Conclusion

Egypt is an alluring country that draws millions of tourists to view its spectacular historical sights. The country has endured climactic changes that threatened its security and transformed its social, religious, and economic structures. Each of these changes brought about a new era in Egyptian history and had a profound effect on the country and its neighbors. This book provided a general overview of Egypt's history and took a look at ancient, medieval, and modern events that left a mark on Egypt's identity.

We explored ancient Egypt and the age of pyramids and pharaohs. We saw how Egypt was irrevocably changed when Alexander the Great arrived on the scene. When he died, his vast empire was divided among his heirs, and Ptolemy I seized his chance to take over Egypt. During this time, Egypt was heavily impacted by the Hellenistic culture, and Alexandria became an intellectual powerhouse in the Mediterranean. The Ptolemies were responsible for building legendary monuments, such as the Library of Alexandria and the Lighthouse of Alexandria.

Eventually, Egypt became a Roman province and later formed a vital part of the Byzantine Empire. By then, Christianity was well established in Egypt and had become the state religion. During the medieval period, Egypt was invaded by the Rashidun Caliphate, which established Islam as the new state religion. Egypt was ruled by various Muslim rulers, including the Abbasids, the Fatimids, the Mamluks, and the Ottomans. Each ruling dynasty left its mark on

Egyptian art and architecture, which led to the complex diversity that still dominates the modern Egyptian landscape.

Egypt is a magnificent country with a powerful history that will be studied for years to come. By learning more about its past, a person can broaden their knowledge about some of the most important events in world history.

Part 2: Egyptian Mythology

An Enthralling Overview of Egyptian Myths, Gods, and Goddesses

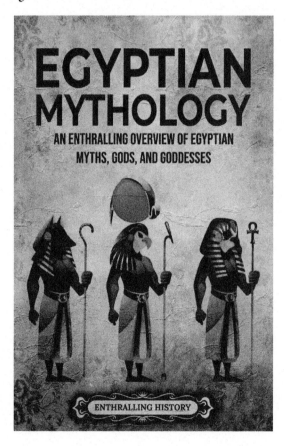

Introduction

Unraveling the mysteries of our existence is one of man's greatest accomplishments. The knowledge we have was made ours by searching, finding, and exploring the world that existed thousands of years before us. Egyptian mythology brings the vivid details of the very distant past to us, and as you are about to discover, there is so much to learn!

Ancient Egypt is synonymous with massive pyramids, the worship of the sun, and their plethora of gods and goddesses. On every page of this book, you will find the multiple, exciting perspectives of their stories. But first, how about getting familiar with some Egyptian mythology lingo?

- **ASPECT:** This seems like a regular word, but watch out for how it is used in ancient mythology, especially when referring to the gods. An "aspect" of a god or goddess means a version of them. If there is one thing to note in advance about the gods and goddesses in Egyptian mythology, it is their ability to shapeshift or manifest in diverse forms. These forms could be animals, inanimate objects, or a separate god altogether. A god could transform into any of these forms or extract a separate god from himself.

- **AMULET:** Amulets are manmade objects or tokens believed to ward off evil. They could be ornaments, charms, crests, jewelry, a small piece of paper with spells written on it, or objects from nature, like claws or shells. An amulet is typically wearable and portable.

- **ANKH:** In nearly every picture of an Egyptian god or goddess, you will see them holding a key-like hook in one hand. This hook is called an ankh, and it was a divine symbol representing the immortality of the gods.

- **DYNASTY:** This was the collective term used to describe pharaohs from the same family line. The end of a dynasty was when a pharaoh from another royal family ascended to the throne. Ancient Egypt had over thirty dynasties, including those of the Greeks and Romans.

- **MIDDLE KINGDOM:** Although the Middle Kingdom is not mentioned very much in this book, it was an era of ancient Egypt. It came between the Old Kingdom and the New Kingdom. The years vary from one history book to another, but a convenient timeline is between c. 2030 BCE and 1640 BCE. Some history textbooks do not acknowledge the Middle Kingdom. Instead, they fuse it with the New Kingdom. An event used to demarcate the Middle Kingdom from the New Kingdom is the Hyksos invasion of Egypt around 1638 BCE, as it caused great political instability.

- **NEW KINGDOM:** The New Kingdom is also regarded as the golden age of ancient Egypt. After getting their land back from the invading foreigners, the pharaohs worked hard to return the nation to its former glory. Impressive structures, magnificent statues, and other antique masterpieces come from this era. Again, the dates differ, but the general consensus is that the New Kingdom typically dates between c. 1550 BCE and 1077 BCE.

- **OLD KINGDOM:** It is all in the name. The Old Kingdom of ancient Egypt is the time before the Middle and New Kingdom eras, dating between c. 2700 BCE and 2200 BCE. At this time, Egypt existed as two regions: Upper and Lower Egypt. The Old Kingdom was also the era of the pyramids. Pharaohs in this era had tall pyramids built to commemorate their reign and serve as royal tombs. The famous Sphinx of Giza was also built in the

Old Kingdom era.

- **PAPYRUS:** This was thick ancient Egyptian paper used as early as the Predynastic era of Egypt. It is named after the plant it was made from. If you lived back then, you could find papyrus in abundance around the Nile River.

- **PRIMEVAL/PRIMORDIAL:** This is used to refer to the mythical timeline of Egypt. It is the oldest, earliest era in Egypt, dating from the creation of the world to the reign of the gods. No years or figures are used to describe this era.

- **PTOLEMAIC ERA:** This is the time after the New Kingdom era when Egypt was invaded and occupied by the Macedonians. This era is named after Ptolemy I, a Macedonian general who served Alexander the Great. By 305 BCE, Ptolemy had defeated anyone with claims to the throne and became the king of Egypt. About 275 years after, Egypt was annexed into the Roman Empire, marking the end of this era. In this book, Egypt during this time is described as Graeco-Roman Egypt. Now that you are ready, it is time to dive in! We begin with the earliest of times in Egyptian mythology and the first story in its chronology: the creation of the world.

SECTION ONE: Cosmology

Chapter 1: The Creation Myths

Of all the creation stories out there, those from ancient Egypt are some of the most intriguing. Stories of where elements of nature and living creatures come from are a part of nearly every ancient civilization in history. The creation of the world has been recounted by many cultures. What you are bound to notice first is that they all allude to chaos or a void before the establishment of the natural order.

The Egyptian creation myths, in all their dynamism, are not exempt from this.

Sometimes, the word "myth" is ascribed to falsehood or uncertainty, but the Egyptians believed every creation myth to be profoundly true. You may read of Egyptian creation myths or any creation myth at all as "cosmological myths" in some texts. It is a synonym. Cosmology studies the totality of the universe, from the origin to its evolution to its eventual fate.

Sources of Egyptian Creation Myths

The multi-versioned Egyptian stories of creation come to us from ancient hieroglyphic compilations from the Old Kingdom, spanning from around 2700 BCE to 2200 BCE.

The Egyptians are world-famous for their elaborate funerals and gravesites. Pharaohs from the Old and Middle Kingdoms were buried in pyramids, with stories from their time told on the tomb walls. These are called Pyramid Texts.

Pyramid text on the tomb walls of Pharaoh Teti of the Sixth Dynasty.

A pyramid was much roomier than your average tomb, and the Egyptians believed that there was no better way to send off their kings to have a blessed afterlife. Pyramids typically had stairs that would lead the deceased king up to the sky (or the sun), guided by protective texts and spells on the walls. These were known as funerary texts. Thousands of years later, multiple excavations of these ancient pyramids practically gifted the world with most of the profound knowledge that exists today about Egyptian creation myths.

Ancient temples were another prominent source. The ancient Egyptians took to carving their stories on a temple's stone walls and ceiling. Perhaps they foresaw the destruction of important religious documents in the soon-to-come conflict-ridden transition of Egypt from polytheistic paganism to Christianity. During this time, the Christians destroyed many documented texts about Egyptian gods and goddesses.

Despite the eventuality of this conversion, creation myths recorded on papyrus paper survived. Such documents, including religious texts written by priests, spell books compiled by magicians, and medical journals written by physicians from the ancient era, have proven to be valuable sources of information about the creation myths and other information about Egypt. They highlight the names of the gods responsible for protection and healing, as well as their roles in creating the world.

Fascinatingly, classical Greek authors also did their bit in making Egyptian creation myths world famous. You probably know of names like Herodotus, Plutarch, and maybe even Diodorus. However, none of these men could speak Egyptian to save their lives, but they proved that a curious mind truly distinguished what made someone an ardent seeker of knowledge.

Their goal was to educate a Greek audience with foreign stories and enrich the Greek culture. But due to the language barrier, these classical authors were at the mercy of interpreters. They relied on the interpreters to read the Egyptian scrolls and carvings on the walls or speak with the Egyptian custodians of knowledge, the priests. Eventually, Greek authors recorded the Egyptian stories based on what they had gleaned from these interpreters. You can imagine that these accounts were imbued with personal and cultural biases. The essence of some stories was lost or diluted in the translation process, resulting in a wide range of differences from the local Egyptian versions. The classical Greek authors could have cared less about these distortions, especially since their accounts practically renamed some of the Egyptian gods. For example, the Egyptian god Amun became Zeus-Ammon (arguably different from Zeus), the Egyptian god Horus was identified with Apollo, and Thoth was combined with the Greek god Hermes.

It seemed as though the classical authors from Greece were not as interested in popularizing the Egyptian creation myths as they were in offering their fellow Greeks a form of entertainment. Barring the inherent inconsistencies, the written stories of classical Greek authors about Egyptian creation myths, which were eventually integrated into ancient Greek culture, have proven to be another key historical source.

Last but certainly not least on the list of sources is word of mouth. This source has been criticized as very unreliable, but Egyptians have always taken pride in telling stories of old. Ancient pharaohs were famed for being excellent storytellers, an ability they shared with their children. Their folktales lauded the exploits of Atum (or Ra) and spoke of the wisdom of Osiris and the beauty of Nut, the sky above them. No doubt, such fervent storytellers would have many versions of a single story, which depended on location and religious perspective. However, these stories had some common ground. Rather than dwell on the inconsistencies of these versions, it is best to think of such dynamic awareness of the universe and its origin as an example of a sophisticated culture.

There is indeed no single tomb, temple, book, or document that paints a whole picture of Egypt's creation myths, but what is mythology without some mystery? After all, the archaeological efforts throughout the years are just enough to put pen to paper.

Accounts of Egyptian Creation Myths

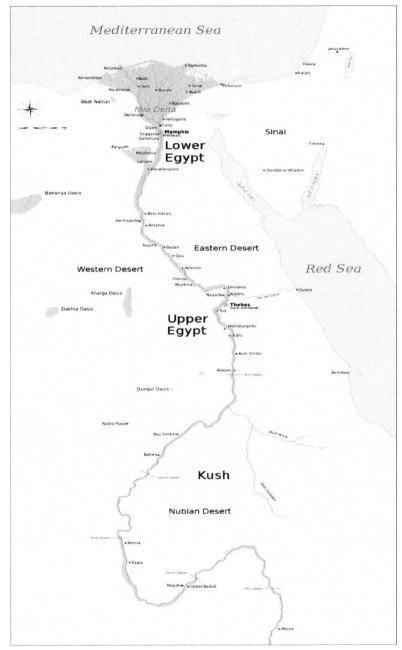

A map of ancient Egypt.

There are four prominent creation stories, which come from four different cities in Egypt. The first one and arguably the most popular is from the ancient city of Heliopolis. The story begins with our beloved universe as nothing but a chaotic, directionless expanse of water known as Nun.

Heliopolis

It is difficult to imagine what nothingness looks like, but a few decent attempts have been made at its portrayal. Nun is the name given to the universe's form before creation, and it bore much semblance to a vast turbulent ocean. It reached everywhere yet went nowhere. There was no night or day, and the only being existent inside the water was a motionless god.

His name was Atum (or Ra in some texts).

Atum must have spent eons in his inert solitude, enough to long for companionship. In time, he decided to put an end to his loneliness. Atum emerged from Nun on a cone-shaped mystical stone called Benben, and in some other accounts, Atum emerged by calling out his own name. As an accessory to his peculiar nature, the god Atum had male and female elements within his being. This enabled him to procreate with himself. He birthed two children: Shu and Tefnut.

Ennead: A Divine Genealogy

Of course, there are variations within our Heliopolitan story as to how Atum conceived his offspring. While some traditions imply an act similar to masturbation, others suggest that Atum mated with his own shadow. Another account tells us that the god Atum sneezed out Shu and spat out Tefnut and that their names are onomatopoeic puns to represent how they were born.

These unique accounts, despite their divergence, unanimously agree that the god Atum was the father of Shu and Tefnut. Shu became the god of air, and his sister Tefnut became the goddess of moisture—the two foundational elements of nature. Together, the twins would embark on a journey to discover their purpose and how to fulfill it.

Atum was unhappy to send his children off into a world pervaded by abysmal darkness and uncertainty, but he could not keep them satisfying their curiosities. So, away they went, but Shu and Tefnut were barely gone before Atum realized that his purpose for creating his children had been defeated.

He was once again lonely.

Desperate for their safety, the god Atum took a part of himself, his eye, and sent it on an important mission to find his tarrying children. Atum's eye, also known as the Eye of Ra, traversed the void until Shu and Tefnut were found and reunited with their father.

Atum received his children with tears of joy. Every teardrop that plopped down from his eyes transformed into a living creature—the first generation of mankind to inhabit a new world.

However, there remained a small challenge. The waters of Nun were not conducive for Atum's latest creation. They needed a place to call home for themselves, somewhere their children could grow. In this dilemma, Shu and Tefnut discovered the purpose they had previously ventured wide and far to find.

The union of Shu and Tefnut birthed the second generation in divinity: the god of the earth, Geb, and the goddess of the sky, Nut. Geb is portrayed in art as a green-skinned man who typically holds up a woman, who is believed to be his sister, Nut. Beautiful Nut arches above her brother, and her body is home to bright glowing dots (stars). It was also believed that Nut swallowed the sun every night and had it reborn to mark the beginning of a new day.

A portrayal of Nut stretching over her brother Geb.
https://commons.wikimedia.org/wiki/File:PSM_V10_D564_Egyptian_representation_of_heaven_and_earth.jpg

Due to sharing such an intimate coexistence, Geb and Nut quickly fell in love with each other, but their father, Shu, disapproved; some believe he might have been jealous of the union. As a consequence, Shu separated the two, forcing them to exist without the other. Ancient Egyptians believed that this is why the earth and sky are parallel elements of nature to this day.

Heartbroken, Geb shed tears of sadness since he could not live with his true love. The Egyptians believed this was where rain and oceans came from.

Before Nut's separation from Geb, she had birthed four children: Osiris, Isis, Set, and Nephthys. A few Egyptian traditions include a fifth child named Horus, but most name Horus as the son of Osiris and Isis, not their brother. A third version alludes to the existence of both: Horus the Elder as their brother and Horus the Younger as their son.

The four (or five) children of Geb and Nut would represent the forces of nature and shape mankind's journey on the earth in stages.

So, from Atum (Ra), the sun god and father of all creation, came Shu and Tefnut; from Shu and Tefnut came Geb and Nut; and from Geb and Nut came four gods and goddesses: Osiris, Isis, Set, and Nephthys.

Together, these nine gods are revered as the Great Ennead of Heliopolis.

Hermopolis

The Hermopolitan version of creation is the oldest, and it does not center around nine gods but eight: the sacred Ogdoad.

The Ogdoad of Hermopolis carved on the wall of a tomb in Deir el-Medina.
(SFEC_2009_POT-0008.JPG: S F-E-Cameronderivative work: JMCC1, CC BY-SA 3.0
https://creativecommons.org/licenses/by-sa/3.0 via Wikimedia Commons;
https://commons.wikimedia.org/wiki/File:Ogdoad_-_The_Place_of_Truth_-_Deir_el_Medina.jpg)

Before the creation of life, these divine beings existed as elements that characterized the world: utter darkness, chaotic waters, mystery, and infinity.

These eight gods were in four pairs, one male and one female. You will find that the male gods had frog heads, while their female counterparts had the heads of serpents. Their names were Nun (or Nu) and Naunet, Hah and Hauhet, Kek and Kauket, and Amun and Amaunet.

Together, they sailed upon the primeval waters that would become a new world. The Hermopolitan creation myth tells of the interaction between these eight gods and their energies, which resulted in a massive explosion; today, it is what scientists call the Big Bang. Consequently, a primordial mound (possibly the Benben) emerged from the waters. This marked the beginning of the golden age on Earth, with the Ogdoad as rulers.

The Four-Way Street

The Hermopolitan creation myth, like that of Heliopolis, has multiple subplots, which are all connected to the Ogdoad. First, a cosmic egg was the source of the universe and everything within it. Some traditions say that the egg was created by the gods themselves, while others say that it was laid by a primeval goose called the Gengen Wer (the Great Cackler), an aspect of the gods Amun and Geb. From this egg came the god Ra (or Atum), who began creating the world.

Another variation of that story involves a mystical lotus that emerged from the primeval waters. This lotus had petals that slowly opened and birthed a bird of light, representing Ra, who began the creation of the world. The third account agrees that the lotus came out of the waters, but instead of Ra, a scarab beetle emerged from the lotus when it opened. It shone as bright as the sun, marking the first sunrise. In some mythological versions, this scarab beetle transformed into a boy named Nefertum. His tears were what created the first human beings to ever walk the earth.

The fourth Hermopolitan version of creation holds that the world came from neither a lotus nor a celestial goose but from an egg laid by a sacred bird known as an ibis. This ibis was Thoth, the god of writing, science, and magic.

The Hermopolitans proudly assert that their creation stories are the oldest since they account for the origin of Ra, the source of the universe. According to them, the god Ra (or Atum) had not just come into existence. He was a creation of the eight gods known as the Ogdoad.

Thebes and Memphis

Many pantheons in ancient Thebes had carvings and statues of Amun, one of the gods in the Ogdoad. This god was worshiped in Thebes as a supreme being and the most important god when it came to creation. The Thebans believed that other gods were the creation of Amun and that the world would not exist without him. He created the goose (the Great Cackler) that broke the void of the primeval waters and summoned the primeval mound (or stone) that would house Atum.

The worshipers of Amun also believed that Thebes, the mighty capital city of Egypt in the 11th century BCE, was founded by Amun, along with the rest of the world. When Thebes rose to prominence in Egypt, Amun became a superior god.

In Memphis, another ancient Egyptian city, a deity named Ptah, the god of crafts and architecture, is believed to have used his expertise in divine speech to form the gods and the world. He was also revered as the protector of what he had created, and he was the only god who had not been created by another.

Wildly varying as these creation stories from ancient Egypt seemed, they share a few fascinating similarities. First is the belief that the world was created by gods, supernatural beings who either created themselves or came into existence through extraordinary means.

Second is the belief that before creation, the universe existed as a watery void. This is symbolic of a state of chaos, emptiness, and the lack of order—that is, until the gods emerge and save the day. The writers of these myths remain to be discovered, but what is certain is that these creation stories have greatly shaped Egyptian culture, both back then and today.

Chapter 2: The Shape of the World and Ma'at

Curiosity is perhaps humanity's greatest gift; otherwise, how would knowledge ever come to us?

The world has been home to humankind for many eons, and as inhabitants of a truly complex environment, the onus of finding the truth has been passed down from one generation to the next. Ancient Egypt is famed for being a center of art, culture, and natural science, which includes cosmology, in which people seek the meaning of the world they live in.

Modern scientific information and technologies were nonexistent at the time, so the Egyptians who sought such knowledge of the universe relied heavily on the supernatural. Gods and goddesses had to have had a hand in how the universe was structured. They also had a hand in the routines of nature, such as dawn and dusk, rain and drought, and wind and storms. Most significant of all, the gods designed the shape of the world.

If you visited the most revered scientists in ancient Egypt, who typically doubled as priests, they would tell you that the earth was flat and oval-shaped. This is evident in the journey of Ra to the underworld, a journey he took every day. It is often described as a descent. This shows the Egyptians thought there was a slope or curve at the edge of the earth from one realm to the other. After his all-night sojourn, the sun god would rise again on the other side, which would be referred to as an ascent.

As you will recall in the Heliopolitan creation myth, the grandchildren of Ra, Geb and Nut, were connected. You will also recall that the goddess Nut is portrayed as a naked woman arched over her brother Geb. She represents the sky (or heavens), through which Ra travels during the daytime.

The arch of Nut speaks to the oval shape theory that ancient Egyptians held. The other half of the oval was the underworld (also known as the Duat), completing a flat oval.

Ma'at: The Order of the World

The world did not just come to be. It had taken the hand of the divine Amun, who turned the desolate waters of Nun into a beautiful home for living creatures of all kinds. With all that work came Ma'at, the order of the universe. Ma'at is a core aspect of Egyptian mythology, cutting across the lives of the gods and their relationship with the mortals.

The exact beginning of Ma'at was creation, and thenceforth, every new king of Egypt had a duty to maintain it. Ma'at would also influence the fate of each soul in the afterlife. Essentially, Ma'at cut across all spheres of existence for both mortals and immortals as a "what" and a "who."

Ma'at: The "What"

First, ancient Egyptian mythology presents Ma'at as a principle, an idea or concept of justice, fairness, order, and harmony. The name itself means "that which is straight." When Amun (or Ra) created the world, his intention was companionship and harmony. The chaotic waters of Nun had long existed, and the creator yearned for peace.

Through the power of divine magic called *heka*, the world was brought to order. The first batch of people who occupied the earth upheld it in honor of their creator. Ancient Egyptians believed that to remain in line with Ma'at, every human had a duty to themself, their fellow humans, their creator, and the earth. Some of these duties, such as humility, self-control, and wisdom, were outlined by an ancient Egyptian vizier named Ptahhotep in his book titled *The Maxims of Ptahhotep.*

These duties were to be followed on the basis of social class, age, and gender. Times and seasons were also associated with Ma'at. Every year, there was a time when the Nile River would flood and a time when it would pull back. This was the order of things, and disruptions in these natural processes were deemed to be a sign of chaos or the anger of the gods. The ascension of a new king was also part of Ma'at.

After the era of being ruled by the gods, Egypt was ruled by men. These men stood as representatives of the gods on Earth, and after the demise of a king, another had to be enthroned to preserve Ma'at. Unrighteous kings would bring misfortune upon the land of Egypt and be condemned to eternal suffering in the afterlife after they died. Ma'at also represented the law but in a more natural and spiritual than legal sense. The kings of Egypt were expected to be models of these laws.

In Egyptian mythology, the principles of justice and order (Ma'at) apply to not just Egypt but also to every nation on the earth. In the ages to come, principles similar to those of Ma'at from other nations would be established in Egypt.

Ma'at: The Who

Reconstructed painting of Ma'at.

In images, Ma'at appears as a beautiful goddess with golden wings, holding an ankh and scepter and wearing an ostrich-feathered headdress. She was born from Amun (Ra) by the power of *heka* (magic) when the world was created.

Ma'at was the reason why the world continued on an orderly path after creation, as all elements of nature were in their place and served their ordained purpose. This goddess was an embodiment of harmony, justice, and continuity. She was the reason why the day was day, the night was night, the sky was the sky, and the earth was the earth as they had been created. Astronomers in ancient Egypt believed that the stars in the night sky chartered their course at the whims of Ma'at.

Of all the goddesses in the ancient Egyptian pantheon, Ma'at had a distinctive nature. She was not a protagonist in any myth like Isis or Hathor. Instead, she was a manifestation of an idea. The people practiced her as a principle rather than worship her as a deity. She represented rules that had to be obeyed rather than a figure who had to be bowed to.

The influence of Ma'at was so ingrained in the structure of Egypt that she was the basis of education. Apart from the pharaoh, scholars, scribes, and other members of the literate elite in Egypt, there were custodians of the knowledge of Ma'at. These bureaucrats were men of high standing in society who worshiped Ma'at alongside her husband Thoth, the god of wisdom.

The scribes were also in charge of educating the people on how to live their lives in accordance with the world order through oral traditions and instructional texts. One of the most famous scribes to write an instructional text in Egypt was Amenemope. His book, titled *Instruction of Amenemope,* was an advanced version of *The Maxims of Ptahhotep,* which had been written many years before Amenemope was born. During the Twentieth Dynasty of ancient Egypt, Amenemope's book became a manual for pleasing the goddess Ma'at.

The book opened by exhorting the people to obedience and a righteous interpretation of his words. It also spoke of the rewards of putting his instructions into practice:

"If you spend a lifetime with these things in your heart,

You will find it good fortune;

You will discover my words to be a treasure house of life,

And your body will flourish upon earth."

Next, the book warned against the ill-treatment of the poor, disrespect for elders, and engaging in shady business. These constituted some of the worst vices in ancient Egypt and were condemned as threats to the preservation of Ma'at.

Amenemope's book hinged largely on the topic of self-control and restraint in the face of provocation. By exhorting the people not to "quarrel with the argumentative man," to "proceed cautiously before an opponent," and to leave such people to themselves, he portrayed compliant people as being worthy examples to their children.

Public behavior and conduct were other topics that the people received clear instructions about in Amenemope's book. In places of worship, they were to be sober and silent. Since land matters were a common source of dispute in antiquity, Amenemope's book spoke against greed and altering land boundaries to accrue ill-gotten wealth or for cultivation:

"And receive the bread from your own threshing floor:

Better is the bushel which God gives you

Than five thousand deceitfully gotten."

Ensuing chapters condemned gluttony among masters and servants and bribery among government officials. He also spoke of Thoth's punishment reserved for corrupt scribes.

"The Ape [Thoth] rests [in] the temple of Khmun,

While his eye travels around the Two Lands;

If he sees one who sins with his finger [that is, a false scribe],

he takes away his provisions by the flood.

As for a scribe who sins with his finger,

His son shall not be enrolled."

Arrogance, trouble-mongering, false witnesses, and mud-slinging were also vehemently rebuked, especially since they were (and still are) common in the practice of law.

The exceptional writing abilities of scribes in antiquity made the principles of Ma'at easily understood and practicable to the people.

Even though the goddess Ma'at had no temples of her own like other goddesses, she was more important than most. Some might argue that she was the most important of all. She represented life itself, and she was omnipresent. Kings offered prayers to her to help them preserve order, and the people prayed for the same in their homes and on the streets. Every mortal in Egypt worshiped her by living their lives, and her influence remained intact for many generations.

In the afterlife, the Egyptians believed that every man's heart would be weighed against Ma'at to determine how much they complied with the principles of justice. This test would take place in the Duat, the famous underworld and the land of the dead.

Chapter 3: The Duat and the Afterlife

The Duat, also known as the underworld or Tuat, was the home of the dead. You can picture it as a dark, chilly place where droves of souls desperately awaited the arrival of Ra to revitalize them, but there was more to it than that. Ironic as it sounds, although the Duat was the "land of the dead," it was a hive of activity.

As staunch believers in life after death, the people of ancient Egypt called the Duat a soul's eternal home, meaning that one would find many souls there. There were also mythical creatures, gods, goddesses, demons, and spirits, each with roles to play.

In earlier texts, the Duat was portrayed as a celestial heaven rather than an "underworld." This was because the pharaohs who died and went to the Duat were said to have gone up to the sky as stars or became part of the sun, which traveled each day through the body of the sky goddess Nut. This makes the concept of the Duat a tad ambiguous, considering that the sky is located above the earth and not under it. Subsequently, during the Middle Kingdom, the Duat became popularized as an underworld where all humans would spend eternity.

The Duat is represented in hieroglyphic texts as a star in a circle, which possibly alludes to its multiple sub-realms. There was the realm where souls were judged, another realm where gods and goddesses lived, another realm where men who had upheld Ma'at would live, and a realm for the unjust. Thus, heaven and hell were in one place, just in different locations.

Geographically, the underworld had features that were recognizable to the souls that called it home. This included lakes and oceans with boats for souls to travel in, as well as mountains and hills. Walls made of iron, lakes of fire, and turquoise trees were slightly out of the ordinary, but the underworld struck an expected balance between normal and spectral.

The Duat: The Land of the Dead

A soul's journey into the Duat began with death.

After death, a person would be embalmed and mummified. During this process, all the internal organs in the corpse would be removed, leaving only the heart in its place. This was because the heart would be needed in the Duat.

Mummification was an important practice in ancient Egypt. It involved the removal of all moisture from a corpse, as it could cause decay. This practice was aimed at preserving much of the deceased's physical form. Although it was the soul of a person that transitioned to the Egyptian afterlife, the physical body was an equally important vessel. This vessel would convey the soul to the gates of the Duat. If the body was broken or rotten, the spirit could get lost.

It is important to emphasize that for the better part of the Old Kingdom, only pharaohs could aspire to find paradise in the afterlife. Subsequently, the people came to the knowledge that even commoners had a place in the afterlife if they were willing to do what it took. Mummification was an expensive process that was not affordable for most commoners, but the practice of drying out a corpse in the desert sun for over seventy days worked as well.

While men were more commonly mummified, noblewomen who could afford the process were mummified too. Fascinatingly, a well-preserved mummy of a pregnant woman from the 1st century BCE was unearthed in the royal tombs of Luxor in 2018.

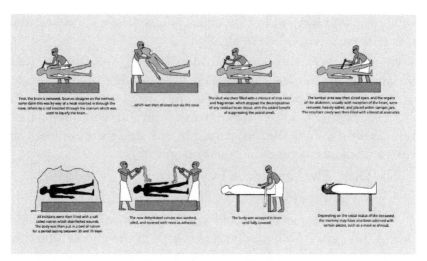

The process of mummification.

The dead were typically buried on the west bank of the Nile River, as it was believed to be the best route to the underworld. Funeral rites included invoking guardian gods and goddesses to assist the soul to the underworld. Apart from magic spells and incantations, these invocations involved such things as burying amulets, figurines, and statues of protection with the deceased.

Then, the deceased would reawaken in the Duat. The Duat was where humans were judged for their deeds on Earth, and as you can imagine, not all would pass the test. If a soul didn't pass, they would be condemned to eternal damnation in the fiery lake of fire, where Ammit, the soul-eating demon of the underworld, resided. The determination to never become prey to Ammit was what propelled the people of ancient Egypt to uphold the Ma'at with their lives.

But before the test took place, souls would be draped in clean robes and given new sandals upon entering the Duat. They were then ferried to the Hall of Truth to be judged. The Hall of Truth was large and magnificent, with souls standing in long lines for trial before Osiris, the god of the underworld.

Osiris would be flanked by the god Anubis and the god Thoth. Forty-two gods (or judges) would also be present in the hall, each representing a district (or nome) in ancient Egypt. When it was a soul's turn to be judged, the soul would step forward and say the "Declaration of Innocence" before each of the forty-two judges. Here is a short example of what they would have said:

1. "Hail Far-strider, who came forth from Heliopolis, I have done no falsehood.
2. Hail Fire-embracer, who came forth from Kheraha, I have not robbed.
3. Hail Nosey, who came forth from Hermopolis, I have not been rapacious.
4. Hail Swallower of Shades, who came forth from the cavern, I have not stolen.
5. Hail Dangerous One, who came forth from Rosetjau, I have not killed men."

These sacred confessions were a soul's testimony of having lived in line with Ma'at, and every confession had to be accepted by the gods, or else the soul was in greater danger of condemnation.

Next, their heart would be handed over for weighing by Anubis on a scale made of gold. The heart represented a person's character, personality, and values they held while on Earth. This is why the heart was typically buried with the dead in ancient Egypt.

On the other side of the golden scale would be a white ostrich feather, an aspect of Ma'at called the Feather of Truth. This test would ultimately determine if the soul was deserving of eternal life or the dreadful opposite. If the soul's heart weighed lighter than the Feather of Truth, then it meant that the soul had indeed lived a life pleasing to the gods. Their reward would be entry into the paradise of the afterlife.

If a soul's heart weighed heavier than the Feather of Truth, it meant that the soul was unjust and unfit for paradise. Their heart would be discarded in a fiery pit of fire or thrown at the soul-eating demon, Ammit. Once devoured, the soul would cease to exist and die a second death.

Ammit, the devourer of souls, as displayed in the British Museum.
https://commons.wikimedia.org/wiki/File:Ammit_BD.jpg

This was the worst fate any mortal could be condemned to, and as a result, surviving the Hall of Truth was more important to the people of Egypt than earthly riches, fame, or glory.

After the Hall of Truth was a lovely lake, known as the Lily Lake or the Lake of Flowers. Only one boat ferried souls across this lake to paradise, and the spirit in charge of the boat was named Hraf-haf. His assistant was named Aken. Hraf-haf was a mystical creature who had his head on backward, and he had a nasty temper. Even after passing the test in the Hall of Truth, the ride to paradise was not for free—at least not on Hraf-haf's watch. Some traditions claim that Hraf-haf would challenge souls to a match of fishing. Losing meant forfeiting their place on his boat and being stranded. Other accounts insist that all it took to convince the foul-tempered ferryman was to be patient and kind, despite his provocative words and glares.

Hraf-haf was not the only obstacle in a soul's path to paradise. There were other perils, such as being attacked by demons who guarded the many gates leading to paradise. These gates were either fifteen or twenty-one in number, and souls had to be on guard to ward off evil spirits.

Aaru, or the Field of Reeds, was the final destination for every soul that survived the ordeals of the Lily Lake. It was located in the east, where the sun rose, and it was usually depicted as a beautiful island with endless fields that stretched breathtakingly to the horizon.

Here, souls could live as they had on Earth. They could have farmlands and harvest crops since the weather and climatic conditions in Aaru were perpetually perfect for cultivation.

Souls could eat and drink and have parties and sex. In Aaru, the social order was preserved. Pharaohs in ancient Egypt were commonly buried with many servants because those servants would assume their duties in Aaru. Possessions that a soul, king or not, needed in the afterlife would be buried with them. These would be given to them in Aaru to be used for their convenience forever.

The Duat: Home of the Gods

You may have heard of Mount Olympus in Greek mythology or Valhalla in Norse mythology. These were the homes of the gods, and so was the Duat of Egyptian mythology. In the earlier perception of Duat as a celestial home above the earth and its eventual perception as an underworld below the earth, ancient Egyptians across all eras agreed on the existence of gods in the Duat.

The first god in the Duat was the god Osiris, following a dreadful incident with his brother Set on Earth. According to ancient texts, Osiris ruled the underworld as brilliantly as he had on Earth. His brilliant knowledge of the underworld was a guiding light for other gods who resided and worked in Duat as judges, guardians, protectors, and friends of mortal souls.

While souls waited to be judged in the Hall of Truth, they were cared for by goddesses like Isis, Nephthys, Hathor, and Qebhet. These goddesses only catered to souls they had been invoked to care for during burial. Apart from Anubis's role as the Weigher of Hearts, the god was the one who stood at the gates of the Duat to usher in souls. His companion, the god Thoth, was a counselor for souls who sought wisdom in the afterlife. They would visit him in his mansion in Aaru for this. The houses of gods and goddesses in the afterlife were more magnificent than their earthly temples, and only the righteous and just would live to see them.

The sun god Ra was another frequent guest in the Duat. Every night, he would come by in his divine boat, the Atet, after an arduous fight with the Serpent of Chaos, Apophis (or Apep). He would spend the ten hours of night revitalizing the souls in the Duat with his solar energy, and at the break of dawn, he would ascend to the sky as the sun.

This was a repeat cycle that was vital to the preservation of Ma'at; it was one that should never be disrupted. Also, with Apophis (Apep) lurking in ambush for the sun god each night, the inhabitants of the underworld would look forward to being witnesses to an epic battle and Ra's victory, something that would always happen to preserve Ma'at.

SECTION TWO: Myths and Legends

Chapter 4: Ra and Apophis

If you have ever wondered how night becomes day, imagine a certain famous god taking eternal trips through a world of dark and the dead and battling a ferocious monster to bring the sun out the next day. Such was the journey of Ra.

By now, you know of Ra, the Egyptian sun god and the sun itself. You also know his status in divinity and his prominence among the gods who laid the foundations of Egypt and the whole world as it has existed for many generations.

One of the core tenets of Egyptian mythology is the emphasis on the intervention of the gods (supernatural beings) in the affairs of humans (mortal beings). This established a complex religious system, and it has been proven to have existed during the Old Kingdom. These beliefs were derived from ancient Egyptian carvings and texts from prehistory. In them were the stories of legendary battles describing the might of the gods and how their victories preserved the earth, its elements, and all who lived on it.

One of these battles was between the sun god Ra and his archenemy, a serpentine villain called Apophis (or Apep). Snakes are creatures both dreaded and revered in Egyptian mythology. You will recall that the goddesses of the Ogdoad were portrayed as having snake heads. Even Ra is often portrayed as having a snake resting on the sun disk on his head. So, snakes did not outrightly symbolize evil.

Apophis, however, was a snake at the foot of the underworld, and he was as evil as they came. He represented chaos, darkness, and utter destruction, and he was known among both gods and men.

The name Apophis is first mentioned in documents from the Egyptian Middle Kingdom (c. 2030 BCE and 1640 BCE), which came right after the Old Kingdom.

Stories of the evil serpent's origins vary from one religious cult and location to the other, but all accounts affirm that Apophis came from Ra. Some even hold that the serpent came forth from Ra's umbilical cord, but no traditions actually refer to Apophis as an offspring of Ra. This is possibly due to Apophis's hatred of Ra and his quest to destroy the sun god by interfering with his earthly responsibilities.

What were these responsibilities, you wonder? Well, since his emergence as the solar god, Ra was chiefly responsible for separating day from night. His daily routine was to travel in the sky in his solar barque (or a chariot of some sort), which was the sun itself. Imagine the sun as a bright flaming barque floating in the clouds and spreading its radiance everywhere it passes; that would be the god Ra at work.

When evening came, Ra would make his slow descent into the underworld on the western horizon; this is why the sun always sets in the west. After spending the night in the underworld, Ra's little ship would rise to the skies again in the east.

Ra never traveled alone. With him on his floating vessel were soldiers (or defenders), such as the god Set (before he turned evil) and the Eye of Ra. They helped protect the sun god.

Midway in their descent to the underworld, Ra and his entourage would be beset by Apophis. Usually, Apophis would lurk around a mountain in the west known as Bakhu at sunset or somewhere in the underworld before the crack of dawn. Ra could never predict where the serpent was waiting to attack, which is why one of Apophis's aliases is the "Encircler of the World." Apophis was a prisoner who could never live on Earth or even in the underworld. He would block the sun god's path to the underworld, and he would not be removed until he was defeated. A few stories suggest that Apophis was bitter since the sun god had overthrown him as the god of gods, but many agree that the serpent was evil from the onset.

Thus, a battle would ensue every night between the sun god and Apophis. Sometimes, the sun god fought alone, and other times, he would have some help from members of his entourage, notably the god Set and Bastet, the fierce goddess of protection. She would take the form of a celestial cat and fight Apophis since cats and snakes were known to be natural enemies.

It should be emphasized that Apophis was a formidable opponent. He was not a mortal creature, so he was incredibly tough to kill, even for a god. He could be repelled, imprisoned, weakened, or dismembered at best. Apophis could eat anything and yet not kill it. Instead, what he ate would be lost forever in a dark abyss, never to taste death or the afterlife. He could prey on the living or dead, gods or mortals. In some accounts, he commanded an army of demons in his likeness. Apophis's eyes held the power of hypnosis, another weapon he wielded in warfare. Ra would sometimes be hypnotized by Apophis, but the gods and goddesses in his company would move swiftly to his rescue.

To mark the start of every battle, Apophis would let out an ear-splitting roar and slither violently toward the sun god. His charge was what caused earthquakes. Every time Set speared Apophis, pinning him to the ground, Apophis would wriggle in brutal rage and roar in pain, causing thunderstorms on the earth.

However, despite Apophis's dreadful outlook, it was never heard of for Ra to lose a battle to the snake. A few times, the sun god would be swallowed by Apophis; this was believed to be the cause of solar eclipses. But in the end, Ra would win the battle. He would tear his way out of the beast's belly and vanquish Apophis, usually with the help of his army of gods and goddesses.

The sun god could not lose to Apophis because that would mark the end of the sun god. If there was no sun god, there would be no sun. And without the sun, there would be no daytime. Without daytime, Earth and mankind would be doomed to perpetual darkness.

Knowing how important Ra's victory was to their existence, mortals would not leave the nightly war between darkness and light to chance.

The Banishment of Apophis

"Get thee back, Apep, thou enemy of Ra, thou winding serpent in the form of an intestine, without arms [and] without legs. Thy body cannot stand upright so that thou mayest have therein being, long is thy tail in front of thy den, thou enemy; retreat before Ra. Thy head shall be cut off, and the slaughter of thee shall be carried out."

-Excerpt from an ancient hieroglyphic spell translated by Sir Wallis Budge

Every year in Egypt, a momentous occasion brought all the worshipers and priests of Ra together in temples throughout the land. The occasion would ensure the victory of the sun god against his vengeful opponent, Apophis, and preserve the order of the world (also known as Ma'at).

Of all the supernatural beings in Egyptian mythology, only Apophis was actively worshiped against. There was no motive for his evil nature, and he had no good side to him. He hated mortals and only sought their annihilation, so rituals and rites had to be adhered to in order to keep Apophis and his wickedness at bay.

The most prominent of these rites was the Banishment of Apophis, also known as the Banishment of Apep or the Banishment of Chaos. This ritual was held in all the provinces of ancient Egypt, as they were all united against a common enemy. The success of this ritual would guarantee the sun god's victory for the next year.

The Banishment of Apophis would begin with the crafting of an effigy or statue representing the serpent. This effigy would be made to bear all the curses and evil of the land and then burned to ashes, which symbolizes the destruction of Apophis. In other temples, images of Apophis would be illustrated on papyruses. They would then be cursed and burned.

These rituals were led by priests, who were guided by a special book titled the "Book of Apophis." The book outlined instructions on other ways to defy Apophis, apart from burning his image. These included spitting on Apophis, trampling on him with the left foot, putting chains on Apophis, and stabbing him with lances or knives. These rites expressed the people's disdain for the evil serpent, and they were believed to give strength to their champion, the sun god, in battle.

Apophis was also an eater of the dead. The Egyptians feared their dead might become prey to the serpent's monstrous appetites, so they buried spells and incantations to repel Apophis with their dead. This would protect their souls in the afterlife from destruction.

The legend of Ra and Apophis had a tremendous influence on the religious affairs of ancient Egypt. It gave the people a sense of duty to preserve their existence by keeping evil under subjugation. Every time the sun rose the next day, they were assured that the sun god Ra had won another victory.

Chapter 5: The Osiris Myth

Pyramids were all the rage in the Old and Middle Kingdoms. Just by looking at pictures of them, you wonder how much time, money, and effort it took to build something so majestic. The answer is a lot. Such resources would not be expended by people who were passive or agnostic about the afterlife.

Egyptians who were not kings were also uniquely buried for a smooth passage to the afterlife. The corpses of nobles were typically mummified: embalmed and wrapped in bandages made from linen, then buried facing the east (where the sun rose). This way, their spirits would rise up and join the sun god on his eternal journey to and from the underworld. Commoners who could not afford the process of mummification left the bodies of their deceased out in the desert sun for more than two months as a method of embalmment. Even though pyramid-building was seen as old-fashioned in the New Kingdom, the Egyptian belief in life after death remained, as did the funeral rites to ensure the deceased's passage.

What was the foundation of this unwavering Egyptian faith, you wonder? It was a myth. The most popular myth in Egyptian mythology at that. It was based on a very intriguing family feud. This chapter puts the spotlight on the myth of Osiris, the god-king who transitioned gloriously to the afterlife despite the rather sordid circumstances.

Family Feud

In the creation story of Heliopolis, the sun god Ra's grandchildren, Geb and Nut, had four to five children before they were forced to separate by their father, Shu, who did not quite approve of their union.

Now, this story begins at a time when Egypt was ruled by Osiris, the first son of Geb and Nut. Our protagonist's earthly form was a handsome bearded young man draped in royal raiment and a feathered headdress (called an Atef) set upon his jet-black hair. His charm and charisma were amplified by his rare wisdom, which he used to rule Egypt.

An image of Osiris.
Unknown author, CC0, via Wikimedia Commons;
https://commons.wikimedia.org/wiki/File:The_Sacred_Books_and_Early_Literature_of_t he_East,_vol._2,_pg._64-65,_Osiris.jpg

The exact time that Osiris was the ruler of Egypt is unknown, which is why historical texts commonly refer to him as a "pre-dynastic" or "primeval" king. At the very least, it can be assumed that Osiris inherited the throne from his father Geb, who was the god of the earth.

Osiris's reign was marked by significant reforms in the lives of the people. First, he outlawed cannibalism in Egypt. In place of such barbarism, Osiris guided his people to look to alternatives like growing their own food on arable land. He blessed all who raised bountiful harvests for their sustenance. This earned Osiris the divine title as the god of fertility, agriculture, and vegetation.

Another highlight of Osiris's reign appears in Plutarch's famous work *Moralia*. This was the improvement of Egypt's artistic culture. Music and dance flourished in Egypt under Osiris's watchful eye, and one day, he embarked on a worldwide voyage to spread this newfound civilization. The god-king visited many lands in Europe and the Near East, bringing the world into a new era of arts and culture. Before leaving home, Osiris entrusted the rulership of Egypt to his wife, who was also his sister, Isis.

Queen Isis adored her husband and held the fort in his absence, despite her secret pains of not having borne him an heir. She had watched her husband administer a kingdom, instilling its people with the virtues of truth, fairness, and justice to the people. She resolved to preserve the standards by being an amiable ruler.

When she received the king's mandate to rule in his stead until he returned, little did she know that a deathly scheme was in the works. This sinister plot was being championed by her other brother, Set.

In the Egyptian corpus, you will find divergent versions of Set's motive for harming a good king. The Greek historian Plutarch suggests that Set had long harbored jealous and envious feelings toward his brother's fortune and peaceful reign over Egypt. He coveted the throne and everything his older brother had. This speaks to a motive that is mostly, if not wholly, influenced by Set's bad nature. After all, he was the god of violent chaos and war. He is represented as a red-haired creature with physical resemblances to multiple animals, including hyenas, jackals, pigs, and foxes.

Other accounts, notably from the Pyramid Texts, infer that Set's hatred toward his brother may have had deeper roots. Some tales say that Osiris slept with Set's wife (and sister), Nephthys, with their illicit affair resulting in the birth of Anubis. In the god-king's defense, Nephthys had deceived him by taking on the form of Osiris's wife, Isis, and he had slept with her thinking it was truly his wife.

Plutarch tells us that Set would not be appeased. Enraged at his brother, Set swore that he would kill Osiris. Set quickly rallied a small group of conspirators. King Osiris was loved by too many people for Set to easily find accomplices, so he bribed a few dishonorable men to his side or manipulated them with words. While the god-king was away on his trip, Set and his men hatched a dark plan.

Soon enough, Set announced he would hold a grand banquet at his place, possibly to celebrate his brother's return from his successful tour of the world. The day came, and it saw the attendance of numerous guests, including King Osiris himself. There was food, wine, and a rather peculiar party favor: a coffin (sometimes written as a chest) fashioned from the highest quality materials in all the land.

Such a coffin would no doubt allow for a most comfortable journey to the afterlife, and nearly every guest in the banquet hall coveted it. Their desire to own the coffin surged when Set announced that the coffin was a prize to be won.

The challenge was simple. One had to step into the coffin and lay inside it. Whoever fit into the coffin perfectly could have it. Set's guests leaped out of their seats for a chance to win it. A good number of them tried to get in the coffin, but none could fit. Guest after guest attempted, and guest after guest failed. This was because the dimensions of the coffin could never fit anyone else in Egypt, save for one: King Osiris himself.

Excited to participate in the game, the king stepped into the coffin and lay inside it. It was a match so perfect that the guests wondered if it was made specifically for the king. In the time it took for them to explore their curiosities, Set swung into action, slamming the coffin shut and coating it with lead.

The reality of Set's evil plan unfolded like a scroll before the people. The coffin had indeed been made for the king. It was all a fatal trap.

Set ordered the coffin be dumped into the depths of the Nile River, sentencing his brother to a most agonizing death. The coffin submerged into the Nile and vanished from sight. All of Egypt was forced to follow a new king.

Redemption and Revenge

Poor Isis learned of the tragedy that had befallen her husband at the hands of Set. Consumed with sorrow, she escaped from the palace and took to searching every inch of the Nile River for the god-king's body. If she could find him, she could heal him with her magical powers, or she could give him a king's funeral if it was too late. The Nile River was a vast expanse of water to search, so the queen must have been at it for a long time. A few traditions say that she ran into Anubis during her journey. He had been cast aside by his mother, Nephthys, and hated by his father, Set, because he was Osiris's son. Queen Isis took Anubis in and raised him as her own.

Meanwhile, Egypt had erupted in anarchy under Set's reign. All of King Osiris's good work had nearly come undone, and the people suffered as a result. They no longer lived peaceful and prosperous lives.

The queen's resilience paid off one auspicious day. Isis heard the news that the coffin had drifted across the Nile to a small city in Phoenicia called Byblos. As it turned out, Osiris's coffin had washed ashore in Byblos. A tamarisk tree grew around it, trapping the coffin in its trunk. King Osiris's residual powers made this deciduous tree flourish season after season while having a distinct fragrance. Some accounts state that the tree could even glow.

It occurred to King Malcander of Byblos and his wife, Queen Astarte (or Ishtar), that it was no ordinary tamarisk tree. The king ordered that the tree be cut down, and he had an ornamental pillar made out of it. This pillar stood in his palace to the envy of all who laid eyes upon it.

The palace of Byblos had many court ladies who tended to the royal family with their skills in child-nursing, grooming, and cloth and perfume making. One day, a frail old woman arrived at the palace gates and pleaded to have an audience with the queen.

Unknown to the people of Byblos, they had just received the goddess Isis, and she was on an important rescue mission. As part of the plan to save Osiris, Isis (in disguise) petitioned Queen Astarte for a job in the palace. If she planned to stay in Byblos, she needed the job to stay near her trapped husband.

The queen of Byblos graciously accepted Isis into her service and entrusted Isis with the care of her son. In gratitude, Isis resolved to immortalize the young prince. It was a magic ritual process that involved bathing the baby in fire to burn away his mortality. A disguised Isis began the ritual that night, but she was interrupted by the boy's mother.

Astarte must have been horrified to find her son's nurse bathing him with fire. She demanded an explanation. It was at that moment that Isis revealed her true identity. The queen of Byblos was entranced to discover that she housed a goddess under her roof. She worshiped Isis, who then revealed her true intent. Without hesitation, the king and queen of Byblos granted Isis's request, and the coffin was removed from inside the pillar.

By then, Osiris was as good as dead, but his wife would not give up. She returned to Egypt and healed him. Many accounts agree that Horus the Younger, the son of Isis and Osiris, was born around this time.

Set, who was ruling Egypt, heard the news of his brother's survival, and he was not pleased. His wife Nephthys had begun to regret her role in the war between her brothers, as well as her abandonment of Anubis.

Set ordered the arrest and detainment of Isis, and for his brother Osiris, he ordered a second death. Plutarch argues that this happened as soon as Isis stepped foot on Egyptian soil with her convalescing husband.

Isis escaped detainment with Anubis's help, but Osiris was not so lucky. Set took advantage of his weakness and violently murdered him. Afterward, Set dismembered Osiris's corpse into fourteen pieces and dispersed them, making sure each piece was far apart from another. Such aggression was Set's twisted way of ensuring that Osiris would not make it back alive again.

Isis mourned Osiris's inhumane demise and set out with her sister, Nephthys, and Horus to find and reassemble Osiris's mutilated body parts. Their quest was a success, at least for the most part. The sisters were able to recover all of Osiris's body parts except his penis. Set had discarded it in the depths of the Nile River, and fish had eaten it. Some stories say that Isis fashioned him a new one made out of wood, while others say she used magic.

With Isis's powers, Osiris came back to life, but he was no longer complete. This made him unfit to reclaim his throne. Instead, he transitioned to the underworld, where he became its god and the judge of the dead.

That was hardly the end of Isis's troubles. Set was still on the rampage, searching high and low for her son Horus. Set sought to take his life just as he had taken his father's.

Isis fled to the marshlands of Egypt with her son, and there, she raised him. Horus grew from boy to man, sharpening his sword of revenge. He learned all about spells and the art of warfare. His archenemy was the god of war himself, and his mother raised him not to be a pushover.

Horus grew to become a mighty warrior and Set's arch-nemesis. Egypt was on the verge of desolation under his cruel rule, and the impoverished people of Egypt found a beacon of hope in Horus. They offered him their support and followed in vast numbers when he led the charge against the tyrant Set.

Set was removed from the throne of Egypt; some say he was killed, while others believe he was exiled into the Red Sea. It is unknown if he reached a new shore or if he continues to drift upon the waves. Most importantly, this tale ends in a resounding victory for the son of Osiris, whose reign would be a soothing balm to a wounded Egypt.

Chapter 6:
Time and the End of Times

Discovering the measurement of time and its passage was a great feat for many ancient civilizations, the ancient Egyptians included.

As you can imagine, there were no wall clocks, wristwatches, or grandfather clocks in the Old and Middle Kingdoms. Still, people needed to keep track of time to figure out how best to apply it to daily living. Only time could separate a day from another day, a week from another week, and a year from another year.

The sun god Ra and his company made trips to and from the underworld every day on his chariot or boat, and the ancient Egyptians got to work themselves to seek the answers of time and space. In the chronology of discoveries, it is agreeable that ancient Egyptians had figured out the "End of Times" first.

The End of Times

The "End of Times" is used to describe the final stage of cosmology: the end of the world as we know it. It refers to an event where the world, humans, and possibly the gods are no longer in existence. In ancient Egypt, it was a time when the world went back to being a void and was supplanted by what had existed in the first place: Nun.

There are two perspectives to the ancient Egyptian belief in the "End of Times." The first perspective was prevalent when the gods ruled the earth as kings. The second perspective slightly reshaped the Egyptian belief system from the Old Kingdom to after the New Kingdom, when Christianity came to Egypt.

The First Perspective: Gods and Men

Compared to other ancient civilizations, such as Mesopotamia and Greece, the ancient Egyptian belief system initially perceived the end of the world as a mistake to be avoided rather than an eventuality.

How you wonder?

Take Greece and Mesopotamia, for instance. Both civilizations believed there would be a flood, similar to the biblical story about Noah, where a flood destroyed the earth. In Mesopotamian mythology, when the flood came, the humans would have to build arks—just like Noah in the Bible did—to save themselves. In the Greek flood myth, only a man named Deucalion and his wife survived the flood by hiding out in a chest.

These flood myths were told in Greece and Mesopotamia as inevitable events and some sort of inescapable punishment for mankind. The nature of the ancient Egyptian perspective on the End of the World (or the apocalypse) was not inevitable.

You are familiar with the sun god's daily routine and how important it is to the preservation of Ma'at. You should also recall that the Egyptians of old played a big role in giving their gods the strength to perform their divine tasks through prayers and worship. Their greatest fear was that if they faltered, the gods could become weak and falter. The eventuality of this would be a disruption in the natural order, but that would be only the tip of a disastrous iceberg. If gods like Ra ever lost their strength and had no worshipers to invigorate them, they could die.

The death of the gods would spell the end of the world, and the murder of the god-king Osiris by his brother Set was a close call. Chaos befell Egypt after Osiris's death, and were it not for the resilience of Queen Isis and the victory of Horus the Younger, the destruction of Ma'at would have been complete. Ma'at had also been shaken to its core when Shu, the son of Ra, had left his throne on Earth and ascended to the sky. A violent storm ravaged the world for nine days, and no god or man could enjoy a moment of clarity until Geb was enthroned.

So, the preservation of Ma'at in the ancient Egyptian belief system was a joint effort by the gods and the humans who worshiped them. As long as each one played their part, the "End of Times" would remain an avoidable consequence.

From another viewpoint, rather than large-scale destruction and the harvesting of souls, the Egyptians perceived the predestined "End of Times" as strictly individualistic. No human could escape death, and after someone died, there was an afterlife where they would spend eternity.

In the Pyramid Texts and other ancient documents, the end of the world was evoked in a peculiar manner. It was seen as a threat to the gods. This is incredibly ironic, considering that ancient Egyptians revered their gods. However, Egyptians were known to threaten the gods with mayhem if their prayers were not answered.

"O Lord of the horizon, make ready a place for me. For if you fail to make ready a place for me, I will lay a curse on my father Geb, and the earth will speak no more, Geb will be unable to protect himself, and whoever I find in my way, I will devour him piecemeal."

Many variants of these kinds of threats can be found in the Coffin Texts (more information on them can be found in Chapter 19), spell books, and medical journals from the Old Kingdom.

Did these threats ever move the gods to action?   Shockingly, they did. The gods wanted Ma'at to be sustained just as much as the mortals. They considered such "worship threats" to be expressions of fervent prayers, and they responded swiftly to all who evoked them. This remains a fascinating aspect of ancient Egyptians' worship of the gods.

The Second Perspective: Men

This saga is set in Early Dynastic Egypt.

The gods no longer ruled men, at least not directly. They were still involved in the affairs of nature and order. Humans still worshiped the gods and looked up to the pharaoh as a guiding light and the messenger of the gods.

The first pharaoh of a united Egypt was Menes (or Narmer, according to some). He established the First Dynasty sometime in the 3000s BCE in ancient Egypt. He is best known for uniting

Upper and Lower Egypt under a single ruler. This made Menes and the other pharaohs after him very powerful.

This became problematic in the long run, though. With the rule of the pharaohs over a united Egypt came an influx of apocalyptic prophecies, each describing a very dramatic "End of Times." These prophecies have been criticized as propaganda-driven, as they typically proffered the reign of a certain pharaoh as the only way to avert the coming danger. However, these stories of a looming apocalypse shifted ancient Egypt's belief system from the god-centric perspective it once held.

First, there was the Prophecy of Neferti.

Sometime in the mid-2000s BCE, the Fourth Dynasty of ancient Egypt was established by the reigning pharaoh, Snefru. King Snefru's kingdom was vast and prosperous, extending to the lands of Libya and Nubia (Sudan). He also commanded a massive labor force and was wealthy in land and cattle.

One day, Pharaoh Snefru was in high spirits and sought to be entertained by an excellent lyrical poet or sage. The men in the king's court recommended a man named Neferti as being best suited for the job.

The king trusted his courtiers and had Neferti brought before him immediately. After paying homage to the pharaoh, Neferti presented the king with two kinds of stories: stories of the past and stories of the future.

It seemed as if Neferti was living up to his reputation. Since Snefru was the pharaoh of Egypt, there was nothing about the past he did not know. He was a revered custodian of knowledge of the gods and the long history of Egypt. But he did not know of the future.

Without hesitation, King Snefru chose to hear stories of the future. Neferti's story, as the king was about to find out, was a prophecy of doom.

"I show you the land in turmoil; what should not be has come to pass. Men will seize weapons of warfare, the land will live in uproar. Men will make arrows of copper, will crave blood for bread, will laugh aloud at distress. None will weep over death, none will wake fasting for death...

Ra will withdraw from mankind: though he will rise at his hour, one will not know when noon has come; no one will discern his shadow, no face will be dazzled by seeing [him], no eyes will moisten with water. He will be in the sky like the moon, his nightly course unchanged, his rays on the face as before."

The first part of Neferti's prophecy described political unrest, civil war, and social anarchy; this is not quite enough to be apocalyptic. It also limited the disaster to Egypt as a nation. However, the second part of the prophecy where Ra is mentioned transformed Neferti's speech from a mere prediction to a prophecy of cosmological bedlam.

King Snefru and his courtiers must have been horrified to hear of such things as the Nile drying up or Ra turning his back on mankind. These events symbolized an age of overwhelming evil and the termination of Ma'at, but there was a resolution: "Then a king will come from the South, Ameny by name...Then Order will return to its seat, while Chaos is driven away."

As it would turn out, this king from the south was Amenemhat I, who would rule Egypt eight dynasties later. Glorifying a pharaoh as the bringer of peace to a disrupted land—and inadvertently the whole world—further established the supremacy of the Egyptian monarchy.

The gods were no longer the sole centerpiece of the people's belief in the "End of Times." Their salvation was now in the hands of a mortal man. Neferti's apocalyptic message surfaced at a time when the kings of Egypt had better positioned themselves as the messiahs of the people. As important intermediaries between the gods and the people, the pharaohs were worshiped and offered the same sacrifices as the gods.

Despite being set hundreds of years earlier, the recovered document containing the Prophecy of Neferti was written around the Twelfth Dynasty, during the reign of the king that was prophesied about. Convenient, don't you think?

This has left historians skeptical about the authenticity of the prophecy. It was possibly a ruse to justify Amenemhat's alleged usurpation of the Egyptian throne from King Mentuhotep IV, whom he had served as a vizier.

The Book of Asclepius: Back to Divinity

In the 1ˢᵗ to 3ʳᵈ centuries CE, ancient Egypt underwent what some might consider a Roman invasion. During this period, ancient Egypt became a Roman province whose political and religious mythical beliefs were fused with Graeco-Roman mythology. This fusion is known as syncretism.

For example, the Greek god Zeus was fused with the Egyptian god Amun, becoming Zeus-Ammon. Ra was the equivalent of Apollo, Aphrodite was the equivalent of Queen Isis, and the Greek god Hermes was the equivalent of the Egyptian god Thoth.

The syncretism of Hermes and Thoth created a mythical author named Hermes Trismegistus, and in the 4ᵗʰ century CE, a sacred apocalyptic text written by this legendary figure was found in Egypt. It was part of a large document called the *Corpus Hermeticum*, and the prophecy inside it was titled the "Book of Asclepius."

This prophecy had a chilling melancholic tone:

"A time will come when it will be seen that in vain the Egyptians served the deity with piety and assiduous service, and all their holy worship will be found fruitless and to no profit. For the deity will retire from earth to heaven, and Egypt will be forsaken; and the land which was the home of religion will be left desolate, bereft of the presence of its gods. Foreigners will fill this country, and not only will the observances be neglected, but even more terrible, it will be made compulsory by so-called laws, under pain of prescribed punishments, to abstain from all religious practices, from any act of piety towards the gods. This most holy land, country of sanctuaries and temples, will be covered with sepulchers and corpses."

This apocalypse, dreadful as it is, ends with a message of hope and rebirth orchestrated by the gods. This prophecy was given by the god Thoth to Asclepius, a demi-god in Graeco-Roman mythology, and it was documented by Hermes Trismegistus. It was a three-pronged message of predestination, and unlike the Prophecy of Neferti, it resonated with the reality of the times. Egypt was under Roman subjugation after a war-torn era, and according to the prophecy, more turbulence lay ahead in order for the world to be cleansed. Most significant of all, the salvation of the world was not in the hands of any man; rather, it was in the hands of a divine being who could neither be bribed nor controlled.

There remains debate as to whether Hermes Trismegistus, the acclaimed author of this apocalyptic prophecy, actually existed. Yet he was an influential figure in Graeco-Roman and Egyptian mythology as a patron of writing.

The Telling of Time

A long time ago, there were no alarm clocks and fashionable wristwatches to tell the time by. Such technologies were not to be discovered until thousands of years later. Still, people had to figure out what time of the day it was or what season was best to do this or that in.

Ancient Egypt had one of the richest civilizations of its time; there is no doubt about that. And Egyptians are credited with some of the earliest innovations of telling the time. This was possible because they believed in the sun god's journey of separating day from night. From as early as 3500 BCE, Egyptians had developed a unique lunar calendar that had thirty days in twelve months: a total of 360 days.

Rather than summer, spring, winter, or autumn, ancient Egypt's seasons were named Akhet, Peret, and Shemu.

Akhet: The Flooding of the Nile

Akhet was also known as the "Season of the Inundation" or the "Season of the Flood." Believed to be the first season in the year, Akhet had four months: *Thout*, named after the ancient Egyptian god of wisdom and science; *Paopi*, named after a famous festival celebrated that month in honor of Ra; *Hathor*, named after the ancient Egyptian goddess of the sky; and *Koiak*, named after a sacred bull in ancient Egypt.

The Akhet season marked the momentous flooding of the Nile River. Since the Nile River was the main source of Egypt's water supply, every time the waters overflowed, the lands would regain their fertility. As you are bound to notice, the Nile River was the centerpiece of the ancient Egyptian calendar in its entirety. The division of time into days, months, and years was an innovation resulting from a close observation of the Nile's patterns. Akhet brought bountiful water to the Nile, more so than any other time of the year, and it marked the start of a new agricultural season.

Akhet also marked colorful religious festivities in honor of the sun god Ra and the goddess Hathor. During the New Kingdom, rituals and festivals in honor of Osiris, Isis, and Nephthys became popular in the month of *Koiak*.

The equivalent of the Akhet season in modern-day calendars falls between September and January.

Peret: The Planting Season

After four months of enriching the soils of Egypt, the Nile River would pull back, leaving the land ripe for planting. Ancient Egyptians called this season Peret or the "Season of Emergence." The word "emergence" refers to the lands along the Nile River, which reemerged after being flooded with water during the Akhet season.

Peret also had four months (approximately between January and May), which gave farmers ample time to plow their lands and plant their seeds. The first month in Peret (or the fifth month in the year) was *Tobi*, named after one of the many forms of the god Ra. Next was *Meshir*, named after the ancient Egyptian god of the wind. *Paremhat* came next, and it was named after a pharaoh who reigned in the 1500s BCE. And the last month of the season, *Pharmouthi* or *Paremoude*, was named in deference to the ancient Egyptian goddess of nourishment and the harvest, Renenutet.

Since the ancient Egyptians were busy cultivating their farmlands, it is no surprise that no elaborate festivals or rituals were celebrated during the Peret season. Instead, they would offer up prayers to Min and Renenutet, the god and goddess of the harvest, to bless their lands and bring them a plentiful harvest in the coming season.

Shemu: A Bountiful Harvest

The harvest season was the most anticipated time of the year in ancient Egypt. The Nile River at this time was at its lowest, and the new crops sprouting from the ground were ready for reaping in the Shemu season, also known as the "Season of Harvest." There would be fresh food in Egypt, a reward for many months of labor.

The Shemu season was also the driest; it would be the equivalent of summer (May to September), with four months marking the end of the year. The first month of the season (and the ninth month of the year) was *Pashons*, a derivative of the god of the moon and son of Ra, Khonsu. After it came *Paoni*, which was named after the festival of the dead (the Valley Festival), which was celebrated during the month. The next month was *Epip*, and after it was *Mesori*, which celebrated the end of the harvest season and the New Year.

Festivities to mark the end of the year were held in honor of Ra, and the thirtieth day of *Mesori* was a special holiday in ancient Egypt. It was the last day of the year, and a series of intriguing events were planned. First, every royal artisan (sculptors, carpenters, painters, smiths, builders, and scribes who lived in the palace) could take the day off work. They joined the townspeople to perform sacred rites. Every temple in Egypt was fortified with spells and torches to ward off evil while the people celebrated. If there were any new pharaohs to be crowned, this was typically the season to do it, and every sitting pharaoh would receive goodwill gifts from his retainers.

As the streets of Egypt lit up in anticipation of the New Year, the people would exchange gifts in good faith. After having harvested and stored enough food in the Shemu season, the people of ancient Egypt would not need to worry about their survival during the coming Akhet season when the Nile would flood again.

Sundials, Shadow Clocks, and Merkhets

The most important highlight in all of the ancient Egyptian seasons was the sun god's preeminence. Every season had a month named after him or one of his forms. The sun, like the Nile River, was a marker of times and seasons. The ancient Egyptians were ahead of their time; they created the first known solar calendar. They discovered the importance of the sun and its cyclical pattern and applied it in the invention of the solar calendar.

More remarkably, the ancient Egyptians were able to use the sun to tell the hours of the day with one of their inventions. The earliest time-telling device was the obelisk, a stone-carved monument with a pointed top and four corners. Obelisks were strategically erected, and their height dimensions were specific enough so they could reflect the motion of the sun. The shadow cast by the sun against a side of the obelisk represented morning or noon.

While obelisks were of tremendous use to the people who lived in Egypt over five thousand years ago, there was a small challenge—obelisks were not mobile. They were not moveable, which meant that people would have to walk miles to the nearest obelisk to be able to tell the time.

It simply would not do.

So, the Egyptians got creative again. The ideal invention had to be portable so that people would be able to tell the time wherever they went. One day, around 1500 BCE, the shadow-casting time-telling technology got a massive upgrade. Someone invented the sundial.

The Egyptian sundial.

The sundial was an intriguing artifact consisting of a flat plate called the dial and something called a gnomon on it. The gnomon was triangle-shaped and protruded out of the dial. It served a similar purpose to hands on a clock by tracing the sun's every move across the sky. Each move would cast a shadow on the dial, which would progress slowly around the plate. This allowed people to tell the hours of the day, but what happened when the sun went down?

Merkhets were used. The merkhet read the journey of stars at night, and it was typically made of wood or bone. Ancient Egyptians used this to track the movement of ten stars across the meridian. Each star represented an hour of the night, totaling ten hours for the night and an hour for the sunrise. Daytime had twelve hours and one hour for sunset, bringing the total to twenty-four hours.

Chapter 7: The Golden Lotus

Another enthralling myth that comes to us from ancient Egypt is that of the Golden Lotus.

Nearly all of the tombs and temples discovered in ancient Egypt had carvings and representations of the lotus flower; in fact, the lotus is regarded as Egypt's national flower today.

The lotus symbolized healing, creation, and spiritual rebirth. This was inspired by how lotuses bloomed in the sunlight and closed their petals to submerge under the water at night. The next morning, the lotuses would reemerge on the water's surface, opening up their petals to herald the sun (or be "reborn"). Lotuses could only be found in ponds and lakes, and they looked as beautiful as they smelled.

In Egypt, you would find blue lotuses adorning the length of the River Nile, and they were famed across the land for their beauty and rejuvenation.

According to the creation myth in Memphis, the god Nefertum emerged as a lotus flower when the world was created by his father, Ptah. Nefertum is depicted as a beautiful young man with a lotus flower on his head, and he was worshiped as the Protector of the Two Lands (Upper and Lower Egypt).

At ancient Egyptian funerals, oil extracted from the lotus flowers was used as an ingredient to mummify the deceased and neutralize the stench of decay. In Egyptian art, there are many depictions of the gods and goddesses holding lotuses to the noses of pharaohs and queens of Egypt, symbolizing their rebirth into the afterlife.

Knowing the significance of these beautiful flowers, the myth of the Golden Lotus can be better appreciated. This story is set during the reign of Snefru (also spelled as Sneferu, the same king who received the Prophecy of Neferti). Snefru is also famed for his strides in ancient Egyptian architecture. This was a legacy continued by his son, Khufu, who built the Great Pyramid of Giza, one of the Seven Wonders of the Ancient World.

The Egyptian myth of the Golden Lotus also originates from the ancient city of Memphis, and it begins with the king feeling rather bored one day. All was well during his reign. There were no civil wars or foreign aggression. The king strolled through his majestic palace, yearning for some sort of entertainment. There were no movies or cinemas in ancient Egypt, but there was music, dancing, and magic.

King Snefru thought of his chief magician, a formidable man named Djadjaemankh. If he invited Djadjaemankh to his palace, the man could perform magic tricks that would lift his spirits. Immediately, he ordered the chief magician to be brought before him.

Djadjaemankh was summoned from his residence, the House of Wisdom. Upon appearing before the king, the chief magician worshiped Snefru and asked how he could be of service. The king expressed his desire to be entertained by a private magic show since all other forms of entertainment had become a bore.

Djadjaemankh, however, had something more outlandish in mind. Instead of a magic show in the palace, he requested the king to take a boat ride on the Nile River with the promise of something wondrous.

The pharaoh saw nothing entertaining about a boat ride—he had been on tons of them with all that time on his hands. Djadjaemankh then introduced a fresh dynamic. Instead of the regular boat rowers, the king was to take twenty beautiful virgins with him as rowers for the trip. These women needed to have long, flowing hair.

This tickled King Snefru's fascination, and he handed over the charge of preparing for the boat ride to Djadjaemankh. The magician ensured that only the most beautiful women were selected. Their oars were fashioned from the finest ebony and coated with gold.

King Snefru's best royal boat was rowed out to the Nile River, and the women, who were dressed in gold-threaded raiment, took their positions to start the journey. From his royal on-boat pavilion, the king was delighted at the view of the sparkling Nile and the beautiful women he was surrounded by. All the women wore ornaments, such as jewelry and hairpins made of pure gold—gifts from the king himself.

As the magnificent royal boat continued along the seemingly endless river, the lead rower on one side of the boat accidentally knocked off the golden lotus that held her hair in place. The golden lotus slipped into the river and was submerged in no time.

Distraught, the rower stopped her rowing, suspending the pharaoh's leisure trip. King Snefru inquired into the disturbance, and the woman narrated her plight to him. She had lost a valuable gift and sought to retrieve it.

The pharaoh, in his magnanimity, entreated the woman to be calm and continue the journey. He also promised that he would replace the lost golden lotus, but the woman refused. She wanted her old lotus back, and she would not go on without it.

Only one man could bring back a submerged lotus, and it was the man who had suggested the trip in the first place. The pharaoh ordered the chief magician to be brought before him on the boat and relayed his dilemma to him:

"Zazamankh [Djadjaemankh], my friend and brother, I have done as you advised. My royal heart is refreshed and my eyes are delighted at the sight of these lovely rowers bending to their task. As we pass up and down on the waters of the lake, and they sing to me, while on the shore I see the trees and the flowers and the birds, I seem to be sailing into the golden days either those of old when Re ruled on earth, or those to come when the good god Osiris shall return from the Duat.

But now a golden lotus has fallen from the hair of one of these maidens fallen to the bottom of the lake. And she has ceased to sing and the rowers on her side cannot keep time with their oars. And she is not to be comforted with promises of other gifts, but weeps for her golden lotus. Zazamankh, I wish to give back the golden lotus to the little one here, and see the joy return to her eyes."

This was Djadjaemankh's cue to perform a most glorious deed. He assured the king and everyone on the boat that the lotus would be retrieved. The magician moved to the back of the boat and faced the vast waters, holding his magic wand. After a recital of spells and incantations, Djadjaemankh stretched out his wand over the water, and a rushing sound shook the currents.

Slowly, the waters gave way "as if a piece had been cut out of it with a great sword." The lake had parted into two halves, and the cut-out part was mounted on each side to make high cliffs of water.

No one on the boat could believe their eyes.

With Djadjaemankh leading the way, the royal boat dived into the open depths of the lake and drifted to the bottom, where it was as dry as land. It did not take too long to spot the golden lotus, and the woman who had lost it quickly retrieved it, overjoyed.

Djadjaemankh levitated the king's boat to the surface and returned the cut-out piece of the lake back to its place, closing up the waters. The pharaoh was beyond impressed by such a show of the supernatural. He applauded Djadjaemankh in the noblest words he had ever spoken to a retainer: "Zazamankh [Djadjaemankh], my brother, you are the greatest and wisest of magicians! You have shown me wonders and delights this day, and your reward shall be all that you desire, and a place next to my own in Egypt."

The king had had enough entertainment to last him the day—and possibly a lifetime—so the royal boat sailed for the palace with songs of the wondrous deeds of Djadjaemankh. The story of the golden lotus was on the lips of all who had witnessed it.

A prominent theme of this famous Egyptian myth is restoration and healing. The golden lotus in this story symbolizes everything valuable: health, wealth, and life itself. The myth also hinges on hope and second chances, possibly alluding to the afterlife. The pharaoh's kindness and that of Djadjaemankh illustrate the kindness of the gods to every believer who earnestly requests their help.

The Golden Lotus myth also bears a resemblance to the biblical story of Moses parting the Red Sea during the exodus of the Hebrews from Egypt. Both stories are parallels, but they share the common theme of faith in the supernatural and the reward of divine intervention.

Chapter 8: The Greek Princess

The precedents of the myth of the Greek princess take us far beyond the shores of ancient Egypt to a foreign land in Greece called Sparta. It was one of the most powerful Greek nations in antiquity, and Spartan King Tyndareus and his wife Leda had a beautiful daughter named Helen.

In Greek mythology, Helen was the daughter of Zeus (equal to the Egyptian sun god Ra), and her beauty was unrivaled. Helen's beauty had attracted a good number of eligible bachelors to King Tyndareus's palace, putting him in a dilemma of who to choose. Eventually, Helen's groom was chosen from among the suitors, and Helen of Sparta was married.

Our story focuses on ancient Egypt during the chaotic reign of Pharaoh Seti II, son of Merneptah and grandson of the most powerful pharaoh of the New Kingdom, Ramesses II.

Pharaoh Seti II was engulfed in the plots to enthrone his half-brother Amenmesse as king over the major cities in Upper Egypt. Egypt had been united almost two thousand years earlier by King Menes, so there was no reason for two kings to rule the land—unless it was mutiny.

A Party of Strangers

As the king repelled the forces that threatened a partition of his kingdom, a strange boat docked on the eastern shores of the Nile River, Canopus. The boat had just weathered a violent storm from the north and had been driven off its course.

The men on the boat had finally found refuge on Egyptian soil after many days at sea, and on the horizon stood the great temple of Hershef, god of the riverbanks. Hershef was also the god who protected strangers and freed slaves from captivity if they bowed to him.

The Egyptian warden in charge of the shores of Canopus was a man named Thonis, and when he learned that strangers had docked in his jurisdiction, he inquired into who they were and where they had come from.

Indeed, they were sailors from Greece, a nation that dominated the Aegean Sea. This was why the Egyptians called Greeks "the people of the sea." Not only were they foreigners, but the ship also belonged to a Trojan royal who had been traveling with his Greek wife.

Fascinated by his discovery, Thonis headed to the temple of Hershef, where the sailors had sought sanctuary and desired to convert to the service of Hershef, thereby gaining their freedom from servitude to the Trojan prince. Their decision seemed odd to Thonis, who thought that they would want to return home above anything else.

Suspicion soon replaced curiosity, and Thonis pried deeper into the matter. The sailors confessed that they were afraid of punishment from their own gods and wanted protection from the consequences of boarding a ship with a cursed man.

The mystery gradually unraveled, and Thonis learned that the Trojan prince had stolen the wife of one of the kings in Greece—a most ignoble deed punishable by the wrath of the gods. The prince had been welcomed into the palace of the Greek king as a diplomatic guest, and yet, he repaid with evil, carting away his host's wife.

Appalled by the actions of the Greek prince, Thonis seized the ship and journeyed to the pharaoh's palace to seek the king's wisdom. Before his departure, Thonis had the Greek princess separated from the Trojan prince and escorted to the temple of Hathor, the goddess of the sky, for her safety.

Pharaoh Seti II granted Thonis an audience and promptly ordered that the Trojan prince be escorted to his presence with his converted men.

Two Lies and a Truth

The Trojan prince was a handsome man who spoke and acted like royalty. He introduced himself as Prince Paris, son of King Priam of Troy. He also revealed the Greek princess's identity as Helen, the daughter of Zeus and his new wife. According to Prince Paris, he had traveled to Sparta for the hand of Helen, which he had won fair and square, and was on his way back to Troy when the storm rerouted his ship.

The converted sailors in the hall murmured among one another, attracting the pharaoh's attention. Seti II gave them room to speak their truth on the matter, reminding them of their freedom granted by the god Hershef to speak freely.

The sailors were, however, hesitant. The prince of Troy was in the hall with them, and regardless of their new status as freemen, they did not want to go against his word.

Pharaoh Seti II took notice of their tension and promised them his protection if they spoke their truth. With this, the sailors spoke up, appraising the princess's ravishing beauty.

As it happened, the prince of Troy had indeed been a guest of Sparta, but he had not come to Sparta for Helen. In fact, the prince was not among the bachelors who had asked King Tyndareus for her hand in marriage. Also, the king had given Helen's hand to Prince Menelaus of Mycenae, not the Trojan Prince Paris, and her wedding to Menelaus had happened many years earlier. The sailor testified that the Trojan prince arrived at the gates of Sparta as an ambassador on a diplomatic mission.

The Trojan prince reportedly stayed in Sparta for the next few days. Menelaus was eventually forced to leave the city for a while on some state affairs. When he was gone, Paris carried off Helen by force, together with much treasure, and sailed away, only to be caught in a storm sent by the angry gods. His boat was swept by a violent tempest to the shores of Egypt.

Prince Paris blatantly denied having forced Helen to leave her husband and home, but the sailors insisted that they spoke the truth. There was no reason for a royal to tell lies, but the sailors sounded equally convincing.

The pharaoh, however, noted variations in the Trojan prince's story. First, he had claimed to have won Helen's hand, but after the sailors' testimony, he claimed that she had escaped with him of her own accord from a loveless marriage to King Menelaus.

Which was it?

From the Horse's Mouth

Caught in his own web of inconsistencies, the prince could no longer speak. As it stood, only one person could tell the truth: the Greek princess, Helen herself. She was safely sheltered in the temple of Hathor.

Pharaoh Seti II offered Prince Paris accommodations in the royal guest house and put his vizier, Paraemheb, in charge of the Trojan prince's welfare. Meanwhile, he would visit the Greek princess lodged in the temple and find out the truth.

With his chief priest and a trusted scribe, the king of Egypt graced the temple of Hathor with his presence and saw Helen for the first time. She was the most beautiful woman in the world. He could easily see how she was the daughter of Zeus.

Helen of Troy by Evelyn De Morgan.
https://commons.wikimedia.org/wiki/File:Helen_of_Troy.jpg

During their private conversation, Princess Helen told her story. Contrary to the Trojan prince's account, she had been happily married to Menelaus, Prince of Mycenae in Greece. She even had two children, Hermione and Nicostraus. Prince Paris had indeed forced her to come away with him after seducing her by taking the form of her husband, Menelaus.

Helen's story confirmed the sailors' version, and the Greek princess begged the pharaoh to save her from her captor, as she felt no affection for him. He was the one obsessed with her and had kidnapped her from her home.

Menelaus had been the suitor chosen by Helen's father, King Tyndareus. The prince of Troy was not even among the men who had sought the Greek princess's hand in marriage; he also did not win her hand fair and square as he had said.

It saddened the pharaoh to hear of Helen's ordeal, and he promised to send the Trojan prince away so that he would not trouble her any longer. It had been the will of the gods to intercept Helen's kidnapper and send the ship to the shores of Egypt. Urgently, the pharaoh sent word to Prince Paris and urged him to sail away from Egypt at the break of dawn. Paris's words had been proven to be lies, but because he was royalty, the pharaoh offered Prince Paris a chance to leave willingly.

The Trojan prince was unhappy to learn of the pharaoh's resolution. He swore that he would come back for Helen since she was his rightful wife. Meanwhile, on the night before his departure, the temple of Hathor (where Helen was hosted) received a divine visitation: a messenger from the sun god Ra.

His name was Thoth.

The Revelation

Thoth appeared to Tausert, Princess of Egypt and High Priestess of the goddess Hathor who lived in the temple. Tausert was so overwhelmed by the presence of Ra's messenger that she fell to her knees. She heard him speak:

"I come hither to work the will of the most high god Amon-Re [Ra], father of us all—and by his command you, who shall one day be Queen of Egypt, must learn of all that is performed this night so that you may bear witness of it in the days to come, when that king of the Aquaiusha [Greece] who is the true husband of Helen shall come to lead her home...

But this night I, whom the Aquaiusha [Greeks] name Hermes the Thrice Great, must draw forth the Ka, the double of Helen, the ghostly likeness of her that shall deceive all eyes and seem to Paris and to all at Troy to be none other than the real woman. For the Ka of Helen and not for Helen herself shall the great war of Troy be fought and the will of the Father of Gods and Men shall be accomplished."

War was coming to Greece—one that would be told and retold throughout the ages. A historic war that would end in victory for the Greeks and a crushing defeat for the city of Troy, Prince Paris's homeland. Most significantly, the war would be fought because of Helen or rather her clone.

This secret, which was revealed to Tausert, High Priestess of Hathor, was not meant for just anyone to hear. Tausert vowed to take the secret to her grave, and Thoth got to work on designing the perfect lookalike of the Greek princess.

The Trojan prince was getting ready to set sail on the Nile when Helen's clone appeared. Unknown to him, the real Helen was still in the temple of Hathor. Prince Paris was excited to have his wife back, and he hurried on his way out of Egypt before the pharaoh changed his mind.

Days rolled into months, and true to the word of Ra's messenger, the Greeks marched to war against Troy due to the actions of Prince Paris. It was a great insult to Menelaus that his wife had been stolen by a guest, and after diplomatic attempts at resolving the conflict failed, the gates of Troy were laid siege.

Menelaus enlisted the help of his older brother, King Agamemnon of Mycenae, for his offensive against Troy. They were joined by the famous war hero Achilles, the sage Odysseus, and other great soldiers, such as Ajax and Nestor. Over one thousand warships from all over Greece sailed across the vast Aegean to contend with Troy and bring Helen back.

It was just as Thoth had told Tausert that night at the temple.

The Trojans were a formidable enemy, and their people were safe behind their high city walls. For a decade, the war would go on, seemingly with no end in sight—all for what was a mere clone of the Greek princess.

Age to Age

Back in Egypt, the people were ignorant of how Helen had come to reside in the temple of Hathor. But because of her beauty and the mystery behind her existence in Egypt, the people thought her to be a human manifestation of the goddess Hathor.

The news spread throughout Memphis and all of Egypt that Hathor had taken the form of a beautiful woman and had descended into the temple to live among the mortals. The people of Egypt flocked to see Helen, whom they referred to as Hathor.

Pharaoh Seti II, who had graciously hosted the Greek princess in his kingdom, soon passed away, and the two pharaohs who came after him reigned for short periods.

Pharaoh Setnakhe, who came third after Seti II, was the first pharaoh of the Twentieth Dynasty. Like Seti II, he was kind to the Greek princess, who had not aged a day as the years whirled by. Unfortunately, Setnakhe reigned for barely three years, after which his stalwart son, Ramesses III, was enthroned.

Ramesses III was different from the other pharaohs who had ruled since Helen's circumstantial arrival in Egypt. It had been almost twenty years, and yet her beauty was unchanging. Ramesses III took one look at Helen and wanted her for himself.

Despite Queen Tausert's pleas that he cease desiring another man's wife, Ramesses III was unmoved in his lust for her. Tausert, who had been the high priestess of Hathor since the time of Helen's arrival, feared that the pharaoh's desire was a recipe for disaster.

Tausert prayed earnestly to Hathor for a solution, and one day, the answer to her prayers docked on the shores of Canopus near the temple.

The Reunion

Helen rushed out of her residence when she heard the news.

She prayed to Hathor that it be true; she had waited for so long. A man stood at the temple entrance, wearing a tired yet happy smile: Menelaus.

There was no containing the Greek princess's joy at being reunited with her husband. Menelaus took her in his arms, entranced and full of stories to tell his wife.

After all those years of war against Troy, the Greeks realized that there was no destroying the Trojans from the outside. Their best soldiers, even the mighty Achilles, had died in the war, and the Greeks were distraught. So, they devised a clever plot to get into the city walls of Troy.

At the behest of Odysseus, one of the wisest men on Menelaus's side, they built a large wooden horse, set it on the shores of Troy, and vanished without a trace. The Trojans came out of their fortress and wondered what the horse was about. The Greeks had left a message for them, stating that they had surrendered and returned to their homeland since the city of Troy was so impenetrable. They had tired of war. The gigantic wooden horse was their symbol of surrender.

The Trojans were initially suspicious, but with no Greek soldier or ship in sight for miles, their doubts faded away. They rolled the large wooden horse into the city, and King Priam of Troy threw an elaborate party to celebrate their victory over the Greeks.

Unknown to the Trojans, there were hundreds of Greek soldiers hiding inside the horse that they had just brought into the city. After a long night of drinking and merrymaking, the Trojans drifted off to sleep. While they snored and slumbered, the Greeks came out of their hiding and opened the city gates for the rest of their troops. Troy was mercilessly sacked, and Menelaus recovered his wife (Helen's clone).

The Trojan Horse.
Adam Jones from Kelowna, BC, Canada, CC BY-SA 2.0
https://creativecommons.org/licenses/by-sa/2.0 via Wikimedia Commons;
https://commons.wikimedia.org/wiki/File:Replica_of_Trojan_Horse_-
Canakkale_Waterfront_-_Dardanelles_-_Turkey_(5747677790).jpg

Menelaus continued with his story, telling Helen that he had been on his way home from Troy with Helen (the clone) when an unforgiving storm wrecked his ship. The clone Helen had vanished in the process, and Menelaus had thought his wife had surely died.

He fell apart in sorrow and was on the verge of committing suicide when the gods revealed to him that the real Helen was safe in Egypt in the temple of Hathor. Prince Paris had recovered a mere clone made by the gods. The Trojan War had been fought over a fake.

Menelaus expressed his bedazzlement at Egyptian magic, and he thanked High Priestess Tausert for keeping his wife safe. He also learned of Pharaoh Ramesses III's rather disturbing plans to marry Helen. The pharaoh had asked her hand in marriage and was on his way for her answer. He had threatened to take her by force if she dared refuse him. So, Helen's husband had returned in the nick of time.

Queen Tausert was not only the priestess of Hathor, but she was also Ramesses's mother. Yet, she promised to help Menelaus and his wife escape safely from Egypt. Running away would raise the ruler's ire, so Tausert came up with a better plan.

The Escape Route

It was a fine evening in Egypt. The pharaoh was in high spirits, anticipating a positive response from the beautiful woman who lived in Hathor's temple. His arrival at the temple was grand and elaborate, but the welcome was short of befitting.

Instead of an excited bride-to-be, Ramesses found Helen dressed in mourning clothes and an unkempt, weary-looking traveler saying words of comfort to her. The king's mother, Tausert, was also there, and the mood in the room was sorrowful.

The king of Egypt demanded to be informed of the situation, and Tausert did the talking. The man comforting Helen was a sailor from Menelaus's boat, which had been destroyed at sea during a turbulent storm. Ramesses questioned the sailor, who, unknown to him, was Menelaus. When the sailor confirmed that he had seen Menelaus's corpse at sea with his own eyes, the pharaoh did not hide his delight. Now, there was no reason for Helen to decline to marry him.

Right there and then, Ramesses asked Helen to marry him. She agreed, but she gave a small condition: the pharaoh would allow her some time to mourn her late husband in accordance with Greek customs. She requested a ship, one well provisioned with the food and wine needed for a good funeral feast. Helen also requested to have all the treasures the Trojan prince had stolen, as well as a bull to sacrifice to the spirit of her husband.

In addition, she requested the pharaoh's permission to take the sailors who had revealed the truth to him. She would need them to perform the funerary rites and sacrifices for her late husband.

She told the pharaoh, "I must accompany them to speak the words and pour the last offering to my husband's spirit—and all this must be done on the sea in which his body lies, for then only can his spirit find rest in the realm of Hades—and only then can I be your bride."

Ramesses saw no reason to refuse, but this was only because he did not realize he was being tricked. With the pharaoh's consent, Helen and Menelaus sailed away from Egypt, never again to return. The couple had traveled far beyond reach before Ramesses learned the truth. In a fit of rage, he sought to kill his mother, Tausert, for masterminding the Greek princess's escape.

That night, Thoth appeared to Pharaoh Ramesses and told him that Tausert had acted in accordance with the will of the gods. The king could do his mother no harm then or after.

Some refer to the myth of the Greek princess as the Egyptian version of the Trojan War. The more commonly known Greek version differs quite a bit. The Egyptian myth is a tale of the predestined journey of a divine mortal and how Egypt was a refuge for her while one of history's most epic wars raged across the Aegean.

Chapter 9: The Treasure Thief

This story begins after the Greek Princess Helen evaded an unwanted marriage to Pharaoh Ramesses III and fled with her husband, Menelaus.

After being cautioned by the gods to bring no harm to his mother, Tausert, the king of Egypt refocused on the politics and economy of his kingdom. In the years that followed, Egypt prospered considerably under Ramesses III. Not only had he conquered the invaders from Libya, Palestine, and other nations along the Mediterranean Sea in his early regnal years, the king of Egypt had established a trade network with neighboring countries to foster harmonious relations.

This helped replenish the coffers in Egypt, which had previously been depleted during the constant wars against foreign aggression. Pharaoh Ramesses not only sought the prosperity of Egypt, but he also desired tremendous wealth of his own. To this end, he began to collect his riches in weights of gold, silver, and gems.

Treasure Bank

One day, the king awoke with a brilliant idea to preserve his fortune. He immediately summoned his finest builder, a man named Horemheb, to share his thoughts. The king envisioned a secret stash for all his wealth, which he fortified against thieves and burglars. Horemheb was delighted to learn of the king's plan and offered himself to receive the king's instructions.

Pharaoh Ramesses ordered his builder to construct a fortress of stone with thick, impenetrable walls and a roof as high as the pyramids. This would be the king's treasure cave, and it would be guarded heavily by soldiers. By then, the king had other construction projects going on, including his magnificent temple in the hills of Thebes, along the western bank of the Nile River.

Horemheb took the king's command and enacted it. He hired the best stoneworkers in all of Egypt, and they mined the best stones from the quarries of Swenett (later called Syene). With these stones, the king's treasure bank was erected, and as Horemheb had promised, it was nothing like any such edifice before it. Its doors were constructed from the finest quality stone, and the inner chamber doors were made of bronze and iron.

Pleased with Horemheb's fine work, Pharaoh Ramesses rewarded him and had all his treasures moved to their new home. The doors to the treasure chamber were sealed shut by the king himself, and he returned to the palace, assured of the safety of his wealth.

What the king didn't know was that his treasures were far from safe.

Mission Impossible

It was night, and all through the land, there was peace and quiet. All of Egypt was asleep, except the men stationed to guard the pharaoh's treasure—and two other men.

They were on a secret, dangerous mission, one that would lead to their deaths if they were discovered. They had slipped past the king's guards and let themselves in through a secret entrance. Now, they were filling their sacks with their share of the loot.

The two men operated in silence and took only a little of the abundance in the room, just as they had the last time and the time before that—and all the many times before that. The king's treasure was visibly reduced, but the thieves would not stop until they had carted away enough or maybe even all of it.

Morning came, and they vanished without a trace, save for the king's missing treasures. Pharaoh Ramesses stormed to his treasure bank and discovered that he had once again been robbed. He was furious. He had lost count of how many times these thieves had made away with his precious fortune.

The only man who knew the intricacies of his treasure bank was the one who had built it: Horemheb. But Horemheb was long dead after completing the construction. He had passed away after a terrible sickness afflicted him.

Who were these thieves, and how had they gotten in so many times without breaking the seal or getting caught by the king's guards?

The pharaoh had had enough of these mysterious delinquents. He needed a plan to catch them in the act and punish them severely. For days, he pondered on a solution, and then it occurred to him: traps.

The robbers were sneaky, like rats, and what better way to catch rats than with strategically positioned traps?

*

It was another perfect night to steal from the king's fortune.

The two sons of Horemheb crept their way into the king's treasure bank and took the secret pathway that their father, Horemheb, had revealed to them on his deathbed shortly before he died. Unknown to the king, the man he had trusted to build his treasure fortress had installed a tiny pathway through the walls to access his fortune. Before his death, Horemheb had summoned his two sons and handed them the mandate of plundering the king's fortune.

It was another night to embark on this deadly mission. There was no getting enough of the king's treasure, and so they had come to steal some more. Unknown to Horemheb's sons, the king had anticipated their move and set a deadly trap inside the treasure chamber near the chests of gold and silver.

The brothers snuck in, wading through the darkness to get to their prize. But one of the brothers fell into the king's trap. He struggled to free himself, but it was of no use. He was going to bleed out. His identity would be revealed. Or worse, he would be captured half-dead and cruelly tortured into naming his accomplice.

To protect himself, his brother, and his family, the trapped brother pleaded for his brother to kill him and cut off his head. That way, he would die painlessly, and with his head gone, no one would recognize his corpse.

The brother blatantly refused. There had to be some other way. He dropped to his knees and attempted to free his entrapped brother several times and in several different ways, but his efforts were futile. The entrapped brother fervently repeated his request and added that they were running out of time. If they were both caught, they would both have to pay with their lives in the most humiliating way.

Hesitantly, the other brother granted the entrapped brother his wish of an honor killing and decapitated him. Afterward, he slipped out of the king's treasure chamber and took his brother's severed head and clothes with him to bury.

The Ultimate Outwitter

Pharaoh Ramesses III was stirred when he heard of the headless unclad corpse caught in his trap. His guards denied being responsible for his death, and whoever did it had expertly left no traces. The seals on the doors remained unbroken, and there were no other signs of a breach.

The king of Egypt took this as a personal challenge, and he garnered his every resolve to outwit the cunning thief. Ramesses could recognize an honor killing when he saw one, and the only way to root out any accomplices was by using the headless corpse.

When morning came, the people murmured among themselves. Those who walked past the palace gates that morning reported a most sordid sight. A naked, headless corpse dangled on a rope in front of the palace. It didn't sound like the body would come down anytime soon, as it was done on the king's orders.

The second brother heard the rumors and had to find out if they were true. They were. His brother's corpse was hung in front of the palace as part of the king's plan to catch him. The king had also stationed his soldiers to observe the reactions of all who saw the corpse. It was highly likely that a family member would come around, see his kinsman hanging, and be unable to contain their sorrow. If such a person turned up at the palace gates to grieve or claim the body, the king had ordered his soldiers to arrest him immediately.

However, the second brother saw through the king's plan, and he decided that he would not fall for it. However, matters quickly became complicated when his mother heard of the gruesome display of her son's corpse. She was maddened with grief and shouted at her other son, ordering him to bring home his brother's corpse. Otherwise, he would never enter the Duat.

The second brother had not anticipated that his mother would cause such a ruckus, and he attempted to comfort her. He assured her that he had properly buried his brother's head with their deceased father and that it was enough for the dead brother to enter the gates of the Duat. But his mother remained thoroughly unconvinced. She cried out louder and threatened to expose his secret to the pharaoh. She was ready to accept whatever consequences came with it, even if it meant the death of her son.

The other brother could perceive that his mother was set in her demands, and he promised to bring home his brother's corpse. He thought up another brilliant scheme.

*

The pharaoh had never been so furious.

How could his own men be so reckless and incompetent as to get drunk while on duty? The men sobered up and explained in detail what had transpired the evening before. An elderly merchant had passed by the palace with two donkeys loaded with wineskins. His donkeys had collided, and their harnesses tore two wineskins open. The wine in the skins leaked out, and the merchant was so upset that he cried out loudly, attracting the soldiers' attention.

Rather than let the wine go to waste, the soldiers helped themselves to the full batches of wine that leaked from the wineskins. The merchant sat with them and shared another wineskin, and they guzzled it greedily. Eventually, they became drunk and drifted off into a deep sleep.

By morning, the merchant had disappeared, and so had the corpse the guards had been assigned to watch over. The merchant had been the second brother, and his plan had worked better than he could have imagined.

Hearing the details made the pharaoh even angrier. He condemned the erring soldiers to a severe flogging and had them dragged out of his sight. Ramesses clenched his fists on his throne, enraged by the audacity of this common thief. He became even more determined to catch this lawbreaker.

It was time to roll out another plan.

*

Another dawn broke in the land of Egypt, and there was fresh news being whispered in the streets. There was an important visitor in the land, and she was the most beautiful woman to arrive on the shores of Egypt after Helen. This woman was an eligible bachelorette, and her hand in marriage would go to any man who told her the best secret.

The men of Egypt trooped to the camp where the beauty was lodged and took turns to win her hand in marriage. The living brother was one of them, and when it was his turn, he saw that she was very beautiful indeed. Even though it was dark, her radiance could not be denied. She offered him a seat and proceeded to ask him about the secret she wanted him to tell. "Tell me the wickedest and cleverest things you have ever done."

If the lady was fascinated by his answer, she would consent to marry him. For the second brother, the answer to this was obvious, so he told it to her. He had beheaded his own brother, who had been caught in the king's trap while they were stealing the king's treasure.

The woman suddenly screamed aloud, alerting her guards that she had caught the treasure thief. She grabbed the second brother's hand and held on to it until the king's guards arrived. But when they turned on the lights, he had vanished. What the woman was holding on to was the severed hand of his dead brother.

Horrified, she screamed and let go of the hand. As it turned out, she was no stranger in the land of Egypt. She was the king's daughter, the princess of Egypt, and like her father, she had been tricked by a man who knew all about their plan.

She returned to the palace and told her father what had happened. This time, the king had a different reaction. He had obsessed so long and hard over catching the treasure thief that he had missed the bigger picture.

The thief was a man of rare genius, and his foresight was second to none. It would be a colossal waste of his talents to punish him. Pharaoh Ramesses issued a decree that announced a pardon for the treasure thief's crimes and a promise of rich rewards if he would join the king's service as a retainer.

In a most unlikely end, the second brother finally revealed himself to the king, and he was given a title in the king's court. He also married the princess of Egypt and never again had to sneak into the king's treasure house.

Chapter 10:
The Tale of Hatshepsut

"A people of ignoble origin from the East, whose country was unforeseen, had the audacity to invade the country, which they had mastered by main force without difficulty or even battle. Having overpowered the chiefs, they then savagely burnt the cities, razed the temples of the gods to the grounds, and treated the whole native population with the utmost cruelty, massacring some, and carrying off the wives and children of others into slavery."

This is the widely debated account of an Egyptian historian named Manetho. In that passage, he describes the Hyksos invasion of Egypt in the 1600s BCE. While modern historians argue that these foreigners took over parts of Egypt as peacefully as possible, lore remains loyal to Manetho's account.

Egypt was reportedly plundered by these Semitic foreigners, and trade routes were disrupted, leaving the succeeding pharaohs struggling to regain Egypt's power. This story is about an unusual pharaoh whose reign is celebrated in history as one of restoration and development.

This pharaoh ascended to the throne of Egypt amid unfavorable odds and left an indelible mark on Egyptian history. This pharaoh was a woman, and her name was Hatshepsut.

The Royally Divine

Set in the Eighteenth Dynasty of Egypt, the story of Hatshepsut mythically begins with the sun god Ra's decision to enthrone a great woman as the pharaoh of Egypt and give her the whole world. The sun god's grand plan would be brought to fruition through the body of a beautiful woman named Ahmose, wife of Pharaoh Thutmose and the queen of Egypt.

The sun god commissioned Thoth to arrange the conception of a baby girl that would grow up to become the pharaoh of Egypt. Thoth obliged and descended to Earth during the night. He headed into the palace. His divine task could not be discovered, so he spelled every mortal in the palace to sleep deeply and possessed the body of Pharaoh Thutmose.

The possessed pharaoh trudged to his queen's bedchamber and found her sound asleep on her lion-shaped couch. The king moved to her and held her up, breathing the divine breath of Ra into her nostrils. He also blessed her and declared that the child that would be born would rule the two lands of Egypt.

Queen Ahmose thought it was all a dream, but she soon gave birth to a beautiful baby girl. She was named Hatshepsut, and the king's household celebrated her arrival in grand style. That night, another divine visitation was paid to the palace. This time, the sun god Ra himself came down, accompanied by the goddess Hathor and her seven daughters (known as the Seven Hathors). The sun god took the baby princess and gave her the kiss of power and his blessing to rule Egypt.

The Takeover

Hatshepsut had the typical upbringing of an Egyptian princess. She was taught to prioritize her familial and sacred duties above all else. She would likely become the wife of a pharaoh and nothing more.

It was unheard of for a woman to become the pharaoh of Egypt. The throne had always been occupied by men, save for Sobekneferu, who had reigned for barely four years with little known achievements.

When Pharaoh Thutmose passed away around 1493 BCE, his son, Thutmose II, became the king of Egypt. Hatshepsut was married off to her brother, Thutmose II, at the age of twelve and became the queen of Egypt. This was a common practice in ancient Egypt, and the new king and queen would reign for the next few years.

Hatshepsut bore a daughter for the King, Princess Neferure, but it seemed she was unable to have any sons. Having an heir was important to the continuation of the dynasty, and no chances could be taken. Eventually, a woman from the pharaoh's harem, who went by the name Iset, gave birth to an heir for the king.

The prince was named Thutmose III, and Queen Hatshepsut adopted him as her stepson. Thutmose III was almost three years old when his father, the king, suddenly died, leaving him next in line for the throne.

Evidently, the prince was too young to be entrusted with affairs of governance and needed a guardian, also known as a regent. Queen Hatshepsut stepped forward and became Thutmose III's regent around 1479 BCE.

In time, Hatshepsut understood what her divine mandate was. She was to be more than this. Beyond the spiritual, she was an ambitious woman who knew all about the state of Egypt and the struggle to recover from the Hyksos invasion that had happened long before she was born. One day, Hatshepsut learned of a plot by the other royal families to usurp the throne from her stepson. This would bring the reign of the Eighteenth Dynasty to an abrupt end.

Hatshepsut would not allow the throne of Egypt to be snatched from her family line, so in the fifth to seventh regnal year of the young Thutmose III, Hatshepsut assumed the throne of Egypt as pharaoh.

The people of Egypt woke up to the most unprecedented news. They had a new king; it was a woman. Aware of her uncanny rise to the throne of Egypt, Pharaoh Hatshepsut proceeded to legitimize her reign by declaring herself the intended heir of her father, the deceased Pharaoh Thutmose I. She handpicked trusted retainers to fill the important positions of government, notably Senenmut, an architect and Pharaoh Hatshepsut's rumored lover.

Next, Pharaoh Hatshepsut tried to convince the people that she was ordained by the gods as the one to unite the two lands of Egypt and restore the country to its former glory. As proof of this, she adopted the name Maatkare, which means "Truth is the soul of the sun god." She also underwent purification rites and observances during her coronation and wore crowns that represented Upper and Lower Egypt.

Before succeeding to the throne, Hatshepsut had only been known as a princess and then queen of Egypt. Her new elevated status required her to carve a new image in the eyes of her people. So, Hatshepsut took things a step further by ordering to be dressed and addressed as a man in person and in pictorial depictions. She took to wearing the male kingly regalia and being portrayed as having a fake beard and a muscular build. She was referenced with respect as "His Majesty."

The Sphinx of Hatshepsut showing her fake beard.

Hatshepsut: The Builder and Trader

Hatshepsut knew that changing her wardrobe was not all there was to be a great pharaoh. One day, she summoned Minister Senenmut and tasked him with overseeing her greatest building projects. Conversely, she embarked on the historic expedition to Punt to revive trade in Egypt.

Many pharaohs before Hatshepsut had shown little commitment to construction projects outside of tombs or pyramids. After the Hyksos had "savagely" invaded Egypt, many temples and monuments were destroyed, leaving the cultural heritage of the land in shambles.

The buildings that Pharaoh Hatshepsut had in mind were no basic relics. She envisioned grand and magnificent structures that would outlive her and become a legacy for many generations. After she consulted with Senenmut, it was agreed that Ineni, an aristocratic architect who had served the past two pharaohs, would be best for the job.

Construction began in multiple locations throughout Upper and Lower Egypt. The Temple of Karnak, which had multiple shrines dedicated to the worship of the Egyptian goddess of the earth, Mut (the Precinct of Mut), was renovated. The Precinct of Mut had fallen to the Hyksos in the Eleventh Dynasty, and its prominence had dwindled over time. With the reconstruction sponsored by Pharaoh Hatshepsut, the Precinct of Mut regained prestige.

Also, in Karnak, Hatshepsut built the Chapelle Rouge, also known as the Red Chapel. This shrine was built in honor of Ra, and it housed the sacred golden barque believed to transport the sun god on his journeys. On festival days, the statue of Ra would be mounted on the barque and carried out of the Karnak shrine by a procession of priests through the streets of Thebes. He would be returned after the festivities. The interior of the shrine was decorated with reliefs and epigraphs of the prosperous reign of the pharaoh.

The Temple of Pakhet, which honored the goddesses Baset and Sekhmet, was also constructed by Pharaoh Hatshepsut as a gesture to revive Egyptian culture. This temple was commissioned in Beni Hasan and came to be renamed the Cave of Artemis by the Greeks (this was because Artemis was the Greek equivalent of Baset and

Sekhmet).

Hatshepsut was also famous for her obelisks. At her behest, High Steward Amenhotep saw to the erection of twin obelisks at the entrance of the Temple of Karnak. At the time, they were the tallest in the world. The pharaoh would have two more obelisks built to mark the celebration of her sixteenth regnal year and a third to replace one of her obelisks in Aswan that had crumbled after its initial construction.

One of Pharaoh Hatshepsut's obelisks at Karnak.

Also significant was the construction of Pharaoh Hatshepsut's grand royal tomb along the west bank of the Nile near Luxor. This site was called Deir el-Bahri, and it would become the entry point to the famous Valley of the Kings. Hatshepsut's royal tomb was also a temple, a complex titled the "Holy of Holies" or Djeser-Djeseru. It was a majestic structure that stood out from the rest because of its lovely gardens and layered terraces, ornamented with statues of Osiris and Hatshepsut, as well as an avenue of sphinxes out front. Mortuary temples in ancient Egypt were designed to honor the sun god and for the posthumous worship of the pharaoh who built them.

Not only was Pharaoh Hatshepsut a master builder, but her reign is also credited with the largest ancient Egyptian trade expedition in history. Following the aggressive occupation of the Hyksos, Egypt had lost plenty of temples and statues. The country's coffers were adversely affected, and the pharaoh sought to replenish Egypt's wealth.

In the ninth year of her reign, five ships departed Egypt in the name of Pharaoh Hatshepsut. Their destination was an African land across the Red Sea called Punt. Prior to the invasion of the Hyksos, the land of Punt had a long history of trade with Egypt, dating back as far as the Fifth Dynasty. One day, the pharaoh heard of Punt and all its riches. It was such a "beautiful land" that the people called it the Land of the Gods.

Pharaoh Hatshepsut charged a Nubian chancellor named Nehsi to lead her ships on a trading mission to Punt. The pharaoh's delegation was well received by the royals of Punt, and their mission was successful. They returned to Egypt with items of ebony, savory resin, ivory, frankincense, gold, and myrrh. Live myrrh trees were harvested from Punt and brought back to Egypt to be planted in the pharaoh's mortuary temple. The pharaoh herself discovered burned frankincense was a useful ingredient in the production of kohl or eye makeup.

While peaceful trade was the theme of Pharaoh Hatshepsut's foreign policy, there are indications that she led strictly military campaigns to Byblos, Canaan, Nubia, and the Sinai Peninsula.

Despite the efforts of erasing her legacy embarked upon by Hatshepsut's successor, Thutmose III, the tale of Pharaoh Hatshepsut and her greatness has survived for generations. She was ordained by divinity, and her tenure restored the wealth and eminence of Egypt.

Chapter 11:
The Doomed Prince

This story begins with the agony of a king without an heir.

He was the king of all Egypt, worshiped as the son of Ra and the father of his people. Yet, he had no son to continue his royal line. Every night, the king would pray earnestly to the gods to make his wife fertile and bear him a son. He also gave many offerings to appease the gods of fertility. One day, he received a promise that his wife would bear a son. And so, she did.

The king called a grand celebration in honor of the gods for answering his prayers. As was the norm, the royal family consulted with the Seven Hathors, deities revered as knowing mortals' fates. They needed to hear what the prince's fate would be.

Unfortunately, the Seven Hathors foretold that a horrible untimely death would befall the prince. He would be killed by a crocodile, dog, or snake.

When the king heard this, he was sorely afraid. He mourned the fate of his son along with his queen. He was as good as heirless, and there was almost no changing their fate. However, the king of Egypt was willing to take his chances.

He immediately ordered for a fortress to be built in the mountains for the prince to live in. It was made from the finest materials in the land and furnished to royal taste. Everything the young prince needed to live in comfort and luxury was provided in the fortress, and the prince was moved there to live out his childhood.

The years passed, and as the prince grew, his curiosity about the world beyond the walls around him grew. He would look from the top of the roof at the horizon, unable to tell what the world felt like. One day, he saw a strange creature wandering outside the walls. He had never seen it before, but it was nothing like a man or a woman.

The young prince asked one of his servants what it was, and he learned that it was a dog. The prince was fascinated by it, and he petitioned his father to let him possess one. The king refused, remembering the prophecy of the Seven Hathors, but the prince was unrelenting until his desire was fulfilled.

That was not the end of it. The prince demanded to know the reason behind his imprisonment and why he could not live with his family.

The king and queen realized that the time had come to tell the prince his destiny. The prince received the knowledge of his fate with bravery. He asked that he be allowed to explore the world for the rest of his days on Earth. The king and queen were reluctant to send off their only son into a world of uncertainty and danger, but once again, they granted him his wish.

So, the prince and his dog set off on an adventure far beyond the shores of Egypt. The prince had no destination in mind, but he went toward the east, led by his own whims. He came to Nahairana, a small town bustling with activity. It seemed to be a festival, as there were many eager young men in the streets. The prince asked one of them what the occasion was. He was told it was a contest. The men of the land were competing to win the hand of the beautiful princess.

The princess lived in a tower that was over one hundred feet high and had seventy windows. Whoever could climb to the highest room in the tower and reach the princess would be the winner of the contest and be allowed to marry her.

Many a brave young man attempted to reach the princess's elevated chamber, but none prevailed. Day after day, the prince of Egypt watched the other young men try, but the task was daunting and seemingly insurmountable.

One bright day, the prince decided to try his luck. Like the princess of Nahairana, he had also lived out his childhood in seclusion. As a result of this, he had picked up considerable climbing skills.

The prince of Egypt succeeded in his quest, but the king would not give his daughter's hand away to a fugitive from Egypt. He remained opposed to the marriage until the princess vowed to take her life if the king would not change his mind. The princess had fallen in love with the prince at first sight, and eventually, her father gave her his blessing. He also gifted servants, land, cattle, property, and precious jewels to the prince. With his new wife, the prince soon longed to return home to Egypt.

Before that, the prince opened up to his wife about the prophecy of the Seven Hathors. He was doomed to be killed by a crocodile, dog, or snake. The princess worried for the safety of her husband and suggested that his pet dog be killed. The prince declined, as the dog had been his companion since he was a boy and had not harmed him even once.

Together, the prince and his wife began their journey back to Egypt. On their way, they came to a large lake, which bordered a quaint town. This lake teemed with crocodiles, and the prince's life was in danger. With the help of a giant who resided in the town near the lake, the prince's life was saved.

The prince and his wife settled in a new home, and he was almost attacked by a snake several times. His wife and servants thwarted every attempt on the prince's life. The prince offered endless prayers and sacrifices to the gods to change his and his wife's fate, as she would be destined to live without her beloved.

One evening, the prince went out hunting with his dog. The dog caught a whiff of game in the forest and chased after it. The prince followed, ready to make his kill until his dog plunged into a nearby river. The prince halted, horrified at what was about to happen. A large crocodile emerged from the river and said, "Behold, I am thy doom, following after thee."

And here, the story ends abruptly. The ancient document where this myth is written was so badly damaged that the end of this story remains unknown.

Did the prince die as he was fated to, or did he escape the grim prophecy of the Seven Hathors?

Chapter 12: The Two Brothers

Bata ran as fast as his legs could carry him.

As he tumbled down the narrow dusty pathway, he could hear Anpu chasing after him with a spear in hand. Only Ra himself could save Bata from being killed for a crime he did not commit.

How did it all begin?

This is the story of "The Two Brothers" from classic Egyptian mythology. It begins with the peaceful coexistence of two brothers; the older was named Anpu, and the younger was named Bata.

Anpu and Bata were born to the same parents, and as the eldest, Anpu owned a house, cattle, and land. He also had a wife, and Bata lived with them. Bata was an excellent farmer. He cultivated the land and planted and harvested crops on his brother's land. He was also the one who fed and worked the cattle. Bata had a supernatural ability to speak to animals.

Every morning, he woke up first to work the field with the oxen, feed the cattle, and bring milk and cheese home for Anpu and his wife. Anpu's farm was in the best hands in Egypt, as Bata was a man who knew of the seasons.

One day in the Season of Emergence, Bata requested Anpu to join in plowing the land. Anpu agreed, and when the next dawn broke, the two brothers went to the farm. They built ridges and planted many seeds. When they ran out of seeds, Anpu sent Bata home to fetch some more, and Bata headed urgently back.

At home, he met Anpu's wife, who was grooming her hair. Bata asked her to get him the seeds, but she declined.

"Go yourself and open the storeroom," she said. "Take whatsoever you desire. If I were to rise for you, my hair would become unruly once more."

Bata obliged and went into the storeroom. On his way out, something unexpected happened. Anpu's wife seduced him and expressed her desire to have sexual relations with him. Bata was repulsed by her advances. He said, "I regard you as a mother, and my brother is like a father to me. You have spoken evil words, and I desire not to hear them again, nor will I repeat to any man what you have spoken."

With this, Bata hurried back to the farm and worked there with Anpu until the evening. Anpu returned home to a surprising twist of events. His wife was in bad shape. She looked beaten and battered by a brute. She lay on the floor in pain, unable to light the lamp or give her husband water to wash his hands with as ancient Egyptian custom required.

Anpu held her in his arms and asked what had happened to her. Anpu's wife spoke that it was Bata who had attacked her when he came home to fetch more seeds. She accused him of threatening to kill her if she told Anpu about any of it.

His wife's words made Anpu violently angry. Armed with a sword and spear, Anpu charged to Bata's quarters to kill him. Meanwhile, Bata was in the barn with the oxen when one of them told him that his brother was on his way to kill him.

Bata peeped through the barn door, and indeed, Anpu was armed and on his way. Bata fled the farm with Anpu hot on his trail. While running for his life, Bata said a loud prayer to Ra, asking for help and vindication.

The god heard Bata's prayer and caused a river to break out from the dry land, separating the two brothers. The river teemed with crocodiles, and Anpu could not get to Bata. From across the river, Bata declared his innocence to Anpu and told his side of the story: the truth. To further prove his innocence, Bata cut a part of himself (his penis, according to some versions of this story) and threw it into the river, where a fish ate it.

As Bata bled, Anpu was convinced, and he was full of regret.

He tried to reach his brother, but he could not cross the river. Bata announced that he was headed for the Valley of Cedars, where he would cut out his heart and hang it on a cedar tree. If the tree was ever cut down, he would die. Bata charged Anpu with a seven-year quest to find his heart and put it inside a vessel of water so that he could come back to life.

Afterward, he bade Anpu farewell and went on his way. Full of regret and anguish, Anpu returned home and killed his wife.

Bata's Woman

Bata found a home in the Valley of Cedars, where he encountered the Ennead of Heliopolis. Ra took pity on Bata for his plight and instructed the god Khnum to create a wife for the man so he would not be lonely anymore.

Bata's new wife was divinely beautiful, and there was no other woman like her in all of Egypt. The Seven Hathors appeared on the scene and looked at her. As the knowers of fate, they foretold that Bata's wife would live a short life. They foretold of her death, just as they had in the myth of the doomed prince.

Sorely afraid of losing his wife, Bata resolved to protect his wife with his last breath. She would not step outside the house or go near the sea or into the forest. This remained the norm for many months until one day, the king of Egypt heard of her and sought her hand in marriage.

He sent countless messengers to deliver his intention to Bata's wife until she agreed to meet him. The king fell in love with Bata's wife and married her, despite knowing that she belonged to another man. When Bata's wife revealed her husband's secret about his heart hanging on a cedar tree, the king sent his soldiers to cut the tree down. Bata died.

A Reunion of Brothers

Anpu got the sign to start his quest and rescue his brother. He darted off to the Valley of Cedars and found Bata in his house, lifeless. Anpu set out to find his brother's heart or some other way to bring him back to life. After four years, he found a seed that had Bata's soul inside it.

He took the seed and dropped it into a jar of water, and Bata came back. He was alive. Anpu restored Bata's soul by having him drink the water with the seed inside it. Bata was revived, and the two brothers joyfully embraced.

Bata transformed into a bull, and Anpu rode it to the palace. The king was so delighted at the creature's display of magical powers that he made it a sacred bull in the temple and rewarded Anpu in gold and silver for it. As a bull, Bata revealed himself to his wife, and she was terrified yet unremorseful for revealing his secret to the king.

Instead, the queen petitioned the king to slaughter the sacred bull and permit her to eat its liver. Bound by an oath to grant whatever she desired, the king reluctantly agreed. The sacred bull—Bata—was sacrificed.

While it was being killed, two drops of the sacred bull's blood fell to the ground, and two magnificent Persea trees sprouted from them. The king's attendants marveled at this mystery and told the king of it. The king pronounced the trees to be sacred.

Again, Bata, in the form of the sacred trees, revealed himself to the queen. She went pale with fright and tricked the king once more into swearing an oath to grant her desire. Then, she asked for the sacred Persea trees to be cut down. The king was unable to refuse. He assigned the most skilled lumberjacks in Egypt to cut the tree down, and they began, with the queen watching. Unknown to her, a tiny splinter from the trees entered her mouth, and she swallowed it.

This splinter caused the queen to become pregnant, and she soon birthed a son, thinking him to be the pharaoh's son. Unknown to the king and queen, the boy was an incarnation of Bata, and he would inherit the Kingdom of Egypt after their death.

When Bata became the king of Egypt, he summoned his brother Anpu and made him next in line to the throne of Egypt. The two brothers were united once more, never to be separated again.

Chapter 13:
Isis and the Seven Scorpions

It was a chilly evening, and the murky marshes of the Nile were no place for a mother and her infant child. Her clothes were no better than rags, and memories of her imprisonment in that spinning mill plagued her mind.

This mysterious woman had an unusual company of bodyguards. They were not able-bodied men or even gods. They were gigantic venomous scorpions. There were seven of them, and they formed a protective circle around her as she made for a mansion on the horizon.

The seven scorpions were named Tefen, Masetetef, Petet, Tjetet, Matet, Mesetet, and Befen. They were assigned by Serket at the behest of the god Thoth to protect the woman and her child from harm. They soon arrived at the mansion, and when the woman knocked desperately, the doors of the mansion opened.

There stood Usert, a wealthy woman who owned and lived in the mansion.

Repulsed by her haggard appearance, Usert showed no compassion for the woman or her baby. Instead, she slammed her door in the faces of these unwanted guests and walked away without remorse.

Little did she know that it was no mere mortal at her door. It was the great and powerful goddess Isis, and her baby was Horus, son of Osiris. Our myth of Isis and the Seven Scorpions is set after the gruesome murder of Osiris and the usurpation of the Egyptian throne by the evil god Set.

Set was on a rampage to wipe out Osiris's bloodline forever, but Thoth, in his wisdom, had helped protect Isis and her son, who was destined to avenge his father. After her escape, Isis concealed her divinity by taking on the form of an ordinary woman to avoid being discovered by Set's hunting dogs.

After being disparaged by Usert, Isis headed for a village behind the mansion to seek help, but her companions, the seven scorpions, would not forgive the insult.

Isis found refuge in the humble home of a poor fisher girl who had only a straw bed and simple food to offer. It was more than enough for Isis and her baby, and they spent the night there, contented.

Meanwhile, the aggrieved companions of Isis held a meeting that night and concocted the ultimate revenge for Usert's insult. One after another, the scorpions transferred all their venom to their leader Tefen and sent him to the mansion.

While the people in the village slept, Tefen crawled in the dead of night and went into Usert's house. The scorpion found Usert's son sound asleep in his chamber and stung him hard. The next morning, Usert found her son on the verge of death. She grabbed him and rushed into the city, crying and seeking help.

Isis was tending to her baby when she heard the ruckus. She was moved with pity for the dying child, and when no one could save him from his suffering, she offered aid.

The boy was in severe pain since the poison in his body tortured him. He cried out in agony. Isis knew that it was the work of her scorpions and took the boy in her arms. She called out each scorpion by name and neutralized its poison in the boy's body with her potent spells.

The goddess then revealed herself to Usert, the one who had rejected her. She also revealed herself to the fisher girl who had shown her generosity. Usert was overcome with guilt and remorse for failing to recognize Isis and being so unwelcoming. She thanked Isis for saving her son and gave all her wealth to the poor fisher girl as a gesture of worship. The myth of Isis and the Seven Scorpions is popular in Egypt since it hinges on kindness, patience, compassion, and forgiveness.

Chapter 14:
The Prince and the Sphinx

The story of the Prince and the Sphinx takes us back to the Eighteenth Dynasty during the reign of Pharaoh Amenhotep, the great-grandson of Thutmose III who succeeded the female Pharaoh Hatshepsut.

Amenhotep had many sons and daughters, but our protagonist is the king's favorite, Prince Thutmose (a different Thutmose from the first three before Hatshepsut). The prince was an athletic young man who had many skills. He was a great hunter and fighter, a charismatic speaker, an expert rider, a wildlife explorer, and excellent in the art of archery.

Despite his status as prince and being beloved by the pharaoh, Thutmose had a problem: all his siblings hated him. Every day, they plotted against the prince in a desperate bid to discourage the pharaoh from naming him the successor to the throne of Egypt. These ploys made Thutmose look unworthy and cruel, and they soon escalated to blatant attempts on his life. Yet no one seemed to notice. Not his father, the king, or his mother, Queen Tiaa.

The worried prince began to keep more to himself and stay away from the pharaoh. Instead, he added one more skill to his long list of abilities—the art of sneaking out of the palace in disguise. To pull this off as frequently as he desired, Prince Thutmose enlisted the assistance of a few trusted servants. He would slip away from the royal court many times to hunt gazelles and wild beasts in the desert. He also yearned for the picturesque view of the pyramids of Saqqara and Giza.

During festivities or sessions at the royal courts where the pharaoh required Thutmose's attendance, he would be around for a minute and gone the next.

One auspicious day, Egypt was in a festive mood for the grand celebration of the sun god Ra. The celebration was to be held in Heliopolis, and every servant in the palace was tasked with readying for the ceremony.

With everyone else distracted, Prince Thutmose saw the perfect chance to sneak out of the palace for another one of his hunting trips. He could not afford to get seen, so he selected two of his most trusted servants to go on the trip with him. At the crack of dawn, the prince and his servants took their secret exit and made their way to the desert on his chariot.

They toiled the entire morning but caught nothing. By afternoon, the infamous baking-hot Egyptian sun was lashing their bodies with its rays. Prince Thutmose and his men rode fast for the north and slowly approached the pyramids of Giza.

These pyramids had been built by the great pharaohs of the Fourth Dynasty (Khufu, Khafra, and Menkaure) over a thousand years before the prince was born. Thutmose was fascinated by the sight of them and yearned to move closer to say a prayer to Harmachis, whose spirit inhabited one of the sphinxes of Giza. In ancient Egypt, a sphinx was revered as the manifestation of Horus and the protector of royal tombs.

The Great Sphinx of Giza.
https://commons.wikimedia.org/wiki/File:DSC_0088_Sphinx01.JPG

Prince Thutmose ordered his servants to wait under the shade of the palm trees while he rode in his chariot toward the pyramids. As the sun shone brighter, the ginormous sphinxes sparkled, and Khafra's pyramid looked different from the others. The head of the sphinx was carved in the likeness of Harmachis, and it protruded from the sea of sand around it while the rest of the sphinx was buried under the sand.

Despising the intense heat, Prince Thutmose dropped to his knees and prayed to the sphinx head shaped like Harmachis. He laid out all his troubles about how his own brothers and sisters were after his life, and he asked for divine help.

Moments later, the prince noticed something rather spooky. The eyes of the sphinx he was praying to moved. He could not believe it, so he continued praying. The eyes of the sphinx were inanimate and made of stone. It had to be all in his head—until it was too obvious to ignore.

Suddenly, the earth began to quake around Thutmose, and the sands drifted violently as the sphinx came alive and tried in vain to wriggle out from the sand. Prince Thutmose was bedazzled by the sight and fell back as the mystic sphinx opened its mouth and spoke with a great voice:

"Look upon me, Thutmose, Prince of Egypt, and know that I am Harmachis your father—the father of all Pharaohs of the Upper and Lower Lands. It rests with you to become Pharaoh indeed and wear upon your head the Double Crown of South and North...

Thutmose, my face is turned towards you, my heart inclines to you to bring you good things, your spirit shall be wrapped in mine. But see how the sand has closed in around me on every side: it smothers me, it holds me down, it hides me from your eyes. Promise me that you will do all that a good son should do for his father; prove to me that you are indeed my son and will help me. Draw near to me, and I will be with you always, I will guide you and make you great."

After this came a blinding bright light that knocked Prince Thutmose unconscious. When his eyes reopened, the sphinx had returned to its former lifeless state, still stuck in the sand.

The sun was setting and casting its sepia rays on the sand from the reddened sky, which means that the prince had been out for many hours. Nonetheless, it was the most extraordinary event that Prince Thutmose had ever experienced, and he vowed to fulfill the wishes of Harmachis if he ever became the pharaoh of Egypt.

"Harmachis, my father! I call upon you and all the gods of Egypt to bear witness to my oath. If I become Pharaoh, the first act of my reign shall be to free this your image from the sand and build a shrine to you and set in it a stone telling in the sacred writing of Khem of your command and how I fulfilled it."

With this, Thutmose mounted his chariot and sped off to find his servants, who had become worried at his long departure. Together, they rode back to the palace in Memphis, with the prince invigorated by his encounter with the divine.

True to Harmachis's words, Thutmose was declared the successor by his father, Amenhotep. The efforts of his royal siblings to besmirch him before the pharaoh, the royal court, and the people of Egypt failed.

From around 1401 to around 1397 BCE, the prince ruled Egypt as King Thutmose IV, the eighth pharaoh of the Eighteenth Dynasty of ancient Egypt.

As pharaoh, Thutmose IV kept his promise to Harmachis. He had the sphinx of Khafre's pyramid dug out from the sand and built a shrine at its feet. The myth of the Prince and the Sphinx was documented in hieroglyphics, etched in a tablet made from red granite and attached to the sphinx.

This ancient tablet was found only two hundred years ago, and its author was none other than Pharaoh Thutmose himself.

Chapter 15:
The Adventures of Sinuhe

You will recall the Prophecy of Neferti that spoke of an apocalypse and how the ascension of a vizier named Amenemhat to the Egyptian throne was the only way to avoid it.

Amenemhat indeed became the pharaoh who founded the Twelfth Dynasty of Egypt, but his reign was not entirely peaceful. For many decades, he was in danger of being overthrown, just as he had overthrown the pharaoh before him, Mentuhotep IV. The king's reign was plagued by civil war and unrest that continued even after he made his son, Prince Senusret, next in line for the throne.

Times were delicate in Egypt, and the king's court reeked of conspiracies and rebellions against the pharaoh.

Our story begins with Prince Senusret, who was away in the east, fighting off foreign invaders, the Temehu tribe of Libya. The prince and his army emerged victorious, and after a bout of celebration, they rode for Egypt with the spoils of war. Among his esteemed officials was a warrior named Sinuhe, a staunch supporter of Pharaoh Amenemhat. Midway to Egypt, the prince and his men were met by messengers from the king's palace.

No one knew what news they had brought, but Sinuhe had a premonition that it was about the king. To ascertain the truth, he eavesdropped on the prince's conversation with the messengers. Indeed, Pharaoh Amenemhat had been murdered in his sleep by one of the many men who sought to end his life, and the prince was to be made the new king in his stead.

The prince was aggrieved to hear of his father's assassination, but Sinuhe was more afraid than sorrowful. If the king of Egypt had been killed by rebels, then they would target all who had supported him next. Sinuhe was also afraid that the prince was in danger of being murdered. No doubt, his reign would be the same as his father's, if not worse.

A Quest of Survival

Sinuhe backed away from the prince's camp and took to his heels. He snuck out of the military encampment under cover of night and traveled along the Nile toward the city of Heliopolis. He arrived at the eastern border of Egypt and advanced to the narrow strip of land between the Mediterranean Sea and the Red Sea called the Isthmus of Suez. From there, he moved quickly to the Desert of Sinai, where his thirst got the better of him.

Sinuhe had never been so dehydrated in his life. His throat was parched, and he could quite literally "taste death" in the middle of his self-imposed exile. His hands were soon numb, along with his knees, yet he crawled on in desperation to stay alive.

Then, he encountered his first stroke of luck: a camp of Asian nomads.

Sinuhe passed out from exhaustion, comforted by some hope that he might be rescued by the nomads. After a long deep sleep, he woke up and found himself cleaned, treated, and fed with milk and water. As it turned out, the nomads were on commercial and cattle grazing business in the Nile Delta area of Egypt, so Sinuhe could not continue with them.

He headed for Syria and arrived at Byblos, the kingdom that had received the goddess Isis when she had come to rescue her husband, Osiris. Sinuhe spent a few nights in Byblos, but it was a land friendly to Egyptians. It was not his destination.

Eventually, he arrived at a kingdom called Retenu (also called Canaan) in Lebanon.

A New Home

The king of Retenu was Ammienshi, and despite the toll that Sinuhe's trip had taken on his appearance, the king could tell that he was an important man from Egypt.

He welcomed Sinuhe to Retenu and offered him a home among the other Egyptians who lived in the kingdom. During their conversation, King Ammienshi inquired into the reason why Sinuhe had come so far from his home. This might have been the king's way of measuring the manner of man that he was. Sinuhe responded by telling the king of Pharaoh Amenemhat's passing and that he had fled Egypt because he feared that a civil war would erupt.

King Ammienshi was aware of the old pharaoh's death and of the ascension of Prince Senusret I as the new king of Egypt. He assured Sinuhe that there had been no revolts against the new pharaoh's reign and sought Sinuhe's counsel on whether or not to support the new pharaoh.

Sinuhe responded by saying noble words about the new pharaoh and entreating King Ammienshi to be loyal. From this, King Ammienshi gathered that Sinuhe was a man of peace and would not pose any threats to his kingdom. Sinuhe was also a man of war, though, which means he could be useful in a military capacity.

So, King Ammienshi made Sinuhe a commander of his armies and consented to his marriage to his first daughter. This elevated Sinuhe's status in Retenu, and he was given an estate called Iaa, which had rich, fertile lands for crops and cattle to flourish.

In his capacity as an army commander and tribal chief, Sinuhe embarked on many military campaigns to protect Retenu from foreign invasions. His services pleased King Ammienshi so much that he decided to make Sinuhe the next king of Retenu.

The Duel of Champions

King Ammienshi's succession plan did not sit well with some of the nobles and commoners in Retenu. They thought the king had spent too many years overcompensating a foreigner for his services, and the throne of Retenu was where they would draw the line.

A wind of rebellion was rumored to soon sweep through the palace, and it was to be championed by an undisclosed war hero in Retenu. Unable to shake off his anxiety, King Ammienshi summoned Sinuhe for a private discussion. He asked if Sinuhe knew the man who was planning a rebellion. Sinuhe answered no, but that would soon change.

There was to be a duel between him and the man who wanted him dead. This duel was to happen in public and in the king's presence. The war hero would reveal himself and fight Sinuhe to determine who was greater.

On the day of the duel, the people of Retenu trooped to the venue of the fight, and many cheered for Sinuhe. They had no doubts about his skills in archery and combatant warfare, and he had all it took to conquer his challenger—until they found out that Sinuhe's opponent was a giant.

The arena fell silent, gasping in awe at the giant's menacing physique. He was armed with arrows, a gigantic battle-ax, and javelins.

Doubts crept into the hearts of some of Sinuhe's supporters, and they feared that this fight would be his last. The battle began in earnest, and as they had feared, the giant was not a walkover. He charged at Sinuhe with every weapon in his armory, and Sinuhe escaped every attack by a hair's breadth.

In the heat of battle, Sinuhe chose an opportune time to hurl a javelin at his opponent. The javelin pierced the giant's neck, and he sank to his knees before dropping dead with a thud.

Jubilation erupted in the arena after Sinuhe cut off his opponent's head, and the king was overjoyed that his successor had won the battle. News traveled throughout the kingdom about the duel, and Sinuhe's greatness was enlarged. It was unlike anything it had been before. He served King Ammienshi for many more years and became king after him.

The Homecoming

"Return to Egypt to look again upon the land where you were born and the palace where you served me so faithfully."

Sinuhe could not contain his happiness upon reading a letter from the king of Egypt. He had sent a letter to ask for forgiveness and to be allowed to visit Egypt at least one more time before he died. It had been many years since Sinuhe left Egypt, and he was not as young as he once was. In his old age, he yearned to go to Egypt and see what his homeland now looked like.

He had not anticipated an express invitation to live out the rest of his days in Egypt, but Pharaoh Senusret I had graciously offered. Sinuhe's self-imposed exile was over, and the dangers of the past were long behind him.

Sinuhe quickly transferred the rulership of Retenu to his oldest son and set off on a long journey back to Egypt. He was welcomed by the king and the royal family. Many of the king's courtiers could not recognize him.

Pharaoh Senusret I was thrilled to be reunited with an old friend. He bore no grudges and mentioned nothing of the past. Instead, he directed that Sinuhe change out of his desert clothes and be given fine linens to wear. He was to be groomed and fed well.

This story ends with Sinuhe living out the rest of his days as a beloved friend of the king. This long-lost fugitive had found his way back home.

SECTION THREE:
Gods and Goddesses

Chapter 16: Amun-Ra

You will recall from the creation myths of ancient Egypt that in Heliopolis, the creator was Atum. Hermopolis, Memphis, and Thebes eventually named Amun as their chief creator god. Atum and Amun are the same; they are both aspects of Ra.

Typically, Amun was worshiped as the morning sun and Atum as the light of night, but things were slightly different in early Egyptian history.

In the Old Kingdom era of ancient Egypt, Amun-Ra was worshiped as two different gods. Amun was the creator deity who had formed the world from the nothingness of Nun and created humans to dwell on the earth. Ra was the sun god who rode through the sky in his barque of light by day and descended to the underworld to defeat the monstrous Apophis (Apep) at night.

In Theban tradition, Amun was only a partner to the female Amaunet and a member of the revered Ogdoad. Unlike Ra, Amun was a spirit form and could only be felt, not seen or touched. Ra was the visible sun and the earth's soldier against the darkness (Apophis or Apep).

Amun was not associated with Ra, the sun god, until the New Kingdom. This may have been a result of the unification of Upper and Lower Egypt and the shifting of the Egyptian capital from Memphis, where Ra was supreme, to Thebes, where Amun was prominent.

The sun god Ra was syncretized with the creator god Amun to become the powerful Amun-Ra. With this, the attributes of the spirit creator god and those of the sun god were fused into a single universal deity.

Amun-Ra: The Creator

In Egyptian mythology, Amun was not born. He emerged from the primordial waters of Nun as a divine, self-created being. He was the first to exist on Earth, and the creation of the world was initiated by him. Amun's first creation was that of *heka*, the magic with which he made the rest of the world. In some traditions, Heka was a god, but in most, he was magic itself, just like Amun-Ra was the sun itself.

Next, Amun created his first children, Shu and Tefnut, who went on to populate the earth with their offspring. After them, Amun created Ma'at, the order of the world. Ma'at, as a goddess, was said to be the daughter of Ra, as were the goddesses Hathor, Sekhmet, and Bastet, who were sisters.

The Eye of Ra is another important aspect of Amun-Ra as a creator god. It is the feminine aspect of Amun. In the creation myth of Heliopolis, the Eye of Ra was sent on a mission to find Shu and Tefnut when they left home. In time, the Eye of Ra became more than just a part of Amun's body. The goddess Sekhmet (or Hathor) was often called the Eye of Ra, the fearsome messenger of Amun-Ra who once destroyed the world as a punishment for the sins of mankind against their creator.

Creation is the first role attributed to Amun-Ra, and in the years that followed the primeval era, the influence of Amun-Ra would only broaden. You will find Amun-Ra, the creator god, depicted in ancient Egyptian texts as a falcon-headed god with a snake-rimmed sun disk on his head. He is also portrayed in creation myths as a scarab beetle named Khepri or a young boy believed to be Horus.

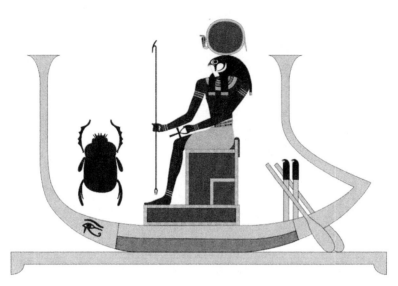

The Forms of Ra: Khepri, the Eye of Ra, and the falcon-headed god.

HarJIT. Derived from files from Jeff Dahl, Rawpixel, Finn Bjørklid, Jasmina El Bouamraoui and Karabo Poppy Moletsane., CC BY-SA 4.0 https://creativecommons.org/licenses/by-sa/4.0 via Wikimedia Commons; https://commons.wikimedia.org/wiki/File:Khepri_Re_Hypocephalus_Scene.svg

Amun-Ra: The Sun God

The most popular depiction of Amun-Ra in Egyptian mythology was as the traveling sun god. When the foundations of the earth were laid and Ma'at took its course, the day was divided from the night, but that did not just happen suddenly.

Indeed, it took the eternal voyages of Amun-Ra to create the miracles of dawn and dusk. The sun god had a shiny boat (or barque) called Atet, and on it, he would course the sky in the daytime as the sun. When evening came, he would descend on the western horizon to the underworld (the Duat) for twelve hours, fighting demons, judging wicked souls, and reviving the needy. In the twelfth hour, the sun god's barque would rise in the east, and the sun would reappear.

In his depiction as a sun god, Amun-Ra was typically shown as a ram-headed god with the sun disk on. He would also have companions on his barque, notably Heka (in his form as a god), Sia, and Hu (gods who represented the divine Ennead). You can also find pictorials of more popular gods like Set and Hathor as being part of Amun-Ra's entourage.

Amun-Ra on his divine barque (Atet) in the underworld.

https://commons.wikimedia.org/wiki/File:Book_of_Gates_Barque_of_Ra.jpg

Despite Amun-Ra's supremacy in the Egyptian pantheon, his journeys were not smooth-sailing. Every day as he descended to the underworld, he would be challenged by an infernal enemy, Apophis (or Apep). Some mythological versions say that Apophis attacked the sun god while he was in the underworld, not when he was descending into it. In any case, Amu-Ra fought off this monster every day and defeated it.

At the gates of the underworld, Amun-Ra would be received by his good friend, Osiris, the god of the underworld. Some Egyptian traditions outrightly fuse Amun-Ra with Osiris, but more generally, they were separate deities. Together, they would condemn the wicked souls of the dead to the Egyptian version of hell and grant the good souls passage to paradise.

Amun-Ra: The Father and King

Long before the era of the pharaohs, the gods ruled the earth. According to the sacred *Book of the Heavenly Cow*, the first king of the earth was Ra. He had just completed his fine work of creation and was the king of mankind—that is, until they began to rebel against him.

In the events that followed, Ra retired to the sky and created the Field of Reeds, the Egyptian version of heaven, for his abode. He also founded Ma'at and commanded humankind to uphold it with their lives.

As the creator of all life and the first in divinity, all other gods and goddesses were descendants of Ra. Apart from the association of Amun and Ra, which led to the emergence of Amun-Ra, or Atum and Ra, which became Atum Ra, there were others. There was the fusion of Ra with Horus, the falcon-headed god. Some depictions of Amun-Ra are as a falcon-headed god. The relationship between the two gods began in creation when Horus was portrayed in some mythological accounts as an aspect of Amun. The syncretism between Amun-Ra and Horus was called Ra-Horakhty.

These associations and his role in creating other deities enthroned Amun-Ra as the father and king of all gods. Naturally, this extended to mortals. Pharaohs of the Fourth Dynasty of the Old Kingdom called themselves the "sons of Ra." Thenceforth, the kings of Egypt became associated with Ra as his sons and divine representatives on Earth, for which they were revered by the people. They were also rumored to have built their pyramids in alignment with the sun as an act of worship.

The cult worship of Amun-Ra in dynastic Egypt began in Heliopolis. By the Second Dynasty, it had spread to the entire land, and the title of the sun god was widely assigned to Amun-Ra. He was the creator, the sun, and the god of the sun. In the Fifth Dynasty, the pharaohs began building temples of Ra, known as sun temples.

Userkaf, the founder of the Fifth Dynasty of ancient Egypt, was the first to commission a sun temple in the plains near Abu Gorab. The sun temple was called Nekhen-Ra, meaning the "Fortress of Ra" or the "Stronghold of Ra," and its remains were unearthed in the early 1840s.

Six other sun temples would be built by Pharaoh Sahure, Pharaoh Neferirkare Kakai, Pharaoh Neferefre, Pharaoh Shepseskare, Pharaoh Nyuserre Ini, and Pharaoh Menkauthor Kaiu, all of them during the Fifth Dynasty.

The Opet Festival was the largest celebration of Amun in ancient Egypt. It peaked in the New Kingdom era around 1539 BCE in Thebes. It began on the fifteenth day in the first season of the year, Akhet (or the Season of the Inundation), and it was celebrated for eleven days during the reign of Pharaoh Thutmose III. It became twenty-four days when Ramesses III was on the throne, and soon after, it took as long as twenty-seven days.

The pharaoh was the most important figure in this celebration since he was the highest prophet of Amun in all the land. The Opet Festival was a time to legitimize his reign and status as the king of Egypt before his people. The pharaoh would be endued with the power of Amun, and as a sign of the god's blessing, the lands of Egypt would be fertile.

As part of the festival rites, a colorful procession of priests would bear the sacred statue of Amun in a gold-coated wooden barque from the temple in Karnak to the Luxor Temple. The people would flock to the streets to see the procession, anticipating the abundance of bread and wine that would soon follow. They would also anticipate their consultations with Amun through his priests for answers to life's problems.

While at Luxor, the pharaoh would enter the innermost room in the temple for the ritual transfer of power and rejuvenation. Afterward, the procession would return the statue to Karnak.

Amun-Ra had his own holiday in Egypt as its national deity. He appeared in every Egyptian myth and sacred book, and his sons and daughters, both mortal and immortal, lived their lives in his service.

The eminence of Amun-Ra remained uncontested throughout the Old and New Kingdom eras of ancient Egypt and even beyond. There was just no unseating the god who caused every new day to emerge and created everything in the world.

Chapter 17:
Isis, Osiris, and Horus

You will recall these three from the famous Myth of Osiris and how their influence stretched from the Old Kingdom to the eras that followed. Isis and Osiris were the first siblings. They were the children of the god Geb and goddess Nut (who were also siblings). They were also the great-grandchildren of the creator god Atum, at least according to the creation myth of Heliopolis, and they became the king and queen of Egypt.

Isis: Goddess of Healing and Magic

Praised as a major goddess in the Egyptian pantheon, Isis was first referenced in texts from the Old Kingdom as a main character in the famous Osiris myth. She fell in love with her brother Osiris from the womb and married him. Together, they ruled Egypt as king and queen.

Isis was born to Geb and Nut, along with her four (sometimes three) other siblings, who were all endowed with divine powers. In the myths of Osiris and that of Isis and the Seven Scorpions, Isis uses her magical powers to heal her husband and a dying child, respectively.

Her hieroglyphic name is often translated as "throne" or "Queen of the Throne," which is why she was regarded as the mother of all pharaohs. Isis is represented as a beautiful woman with black hair and cow horns on her head. She wears a red sheath dress and holds an ankh and a staff. Her symbols are the tyet (also known as the Knot or Girdle of Isis), the moon and solar disks, and sycamore trees. She is also portrayed as a majestic figure with outstretched wings or as a scorpion.

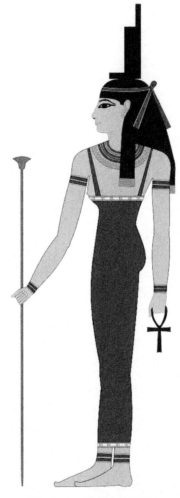

Isis, the goddess of healing.
Jeff Dahl, CC BY-SA 4.0 https://creativecommons.org/licenses/by-sa/4.0 *via Wikimedia Commons;* https://commons.wikimedia.org/wiki/File:Isis.svg

The tyet is Isis's most prominent symbol, and it stands for life and well-being. The goddess Isis was not among the Egyptian gods and goddesses of creation, but her status grew over time. By the Roman era, the worship of Isis had reached its peak. She was honored as a queen, healer, mourner, mother, wife, and protector.

As the wife of Osiris, Isis showed tremendous support to her husband before he became the god of the underworld. When Set came after Osiris and killed him more than once, Isis never gave up on him. She rescued him and healed him with her magic powers, even when his body was mutilated. Isis soon became a model for the virtuous Egyptian woman. She was devoted and faithful to her husband, no matter the circumstance.

Isis's son, Horus, became associated with the pharaohs of Egypt, which made Isis become the queen mother of all the kings of Egypt. She became a significant divinity of protection, nourishment, and companionship for pharaohs from the Fifth Dynasty onward.

Besides her royal importance, the goddess Isis was worshiped as the protector of women and children. During her reign with Osiris, Isis was known to teach the women of Egypt how to master baking, weaving, and wine-making. This endeared Isis to the women, and they prayed to her for the preservation of their marriages and children. As shown in the myth of Isis and the Seven Scorpions, Isis had a soft spot for children. She also protected her own son Horus from the wrath of Set until he was old enough to avenge his father.

Another important aspect of Isis was her power of healing. She had brought Osiris back from the dead twice and healed Usert's young son in Egyptian mythology, earning her a prominent spot in the mystical matters of ancient Egypt. An ancient Egyptian book of spells tells the story of Isis healing the sun god from a snakebite wound in exchange for the knowledge of his "true secret name." This secret name of Ra is believed to carry immeasurable power, and Isis's possession of it was what made her the most powerful magical healer in the world.

In the myth of Osiris, Isis sorrowfully restored the king's broken body and helped him transition to the afterlife as the god of the underworld. This act made Isis a worshiped mourner and guide to the afterlife. During funerary rites, Isis would be invoked to make the deceased whole and preserve their soul in the afterlife.

Despite her fame across Egypt, it was not until the early to mid-300 BCE that the first temple of Isis was built. This happened during the reign of Pharaoh Nectanebo II, the last native ruler of

Egypt. The Macedonian pharaohs who subsequently ruled Egypt carried on the legacy, erecting more structures for the worship of Isis throughout the land.

This made the cult of Isis, which had existed as early as the Fifth Dynasty, spread throughout the Mediterranean. Foreign sailors began worshiping Isis as their protector at sea, and her fame soon reached the shores of Rome, Greece, and other parts of Asia Minor. Travelers and merchants who joined the cult of Isis spread her worship in the cities and kingdoms of the Middle East, including Iran.

It had taken a long time for Isis to be independently worshiped within and outside Egypt and Nubia, but attributes of her care, empathy, and compassion soon attracted men, women, and children in the thousands to kneel at her feet.

Osiris: The God of the Underworld

When Osiris was born to his parents, Geb and Nut, he was predestined for greatness. Not only was he the firstborn and the heir to the throne of predynastic Egypt, but an epic clash with his brother would change the course of his life for all eternity.

The name Osiris has a rich debated etymology. While it is commonly agreed that the name "Osiris" is the Latin translation of the Egyptian name Asar, there are many meanings of the name itself, including "Seat of the eye (of Ra)," "the Mighty One," "the Beautiful One," and "the Created One."

You will find depictions of Osiris as a green-skinned man (like his father Geb) with a beard. He wears a long ostrich-feathered crown called the Atef and holds the royal crook and flail. Instead of a royal robe, his lower torso is wrapped like a mummy. In a few depictions, he is portrayed as having black skin instead of green, representing the fertile marshes of the Nile River.

Osiris was the god of life and the god of death. He was also the god of the afterlife since he was the judge of the dead, and he was the god of resurrection. These rather contrasting aspects allude to his journey as an earthly king and how it was renavigated to a reign of the underworld.

It's all in the legendary myth of Osiris.

During his reign in Egypt, Osiris was loved by his people for bringing peace and prosperity to the kingdom. As the god of fertility and agriculture, he taught his people how to cultivate the land and harvest food for their survival. With his wife and sister Isis, Osiris ruled Egypt with unmatched wisdom, much to the envy of his brother Set, who eventually murdered him twice.

After being raised from the dead by his wife, Osiris assumed his throne in the underworld as the judge of the dead. His death and resurrection were the dawn of a new era of worship, one that would transcend predynastic Egypt.

In line with his contrasting roles as an earthly king and the king of the underworld, Osiris is portrayed as both a kind, generous god and a dreadful deity who commanded demons of the underworld. He also had the powers to decide whether a soul would live on in the afterlife or be destroyed.

As an important figure in the afterlife, Osiris's worship spanned from around 6000 BCE to the Ptolemaic Dynasty (323 BCE-30 BCE). Annual festivals to commemorate his death and resurrection were held, and a city in Upper Egypt called Abydos became the center of the cult of Osiris.

During the festivities, the people would perform plays, telling the story of Osiris's murder and dismemberment, how Isis revived him and helped him transition to the afterlife, and the revenge of Horus. They would also build ridges on their farms called "Osiris Beds" and planted seeds of grain. The germination of these seeds was symbolic of the resurrection of Osiris, and it was heralded with rejoicing. Reliefs of this festival were carved on the tomb walls of Pharaoh Tutankhamun.

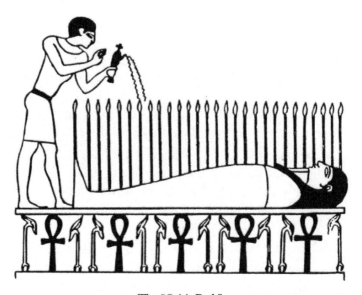

The "Osiris Bed."
https://commons.wikimedia.org/wiki/File:Osiris_Philae.jpg

By the Twelfth Dynasty, a five-day funeral ritual was held every year in Abydos, the worship center of Osiris. The events for each day were outlined on the Ikhernofret Stela, a scared stone slab in Osiris's temple. On the first day was a procession led by the god Wepwawet, the Opener of Ways. At this time, the people would perform a battle play where Osiris would triumph over his enemies. The second day was the Great Procession of Osiris. A statue of Osiris (representing his body) would be moved from the temple to his tomb in a boat. On the third day, the people would mourn the death of Osiris, and on the fourth day, the people would pray while funeral rites were performed. On the fifth day, the people of Egypt would celebrate the rebirth of Osiris at dawn and move the statue back to the temple in a celebratory style. This represented Osiris becoming ruler of the underworld and restoring Ma'at.

The Greek author Plutarch makes a different observation of the festivals of Osiris. He describes them as being gloomier and solemn, often restricted to the temple premises. He also tells of rituals of clay performed by the priests of Osiris. It involved mixing fertile soil with water in small golden coffers and molding crescent-shaped figures representing Osiris and Isis. Other accounts describe the baking of divine wheat bread and cakes from wheat grain grown in the temples of Osiris.

The ancient Egyptians believed that after death, every person qualified for the afterlife would be welcomed by Osiris. If not, a soul was damned to be devoured by the demon Ammit or cast into a fiery lake.

Osiris retained influence in the religious realms of ancient Egypt well into the Hellenistic Period (c. 323 BCE). This era fused Osiris with a Greek god named Serapis, and temples were constructed for their cults in Memphis and Philae.

Horus: God of the Sky

You may have seen pictures or depictions of a falcon-headed god from ancient Egypt. His name is Horus, and he was the son of the god Osiris and the goddess Isis. Not only was Horus a member of the beloved trinity of ancient Egypt, but he was also worshiped as the "Pharaoh of All Pharaohs."

Horus had an unusual childhood. He had been born to a mother who was on the run from a man who had killed his father and snatched his birthright. This shaped the nature of Horus's upbringing. He lived out his growing years in the swamps of the Nile Delta, hiding from his uncle. This is why many Ptolemaic figurines of Horus as a child are a young boy with a finger to his lips, indicative of silence. Under the protection of his mother, Horus was trained in the art of magic, and his father, who had transitioned to the underworld, taught him the art of warfare.

The man who had disrupted his family was none other than his uncle Set, and it was Horus's destiny to destroy Set and save Egypt from a tumultuous reign. After years of battle against Set, Horus was victorious, and he reclaimed the throne of Egypt. Thereafter, the fame of Horus spread, and he made worshipers of many men and women throughout the land and in the generations to come.

The symbol of Horus is a falcon, and the Eye of Horus is believed to signify good health, healing, and protection. The Eye of Horus originates from a version of his conflict with Set, where Horus's eye was gouged out in the heat of battle. Horus's eye healed after the encounter, and he offered it to his father, Osiris, as a keepsake for the afterlife. Some ancient Egyptian traditions used the Eye of Horus and the Eye of Ra interchangeably since Horus was the offspring of the sun god.

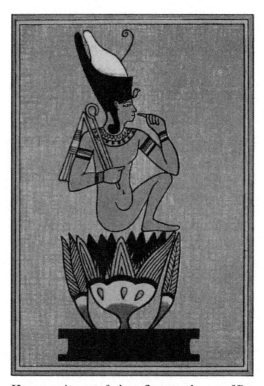

Horus coming out of a lotus flower as the son of Ra.
Unknown author, CC0, via Wikimedia Commons;
*https://commons.wikimedia.org/wiki/File:The_Sacred_Books_and_Early_Literature_of_t
he_East,_vol._2,_pg._272-273,_Horus.jpg*

Horus was worshiped as the sky god, whose right eye was the sun and the left was the moon. He was also the falcon that soared in the sky, representing his status as "he who is above" or his kingship. This explains why Horus was associated with kingship, and all the pharaohs of dynastic Egypt proudly called themselves the descendants of Horus. They associated with him while they were alive, and in death, they were associated with Osiris.

Cults of Horus emerged in Edfu and Nekhen, the capital of Upper Egypt in predynastic Egypt. His temples were beautiful edifices with courtyards, lakes, and gardens. While only the priests could enter the innermost rooms that housed the statues of Horus, people from all over Egypt flocked to the temples to offer prayers, give and receive alms, and receive interpretations of dreams and signs.

The Festival of Victory was the most important celebration dedicated to Horus. It was a colorful event that was held in the month of *Meshir*, the second month in the Season of Emergence (the sixth month in the ancient Egyptian calendar). The people would converge in Horus's temple at Edfu and begin the festivities with a drama depicting Horus's triumph over his evil uncle Set. The pharaoh would play the part of Horus, and he would wrestle a hippopotamus, which represented Set.

If the pharaoh killed the hippopotamus, he would be respected by the people as the legitimate owner of the throne. If the king could not attend the festival in person, he could assign a priest to fill the role. It was important to put on a delightful show and display the power of Horus and his supremacy over Set.

The name "Horus" is arguably the name of the fifth son of Geb and Nut. This variation of Horus is known as Horus the Elder by those traditions that believe in his existence. Horus the Elder was the brother of Osiris, Isis, Set, and Nephthys. Other ancient Egyptian traditions name Hathor as the mother of Horus the Elder and further assert that he was the falcon god and the "Distant One." He was a messenger from Ra to guide humans and comfort them until he transformed into the child of Osiris and Isis as Horus the Younger.

In Graeco-Roman Egypt, Horus became the equivalent of the Greek god Apollo, and Edfu, the city of Horus, was renamed Apollinopolis (the city of Apollo).

Chapter 18: Set and Nephthys

Just like Osiris and Isis, the god of chaos Set and the goddess of death Nephthys were siblings who got married. This couple had vital roles in the Osiris myth, and in the end, they turned out to be a most unlikely pair. Were they ever in love? What happened to their marriage in the course of events involving their other siblings? What was their place in the Egyptian pantheon?

You are about to find out.

Set: The God of Chaos

Everything there is to know about this god from ancient Egypt is in the name. Every time there was a storm or a violent earthquake, the people of ancient Egypt would whisper to one another that it was Set at work. He represented everything foreign or disruptive to order, and he was the villain in nearly every story he was a part of.

Set, god of chaos.

Set was born to Geb and Nut, along with three (or four) others, and the myths agree that he had been a troublemaker from birth. He was even said to have had torn out of his mother's womb! Geb and Nut must have suspected that their new son would do great yet terrible things.

His childhood was set in predynastic Egypt, and one day, his parents announced Osiris as the crown prince of Egypt. Since Osiris was the firstborn, he was the first in line, with Set behind him. This made Set envious, but there was little to be done at the time. It was the natural order anyway, and their father Geb was going to be around for a while.

It was not long enough after that Geb abdicated the throne of Egypt and gave it to Osiris. The young king had many bright ideas to make the land prosper under his reign, and there was Set, who was unable to quell his growing bitterness and jealousy. While Osiris took Isis for his wife, Set asked for the hand of Nephthys.

With this, Set and Nephthys were married, but little is known about their love story or if it even existed. On the contrary, the union of Set and Nephthys has been described as loveless and unhappy, while that of Osiris and Isis flourished. This did not help Set feel any more love toward his brother, who was now the king. From the shadows, Set watched his older brother transform Egypt and bring the people knowledge of agriculture, arts, and civility. The queen was also loved by the people for teaching the women the art of weaving, baking, and making wine.

Through it all, Set desired the throne, and it grew increasingly difficult to turn the hearts of the people against his brother. Eventually, he managed to form a small group of traitors, but their collective influence was barely enough to oust Osiris.

As the years went by, Set wallowed in his desperation to disrupt the succession order of Egypt.

It must have been a long day of plotting against Osiris and failing woefully. Set returned home to more enraging news. Osiris had slept with his wife Nephthys, and the young Anubis, whom Set had taken for his own son, was actually Osiris's son.

The news that he had been tricked by the king pushed Set further into the hot depths of his anger and hatred. Set stormed to the palace and confronted the king about the scandal with his wife. Osiris was shocked to hear about Anubis, but he had an explanation about the night with Nephthys. Nephthys had actually tricked the king into sleeping with her by disguising herself as Queen Isis that night. Osiris was regretful about the incident and apologized to Set.

Set took the king's words with a grain of salt. Now, he had all the more reason to hate Osiris, and as it stood, killing the king was the only way he could get the throne. After all, Queen Isis had yet to give birth to an heir.

Upon returning home, Set found Anubis waiting to welcome him. Everything about the boy reminded him of Osiris and Nephthys. It reminded him of treachery. That night, Set rejected Anubis and had him exiled from his sight. He would no longer treat Anubis as his son again. It was Set's first real act as the god of chaos and violence.

Next, he conjured up another evil scheme to get rid of the king, and for the first time, Set achieved his aim. He had Osiris trapped in a coffin and submerged the coffin in the Nile River. He also took his followers and invaded the palace of Egypt, forcing Queen Isis to flee for her life.

Set took the crown of Egypt and put it on his head. His reign was marked with mercilessness and terror, and the once peaceful and prosperous Egypt became a warzone. Set relished every moment of it. He was nothing like his brother, and he cared little for the love or adoration of the people when they could fear and tremble before him instead.

King Set took on as many concubines as he could since Queen Nephthys had betrayed him, and he enjoyed his dark reign for some time. Except, one day, bad news came knocking.

Isis had somehow found her husband. She had brought him back to life, and she was pregnant with an heir! Set was maddened by what was a twofold disaster, and he could not spare a moment of inaction. He set off immediately to search for his brother and found him recovering around the marshes of the Nile. Set murdered Osiris again, and this time, he was going to make it impossible for Osiris to recover.

He dismembered Osiris's corpse into fourteen pieces and buried each part far away from the other. He also found Isis and had her imprisoned to await the same fate that had befallen her husband.

Little did Set know that he had run out of luck.

Before he could harm Isis, she escaped from captivity and continued the search for her husband's body parts. Worse still, Isis was being helped by Set's wife, Nephthys, and Anubis, whom Set had disowned.

With the birth of Horus, Osiris's son, Set could feel the end of his reign lurking, but he would do everything to prevent it, even if it meant killing his nephew.

The story of Set is not complete without his epic battle with his nephew Horus. It was the most significant battle in predynastic Egypt, and it was indeed one for the ages. You know the background, but the progression of the war, as described in an ancient myth titled "The Contendings of Horus and Set," gives more gory details.

It all began with Horus and Set embarking on extreme tasks for competition. The prize was the throne of Egypt, so both Horus and Set were ruthless in their endeavors. At the end of every mission, none was willing to concede to the other. Set was the god of chaos, and brute strength was one of his abilities. Horus was his equal, having been trained by his father, Osiris, who had become king of the underworld after being murdered the second time. Horus was also a master sorcerer. He learned these skills from his mother, Isis.

Their competition soon escalated to open assaults and destructive battles, which provoked concern from the other gods and goddesses of ancient Egypt. This led to a congress presided over by the Ennead (nine gods) of Heliopolis to determine the rightful owner of the throne of Egypt. In some accounts, the council was unable to reach a consensus, and the rift between Horus and Set dragged on painfully for eighty years. Horus and Set tore away at each other, and Set used every trick he had in his evil book, including mutilating Horus's eyes and attempting to defile him sexually. Horus had his eyes restored, and in some accounts, Horus caught Set's semen in his hands and tore off Set's testicles for revenge.

In the end, Horus emerged victorious, while Set took a shameful exit from the throne of Egypt. But was this the end of the road for Set?

With Set's villainous role in Egyptian mythology, especially in the stories of Osiris and Horus, you would expect that Set was treated similarly to Apophis (or Apep), the hated evil serpent who challenged the sun god Ra.

Despite his dark nature, Set had a surprisingly positive side to him. He was part of the entourage who traveled with Ra to and from the underworld every day. This epic twist created a place in the hearts of the people, and they worshiped Set. Some historians even argue that Set was a thoroughly misrepresented god and that he may not have been so evil after all.

As a glimpse into the good side of the god of chaos, we have the barque of Ra: the divine boat that ferries through the sky in the daytime and descends to the underworld at night. It also doubles as a warship for the sun god's encounter with the all-dreadful Apophis.

Set was almost always on this barque because no other god could fill the shoes of the "Protector of Ra." He was also known to slay Apophis on many occasions and rescue the sun god whenever he got hypnotized by the serpent. Apophis found a fierce opponent in Set, as they were both masters of trickery and shared a frightful thirst to win battles.

Set fighting Apophis to protect the sun god Ra.
https://commons.wikimedia.org/wiki/File:Set_speared_Apep.jpg

As a warrior and defender, Set was also believed to strengthen pilgrims on their journey to the afterlife. As it turned out, Set worked with Horus to guide the souls of the deceased into the afterlife, which is yet another thoroughly ironic aspect of his being. You should know that chronologically, the positive aspect of Set came first. He was first revered as the "Protector of Ra" and, in some traditions, as the god of love. He was a hero-god.

The cult of Set and his temples in Avaris and Ombus was widely attended by the people of Upper Egypt. He was highly venerated and popularized by the Nineteenth Dynasty Pharaoh Seti I (who was named after Set) and his successor Ramesses II. They openly associated with Set as their father and protector. In his temples, only the priests of Set could be near his statues or enter the inner rooms. Others could only pray in the outer parts of the temple, and priests were designated to help the people with offerings, prayers, weddings, funerals, or consultations.

Not long after Ramesses II's reign, especially with the incursion of foreigners into Egypt, Set's reputation transformed radically. More emphasis shifted to his role in Osiris's death and his evil tenure as the king of Egypt, leading to the gradual demonization of a once-loved god.

Set became the god of foreigners, god of the desert, and god of chaos at the end of the New Kingdom. He became associated with aggressive foreigners from Asia Minor who invaded and enforced their rule by proxy on Egypt. Set's Greek equivalent was Typhon, a hideous evil beast who fought against Zeus for control of the universe but was defeated and locked away in Tartarus forever.

Fascinatingly, Set's demonization did not end the worship of him. Rather than hate him, the people of ancient Egypt prayed to Set to ward off evil, especially in the afterlife. As he had been a protector of Ra, they earnestly prayed for his protection.

Another perspective to this reaction was the Egyptians' belief in Ma'at. For order to exist and be appreciated, there had to be disorder. For peace to be valued, there had to be chaos. Set existed to balance the scale of harmony in the world; otherwise, life would have no meaning.

Symbolically, Set had many forms, possibly because of his contrasting nature. He is depicted as a muscular man with brown skin and the head of a composite animal in some documents and as a fork-tailed beast with red hair in others.

The god of chaos retained influence well beyond the era he was demonized in, and this distinguishes him from the league of villains in Egyptian mythology.

Nephthys: The Goddess of Death and Darkness

Beyond the myth of Osiris, the goddess Nephthys does not make much of an appearance. Nonetheless, she was one of the Ennead, and her actions, although seemingly insignificant from an outside view today, largely affected the course of events in her family and in Egyptian mythology and even history.

Nephthys was born to Geb and Nut. Like Set, she must have found herself ever in the shadows of her famous sister Isis. She could relate to how Set felt about Osiris, and that may have been the attraction. Her marriage to Set was not said to be happy, especially since she secretly wanted Osiris.

There is no telling if her desire for Osiris had anything to do with the fact that she wanted what Isis had or if it was all just lust. However, we know that Nephthys was set in her ways to make Osiris look her way. Nephthys knew that Osiris only had eyes for his queen, which means there was only one way to seduce him.

That night, Nephthys took on a foolproof disguise and appeared before Osiris in the exact likeness of his beloved queen. Osiris had no reason to suspect that it was Nephthys in disguise, so he slept with her. Nephthys's sinister plan succeeded. She returned home to Set, who had been too occupied with his endeavors to notice her absence.

In time, Nephthys realized that her actions had provided Set with the justification he sorely needed to harm King Osiris. Set also discovered that her son, Anubis, was formed after she slept with Osiris, and he cruelly expelled the boy from his household. This marked a turning point in the story of Nephthys, as her actions thenceforth reflected remorse for the damage she had caused.

After Set killed Osiris so brutally, Nephthys helped her sister Isis find the king's body parts. They searched for a long time, and they were assisted by Anubis. After the sisters found the parts, Nephthys stayed to help revive Osiris. She also stayed to help nurse young Horus after he was born. He would grow to bring her husband to his doom.

Very little is known about Nephthys as the queen of Egypt, perhaps because she was hardly ever in the palace. Set also had enough concubines to take Nephthys's place while she sought to atone for her actions against Osiris and Isis. Nephthys spent so much time with Isis that they became twin goddesses, closely associated with each other in divinity.

The name Nephthys is often translated to mean "Mistress of the Temple Enclosure" or "Lady of the House." The goddess is portrayed in paintings and sculptures as a young woman wearing a headdress shaped like a house with a basket atop it, yet she was not a model housewife or homemaker. The house stands for the temple and priesthood. Because of her service to Osiris, Isis, and Horus, Nephthys was honored as a divine helper of the weak and the dead in ancient Egypt.

An image of Nephthys.
https://commons.wikimedia.org/wiki/File:Nephthys2.png

As the nursing mother of Horus, Nephthys was adored as the nursing mother of all pharaohs. She was also their protector and the breather of fire upon their enemies. As the wife of Set, Nephthys's worship peaked at the same time as Set's. There were no significant temples of Nephthys until the Nineteenth Dynasty, which was when Ramesses II and his father made Set a more famous god. A temple of Nephthys was built in Sepermeru, Upper Egypt, close to the temple of Set. As the sister and comforter of Isis, Nephthys was honored in Abydos as a helper of the dead. She helped the dead transition to the afterlife, she mourned for the grieving, and she comforted women during childbirth.

Like Isis, Nephthys possessed magical healing powers, and you would find ancient Egyptians wearing amulets of Nephthys in good faith that she would heal them of their illnesses. She was also invoked with Isis during embalmment and other preparatory funeral rites.

Finally, a twist to Nephthys's personality was her being a goddess who enjoyed offerings of beer during festivities. For one associated with death, mourning, and darkness, Nephthys's association with celebratory wine was ironic. It may have been another accessory to her compatibility with Set, whose reputation was just as dynamic.

Chapter 19: Anubis and Thoth

The ancient Egyptian pantheon had well over a thousand gods and goddesses who were worshiped throughout the land. Their shrines, temples, and festivals in Egypt were world-famous, and the greatest legends of history were woven around these divine beings. From the primordial era to creation and after, the relationships that Egyptian gods and goddesses had with humans and with one another are the unique stories that shaped the history of ancient Egypt. Among these players were the gods Anubis, the patron of lost souls, and Thoth, the god of wisdom and magic.

This is their story.

Anubis: The Patron of Lost Souls

You can't talk about the gods of ancient Egypt without mentioning a certain god shaped as a man with the head of a jackal (or a dog). He was one of the most famous gods worshiped in ancient Egypt, and he stood at the gates of the afterlife to usher in souls. In the Pyramid Texts, he is depicted as one who stands with Osiris. He weighs the heart of every soul in the Hall of Truth to determine if they are worthy of the afterlife.

His name is Anubis.

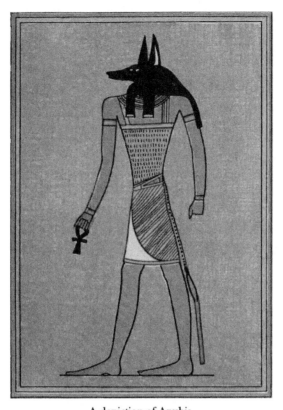

A depiction of Anubis.
Unknown author, CC0, via Wikimedia Commons;

Before the popularization of the myth of Osiris, Anubis was believed to be the son of Ra, the sun god. Subsequently, Anubis's origin found roots in more interesting circumstances. He was the lovechild of Osiris and Nephthys, and he was raised as a son of Set until the latter discovered his true pedigree.

The name "Anubis" is Greek, and he was called "Anpu" before the Greeks came to Egypt. Anpu translated to "royal child" in ancient Egyptian, and this may have been in deference to Anubis's status as the son of a king.

Osiris's myth provides a glimpse into what could have been Anubis's childhood. Born to a father who was ever scheming against the king of Egypt and a mother who was either still obsessed with seducing the king of Egypt or regretting her actions, Anubis's childhood might have been lonely.

Ultimately, he was discarded without hesitation by Set, and Anubis left what he once called home. The Greek author Plutarch narrates that Anubis was abandoned by his mother Nephthys as a helpless infant and left without a parent until a certain goddess adopted him.

Whether Anubis was adopted as a helpless infant or a much older child, he became the son of Isis, who was on the run from Set. Many versions of the myth of Osiris cite Anubis as the one who saved Isis from prison after Set captured her. With his mother, Nephthys, he helped Isis assemble the dismembered body parts of Osiris. This action warmed the hearts of the ancient people of Egypt, and they saw Anubis as a protector, guide, and helper. And his roles in the afterlife were not far off from that.

First, Anubis was the "Embalmer-in-Chief" of ancient Egypt. In fact, he was credited with being the first to ever embalm a corpse in the history of Egypt. The corpse was that of Osiris after he had been killed by Set. As the inventor of this sacred Egyptian practice of preparing the dead for their new lives in the underworld, Anubis was commonly featured in funerary art. During mummification, one of the priests would wear a wooden wolf mask to physically represent Anubis while saying prayers for a successful preparation process.

Anubis was also the "Guardian of the Scales." After Osiris's descent to the afterlife and assumption of the throne as the king of the underworld (the Duat), he had much to do. Not every mortal was righteous enough to pass on to the afterlife. Some were to be condemned to hell as prey of Ammit. To determine the fate of each man, tests had to be done, and Anubis was commissioned with this process.

Each mortal's heart would be weighed on a scale in the Hall of Truth. On one side of the scale would be an ostrich feather, which signified Ma'at, order and truth. If the heart weighed lighter than the feather, the soul would be ushered into the heavenly afterlife, but if the heart weighed heavier than the feather, the soul would be condemned to Ammit's belly or an eternal lake of fire.

Man and woman, young and old, noble and commoner, no one was exempt from this trial. The gates of the afterlife were guarded righteously by Anubis, and only the light-hearted could gain entry.

Anubis was also called the "Protector of the Graves." It was a tradition in ancient Egypt to bury the dead on the western bank of the Nile River since it was seen as the gateway to the underworld. Anubis, being the "Foremost of the Westerners," was in charge of keeping the souls buried on the western bank safe, just as he had protected Osiris's body from Set once. In this legend, Set transformed into a vicious leopard to assault Osiris's corpse, but he was repelled and skinned by Anubis with a hot iron rod.

In deference to Anubis's heroic act, the priests of ancient Egypt would wear leopard skins when preparing a corpse. They would also send off the deceased with prayers to Anubis to guide them to the afterlife, which brings us to another one of Anubis's sacred duties; he was the patron of lost souls.

Whenever a person died in ancient Egypt, it was believed that unless they were guided into the afterlife, they could be lost forever. As another one of his many titles, Anubis was venerated as the "Master of the Secrets," for only he knew the road to the afterlife and what lay at its gates and beyond. In ancient royal tombs, depictions of Anubis leading the deceased mortal by the hand into the Hall of Truth were popular.

Anubis's sacred duties were a part of every crucial step into the afterlife. Anubis protected the dead, led them to judgment, administered their judgment, and welcomed them to the afterlife. He was an incredibly important deity. A few ancient traditions posit that he had been the first ruler of the underworld, but he became Osiris's righthand man when he took the throne. Considering the times when Anubis was born and his journey with Isis, the plausibility of this account remains widely debated.

Symbolically, Anubis was the black jackal god. The color black represented the discoloration of a corpse after being cleaned with a chemical called natron during mummification. Black also symbolized the color of the shores of the Nile River, as well as aspects of life, death, and rebirth in the afterlife—things that were all associated with the god Anubis.

Anubis was known to hate injustice and troublemakers, which is possibly one of the reasons he soon became an enemy of the god of chaos, Set. While he did not take center stage in any of the popular ancient Egyptian myths, Anubis's fame stretched from predynastic Egypt well into the era of Graeco-Roman Egypt. The Greeks compared him to their god Hermes, and as fellow believers in the concept of the afterlife, the Greeks shared reverence for Anubis. He was worshiped throughout the land, and many shrines were built in his name.

Cynopolis, an ancient city in Upper Egypt, was home to the esteemed cult of Anubis, and the cult had a vast followership. Every man and woman was keen on the preservation of their souls and a smooth transition to the afterlife. What better way to be assured of a place in eternity than worshiping the one who stood at the gates of the underworld and knew all its secrets?

Thoth: The God of Wisdom, Magic, and the Moon

Many gods and goddesses in ancient Egyptian mythology were in charge of things that were mostly spiritual and sacred, but this ibis-headed god who comes to us from the city of Hermopolis had more intellectual associations.

He was the god and inventor of writing, the one who created the many languages in the world. He was the righthand man of Ra, the arbiter of the gods, and the chief of the famous cosmological Ogdoad of Hermopolis. He was Thoth.

You will find illustrations of Thoth as a man with the head of an ibis or occasionally a baboon. Like many other gods, including Anubis, Thoth is portrayed as holding an ankh, also known as the "key of life," as it symbolizes the immortality of the gods. Thoth is also commonly shown as wearing a royal crown or headdress, demonstrating his association with the god Shu, the son of Ra.

Thoth, the god of wisdom.

In the creation myth of Hermopolis, Thoth is the self-begotten creator of the world order or Ma'at. In other accounts, he is the husband of the goddess Ma'at, who, with Anubis, weighed the hearts of souls against Ma'at and recorded the results. Thoth's association with Ma'at is the foundation of his existence as the god of wisdom.

In early Egyptian mythology, Thoth went from being the head of the Ogdoad of Hermopolis to being part of the sun god Ra's barque entourage. He would counsel the sun god and keep journals of their voyage. Thoth was believed to be the source of hieroglyphics, and he became the "Lord of the Scribes" and the partner of Seshat, the Egyptian goddess of writing, wisdom, and knowledge.

Thoth's intellect created other diverse forms of human knowledge, such as law, science, and the art of worship. He was a god of perfection and diplomacy who could never make mistakes in his judgment. This made him a confidant of Ra, as illustrated in the Hermopolitan myth of "Thoth and the Distant Goddess."

This myth began with a dispute between Ra and his daughter. This dispute was long, and eventually, Ra's daughter stormed out of his sight and went far away from him into the deserts. In time, Ra became concerned that his daughter had been away for too long and sent many messengers to bring her back. The most famous eventuality of this was that the sun god sent his eye, the Eye of Ra, to find his daughter and bring her back home, which was a success.

In another account, however, things were not so simple. Ra's daughter was too powerful to be brought home. Ra needed an intervention, and that was when he thought of Thoth. No other god was wise enough to bring home the Distant Goddess. He summoned Thoth and charged him with the task. In the end, Thoth returned with Ra's daughter, and as a reward, he was given a wife named Nehemtawy.

Another one of Thoth's golden achievements was what led to his becoming the god of the moon. Back in predynastic Egypt, the average year had only 360 days. The sky goddess Nut was pregnant from the actions of her brother and lover Geb, and their father, Shu, was not the only one who was unhappy about it. Her grandfather Ra was just as furious, and with his divine power, he cursed Nut so that she would not give birth on any day of the year.

It was a harsh punishment, and Nut was distraught until Thoth learned of her plight and came to her rescue. He visited Iah, the god of the moon (or the moon itself), and requested Iah to give him some moonlight time. The moon god was intrigued by Thoth's request, but such a favor could not be granted so easily. So, the two gods made a gamble, and Thoth won, earning him the prize of moonlight time. Iah let Thoth have the moonlight time he needed, which was about five days.

With this, Thoth added five days to the year, allowing Nut to bypass Ra's punishment and give birth to her children, one on each day: Osiris, Isis, Set, Nephthys (and Horus in some accounts). Ra heard of Thoth's wisdom and was more impressed than enraged. This is believed to be the beginning of Thoth's relationship with the sun god. Ra gave Thoth an elevated place on his sacred barque and sought his counsel to defeat the evil Apophis (Apep).

In the myth of Osiris, Thoth played the role of a counselor and mediator. He was the one who suggested to Isis to find her husband's body parts and told her the magic words to say to bring him back to life. He also guided Anubis when he helped Isis escape from Set's captivity.

When the war between Horus and Set broke out, Thoth took on the role of the arbitrator, adding "God of Equilibrium' to his many titles.

Thoth was the one who ensured that each battle was fair, and he guided Horus on how to heal his eye when it was ripped out by Set in the heat of battle. "The Contendings of Horus and Set" negates the existence of Thoth before this war. Instead, Thoth was born from Set's forehead after Set's accidental contact with Horus's semen. He became a mediator thenceforth.

The influence of Thoth in ancient Egypt was propagated by the authors, librarians, and scholars of the time, who doubled as his priests. They honored him as the father of writing and the inventor of words. They also used the ibis, the symbol of Thoth, as their emblem and were versed in magic spells in the name of Thoth. The cult of Thoth soon emerged from the city of Hermopolis, and his worship had spread throughout the land by the end of the New Kingdom. During the festivals of Thoth, thousands of ibises and baboons would be mummified and sold to worshipers to give as offerings to Thoth. An excavation of the ancient sites around these worship centers, notably in Hermopolis, revealed a large number of these mummified animals.

"Thutmose," meaning "born of Thoth" or "Thoth is born," was the name of five pharaohs, three known viziers, and a famous sculptor in ancient Egypt. The wide association with Thoth by the nobility shows his influence, which held its momentum from predynastic Egypt until the emergence of early Christianity in Roman Egypt.

Being lovers of all things artsy and civilized, it was no wonder that the Greeks highly revered Thoth. Like Anubis, he was equated with Hermes and syncretized to become Hermes Trismegistus in the Hellenistic era. Hermes Trismegistus represented a holy blend of spiritual and material wisdom, as personified by Thoth and

Hermes, and he was believed to author many books, collectively called the *Corpus Hermetica.*

Finally, ancient Egypt's god of wisdom was a secretary in the afterlife who stood next to Osiris and Anubis in the Hall of Truth, keeping account of every heart weighed against the feather of Ma'at. Thoth was also famous among the souls in the afterlife as a hospitable host for those who sought rest at his residence, the Mansion of Thoth. He also granted protective spells against the demons that lurked in eternity.

Chapter 20: Hathor and Bastet

Two other goddesses who enjoyed reverence and relevance in ancient Egypt were Hathor and Bastet. In the Metropolitan Museum in New York City, you can find a plaque of Hathor and Bastet on display.

This artifact is traced to the Eighteenth or Nineteenth Dynasty, sometime between the reign of Pharaoh Ahmose I and Pharaoh Ramesses I. The artifact portrays Hathor as a sistrum, a musical instrument from ancient Egypt, playing to a cat, a symbol of Bastet. These two goddesses were associated with the arts and joy in ancient Egypt, but there was a lot more to them.

Hathor: The Mother of the Sky

Hathor's origins are as multi-versioned and dynamic as her attributes, but every story establishes her connection with the sun god Ra. Before Isis became popular as the "Queen Mother of all Pharaohs," Hathor held that title. After all, she was the mother of the sun god himself or, in other accounts, his daughter or consort and companion on the divine barque. Alternately, she was seen as the mother of Horus who symbolized rebirth, rejuvenation, and beauty.

Her most popular title was the "Mother of the Sky," which had been conferred on her because of her association with Ra. The ancient Egyptians believed that the sky was where the sun journeyed through each day and that the sky was where the sun was reborn at the break of every dawn. This translated to their belief in

Hathor as the mother of Ra, who gave birth to the sun every day—a cosmic mother. "The Golden One" was in deference to Hathor's status as an important member of Ra's company on his divine barque. She was the reason that the sun shone so bright and gave the world resplendence.

The cow is Hathor's animal, and depictions of her are a woman with the head of a cow or wearing a headdress with crown horns protruding from it and a sun disk in the middle.

An image of Hathor.
Jeff Dahl, CC BY-SA 4.0 https://creativecommons.org/licenses/by-sa/4.0 via Wikimedia Commons; https://commons.wikimedia.org/wiki/File:Hathor.svg

In other representations, Hathor is a cow or a sistrum, a percussion instrument she used to rid the land of Egypt of misfortune and sadness. She was also represented as a sycamore tree whose milky sap alluded to life and fertility.

As an equal of the Greek goddess Aphrodite and the Roman goddess Venus, Hathor was revered as a goddess of beauty and love in ancient Egypt. She was popular among the women as a representation of spiritual and physical femininity and as a divine midwife. Her role in femininity often leads to Hathor being compared with Isis, the wife of Osiris, and Mut, the partner of the god Amun. These three shared similar aspects, but Isis represented a more conservative side of femininity: the model mother and wife. Mut represented a more assertive feminine aspect, as she was typically independent. Hathor was free-spirited, openly sexual, and fun-loving, and, as you are about to find out, Hathor's reputation wasn't always that of a happy and benevolent deity.

In ancient texts from the Middle Kingdom to the New Kingdom, Hathor was the feminine aspect of the Eye of Ra, which was seen as Ra's messenger and harbinger of doom. According to an ancient legend, the sun god grew displeased with the state of moral decadence in the world he had created. Humankind no longer worshiped him and blatantly rebelled against him. As a punishment, Ra sent his daughter, Hathor, to wreak destruction on humanity. For this, she transformed into Sekhmet, the lioness-headed goddess of war, and she destroyed the world as instructed.

As she ravaged the earth with her hot breath of fire, the other gods were worried about Sekhmet's surging bloodlust. They asked the sun god to show mercy and call Sekhmet back from her sinister mission. If she was not stopped, she would wipe out every human alive, and the world would be empty and meaningless again.

Ra saw reason and decided that he would stop Sekhmet, but she was too far gone in her destructive spiral. There was one other way to stop her. Ra instructed for a special kind of beer to be made for Sekhmet. It was made with extra alcohol and blended with red dye to give it the appearance of blood. Sekhmet received the beer and, mistaking it for blood, took several gulps of it all at once.

Moments later, she was overcome with dizziness and fell into a deep sleep. Three days after, Sekhmet woke up as Hathor, the kind and gracious goddess. She became popular since she was the opposite of what she had been as Sekhmet. The story ends here in many versions. However, a variation of this myth does not end with Sekhmet turning good just yet.

Instead, it provides a fascinating prequel to "Thoth and the Distant Goddess," in which Thoth is sent to bring a daughter of Ra back home. Legend tells that the daughter of Ra was actually Hathor (or Sekhmet). She had woken up from her deep sleep and realized that she had been tricked by Ra. Her wrath knew no bounds.

A heated argument ensued between father and daughter, and Hathor left home for a faraway land as a sign of rebellion against the sun god for his trickery. Unable to bring her home, Ra sought the services of Thoth, the god of wisdom. Only he was able to get the job done, but he had to convince Hathor 1,077 times before that happened. The daughter of Ra may have started on her path of becoming good after coming home.

"Goddess of Love" was another one of Hathor's titles, and it told of the sexual aspect of this goddess. Even the gods were not immune to erotic pleasure, and as a consort of Ra, Hathor is depicted to have stimulated the sun god sexually to lift his spirits on many occasions. In other depictions, she is a beautiful woman with gorgeous hair, with each lock representing irresistible charm. Hathor may also have appeared to mortal men as a naked, attractive woman.

Ancient Egypt was a center for the arts, music, and dancing—an integral feature of their religious festivities. Hathor relished the view of celebration, whether it be eating, drinking, singing, dancing, or the women looking their best and smelling exquisite. Hathor could not resist the fragrance of incense any more than she could resist a good drink of wine. Like Nephthys, Hathor would get drunk while hearing the sistrum play.

Musical instruments were the keynote in the worship of Hathor. Apart from her favorite, the sistrum, the people worshiped the goddess of joy by singing hymns and playing lutes, harps, and tambourines. Every year, the people of Egypt celebrated Hathor by bringing flowers and dancing all the way to her temple in Dendera.

Hathor was fun-loving and dangerously adventurous, but she was also the goddess of tourism and trade. She was believed to be ancient Egypt's border protector who ensured that every ship on the Nile and Egyptian ships on other rivers and seas were safe. If you recall in the myth of the Greek princess, the temple of Hathor was where Helen sought refuge, and it was located near the shores of Egypt. In the myth of "Thoth and the Distant Goddess," Hathor left home for a faraway place, possibly Libya or Nubia, and became famous in these lands.

Through ancient Egypt's foreign trade relations, Hathor's fame spread to Canaan, Punt, Syria, and parts of Sinai. At the time, the vast turquoise and malachite reserves in the Sinai Peninsula made it a mining hot spot. With the spread of Hathor's worship into Sinai, she became the "Lady of Turquoise" and "Lady of Malachite." Egyptian traders who traveled to these foreign lands returned home with exotic items, which they called Hathor's gifts to Egypt (or to the pharaoh), as many mining sites were worship grounds in honor of Hathor.

As you would expect, the goddess Hathor was not without a role in the afterlife. Funerary art and literature from the earliest times in Egyptian history describe Hathor's first visit to the afterlife as a stopover between Egypt and foreign lands.

The Duat was crowded as could be, and many souls needed guidance in the afterlife. Hathor offered a helping hand and manifested as Imentet, the goddess of the west. She then joined the league of gods and goddesses who participated in the transition of souls. As Imentet, Hathor cared for the souls of the dead by nourishing them with food and drink. This shows Hathor's motherly nature, as well as her attributes as a protector and guide.

Pharaoh Horemheb with the gods Hathor, Osiris, Horus, and Anubis.
Jean-Pierre Dalbéra, CC BY 2.0 https://creativecommons.org/licenses/by/2.0 *via*
Wikimedia Commons
https://commons.wikimedia.org/wiki/File:La_tombe_de_Horemheb_(KV.57)_(Vall%C3
%A9e_des_Rois_Th%C3%A8bes_ouest)_-4.jpg

The myths of the doomed prince and the two brothers portray the Seven Hathors, another aspect of Hathor. They were the knowers of fate.

Bastet: The Goddess of Protection

Like Anubis, there is no misrecognizing the cat-headed goddess of ancient Egypt and her slender body. She often holds an ankh and a sistrum. Her name is Bastet (or just Bast), and she was the rave of Lower Egypt for a considerable length of time.

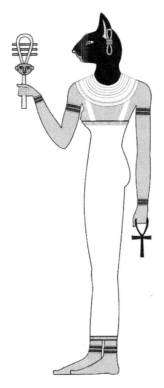

A depiction of Bastet.

It is important to emphasize how much the ancient Egyptians adored cats; they practically worshiped them. The royal household of Egypt would dress up their cats in golden earrings, nose rings, and neckpieces. These cats would also eat with them at their tables. Among commoners, cats were not treated much differently. Even if they could not afford expensive ornaments, they did not take the creatures for granted. After all, cats protected the household by keeping destructive pests such as mice and snakes away. Excavations of the temple of Bastet revealed hundreds of mummified cats, and historians suggest that giving cats the same burial as humans may have been a thing in ancient Egypt.

The earliest origins of Bastet were as a lioness-headed goddess. She was believed to be the daughter of Ra and skilled in the art of warfare. She became associated with cats in the Twentieth Dynasty, which was in the New Kingdom. Her association with Ra meant an association with Hathor as Sekhmet, which is why Bastet and Sekhmet are described as sisters.

Like Sekhmet, Bastet manifested as the initially terrifying Eye of Ra but subsequently softened her reputation by becoming the scourge of Apophis (Apep) on the sun god's divine barque. Legend has it that at the behest of Ra, Bastet, in the form of a cat, would defeat Apophis by beheading the serpent with a sword in her paw.

Apart from Ra and Sekhmet, Bastet was associated with Isis for her protective nature. You will find many alabaster sculptures of Bastet with a litter of kittens at her feet. This alluded to her status in divinity as the goddess of fertility, pregnancy, and childbirth. Cats are known to be highly protective of their offspring, and this nature was conferred on Bastet following her transformation. She was revered as a mother and protector against sicknesses and misfortune. She was seen as being equal to the Greek goddess Artemis.

The worship of the cat goddess began in Bubastis, where her cult was established. Bubastis was a Nile Delta city in Lower Egypt that became the eighteenth regional capital of ancient Egypt. This brought the worship of Bastet more into the spotlight, spreading to Upper Egypt from Bubastis and Memphis. The Greek writer Herodotus in his work, the *Histories*, describes the mass transit of people from all over Egypt to Bubastis for the grand festivals in honor of Bastet:

"When the people are on their way to Bubastis, they go by river, a great number in every boat, men, and women together. Some of the women make a noise with rattles [sistrums], others play flutes all the way, while the rest of the women, and the men, sing and clap their hands...When they have reached Bubastis, they make a festival with great sacrifices, and more wine is drunk at this feast than in the whole year besides. It is customary for men and women [but not children] to assemble there to the number of seven hundred thousand, as the people of the place say."

The magnificence of Bastet's temple in Bubastis further spurred Herodotus to describe it. It was situated on an island, accessible via two routes from the Nile River. The temple was built in a central location in the city, so there was no missing its resplendent view. It had majestic stone carvings and was surrounded by tall grove trees that "reached to heaven."

The people would wear protective amulets that depicted cats, signifying Bastet's protection. They would also exchange gifts of kittens on New Year's Day. It was believed that these acts would rid the year of evil and herald prosperity.

Bastet did not have as many attributes as Sekhmet, and she was also not a part of the primordial Ennead like Isis. Yet, she remained an influential deity well into the Persian invasion of Egypt in the late 500s BCE and beyond. Roman Egypt also saw decades of her relevance, and for most of those years, the goddess of cats was an immense joy to the people.

SECTION FOUR:
The Sacred Books

Chapter 21: The Coffin Texts and the Book of the Dead

By now, you know all about the importance of life after death in ancient Egypt and how this belief shaped the lives of the people for many years. You also know that funerals in Egypt were not simple or rushed. Deliberate spiritual processes were undergone to seal the transition of the dead to the Duat in the hopes that they had followed Ma'at their whole life, or at least enough to qualify for paradise.

In Chapter 1, you read about the ancient sources that provided us with all the knowledge of Egyptian antiquity there is. A few names like the Pyramid Texts come to mind, but in this chapter, the spotlight is on two other important sources that came after the Pyramid Texts.

Coffin Texts

For a long time in the Old Kingdom, only pharaohs were buried with funerary art in their tombs. The walls of kings like Unas, Pepi I and Pepi II, and Menkaure I, and even queens like Neithhotep, Behenu, and Ankhesenpepi II had corpuses of texts carved into them to hasten the royal's journey to the Duat, which was at the time believed to be in the sky.

There was no book titled "Coffin Texts" in ancient Egypt. What exists as the Coffin Texts are compilations of texts recovered from multiple coffins during excavations by 19th-century archaeologists.

These texts were translated from their originally written form to hieroglyphics by Dutch Egyptologist Adriaan de Buck, and they are valuable sources when studying ancient Egyptology.

Much of what made up the Coffin Texts were spells that were carefully etched into the inner part of the coffin before putting the corpse inside it. These spells currently number 1,185, and most make references to mythical stories from predynastic Egypt, such as Osiris's myth. This myth is the most recurring story in the Coffin Texts.

Before its popularization, the afterlife was perceived as the eternal home of the kings alone, as well as a few privileged queens. Old Kingdom nobles, scribes, and commoners did not believe that they could share such glorious eternity with their leader.

However, with the phenomenal discovery of Osiris's descent, not ascent, into the afterlife (or the Duat), the people realized that they had been wrong. The Duat was not in the sky or beyond their reach. Every person, king or not, who believed in Osiris and lived their lives in accordance with Ma'at could enter paradise. The cult of Osiris propagated this belief throughout the late Old Kingdom.

Consequently, from 2100 BCE, the Coffin Texts gradually replaced the Pyramid Texts, and the concept of the afterlife became far less exclusive. With this, non-royals could afford fairly elaborate funerals and all the materials required to make them so. Effigies, figurines, ceramics for burial vessels, precious metals, granite, and materials for mummification were no longer for pharaohs only. Production efforts were geared at making slightly inferior quality versions of these materials for commoners to use.

This impact on the spiritual and cultural outlook of ancient Egypt made Osiris's myth and its protagonist a most famous highlight of many Coffin Text spells.

"Ah Helpless One!

Ah Helpless One Asleep!

Ah Helpless One in this place

which you know not, yet I know it!

Behold, I have found you [lying] on your side

the great Listless One.

'Ah, Sister!' says Isis to Nephthys,

'This is our brother,

Come, let us lift up his head,

Come, let us [rejoin] his bones,

Come, let us reassemble his limbs,

Come, let us put an end to all his woe,

that, as far as we can help, he will weary no more.

May the moisture begin to mount for this spirit!

May the canals be filled through you!

May the names of the rivers be created through you!

Osiris, live!

Osiris, let the great Listless One arise!'"

This excerpt was a popular protective spell in many Coffin Texts. While it told of how Isis and Nephthys revived Osiris after he was killed by Set, it also invoked the two goddesses to protect the deceased on their journey to the afterlife.

Descriptions and invocations of guardian gods and goddesses were also found in the Coffin Texts. These were believed to help the deceased soul recognize guardians in the afterlife and submit to their protection. With demons, snares, and traps lurking at every stop, a soul needed divine help to navigate the Duat until they reached paradise. An unguarded soul was at risk of dying a second death or getting lost forever, so you can imagine that ancient Egyptians were finicky about the content in their coffins.

With the growing fame of Osiris as the judge of the underworld, the Coffin Texts provided the earliest known sources of events in the Duat, such as the judgment of the dead in the Hall of Truth. The most famous source from this era was the *Book of Two Ways*, which has an intricate map of the Duat and is, so far, the oldest illustrated book in history.

The author of the *Book of Two Ways* may never be known, but copies of the document were carved onto some ancient coffins from a village called Deir el-Bersha. No doubt, the people had copied this map from an original in the belief that the map would guide the deceased soul through the realms of the Duat. The oldest copy of this book was found in the tomb of a woman named Ankh, who was presumed to have lived during the Eleventh or Twelfth

Dynasty.

In this book, there were two routes to paradise, which is why it is called the *Book of Two Ways*. The two routes were by the sea and land, which were separated by a fiery lake and hideous monsters. Both routes were riddled with perilous obstacles through which the soul must endure before appearing before Osiris.

As the most advanced version of the Coffin Texts, the *Book of Two Ways* would be replaced with the *Book of the Dead* in the Middle and New Kingdoms.

The Book of The Dead

The evolution of the Egyptian belief in the afterlife and its intricacies began with the Pyramid Texts, which dominated most of the Old Kingdom. Subsequently, the Coffin Texts, which drew on the Pyramid Texts but were more generally accessible, became more dominant. The highlight of the Coffin Texts was the *Book of the Dead*, which many Middle Kingdom Egyptians adapted to their funerary practices.

The emergence of the New Kingdom flagged a new stage in this evolution, and the *Book of the Dead* was the latest rage. Unlike the Coffin Texts, which were only drawn or carved on coffins, Twelfth Dynasty copies of the *Book of the Dead* could be written on papyrus and buried with the dead.

Like the Coffin Texts, there is no single *Book of the Dead*. Instead, there are compilations of many copies found in ancient tomb sites and coffins. A total of two hundred spells, hymns, and recitals were translated from their original hieroglyphic versions.

As the name implies, the *Book of the Dead* was written for the dead. It was a manual for overcoming dangers in the afterlife. The first spell was a prayer to Ra (or Atum) for the dead to successfully transition to the Duat. Also compiled in the *Book of the Dead* were spells to be recited by the deceased for the preservation of their bodies and protection from evil in the form of serpents like Apep:

"O you waxen one [Apep], who take by robbery and who live on the inert ones, I will not be inert for you, I will not be weak for you, your poison shall not enter my members, for my members are the member of Atum. If I am not weak for you, suffering from you shall not enter into these members of mine. I am Atum at the head of the Abyss, my protection is from the gods, the lords of eternity, I am He whose name is secret, more Holy of a throne than the Chaos-gods; I am among them, I have gone forth with Atum, I am one who's not examined, I am hale, I am hale!"

Some spells allowed the deceased to shapeshift into the forms of gods to fight against attackers. With one spell, for example, the deceased could transform into the sun god Ra to fight off savage crocodiles:

"Get back! Retreat! Get back, you dangerous one! Do not come against me, do not live by my magic...O you with a spine who would work your mouth against this magic of mine, no crocodile which lives by magic shall take it away."

There were also spells in the *Book of the Dead* that were meant to empower the dead to board the safest ferries in the underworld:

"O bringers of the ferry over this difficult sandbank

Bring me the ferry, tie for me the cords, in peace, in peace

Come, come, hasten, hasten, I have come to see my father Osiris."

The longest and most popular spell, Spell 125, described the judgment of souls in the Hall of Truth lucidly. It portrayed the jackal-headed god Anubis as the one who weighed the hearts of every man, with Thoth by his side and Osiris as the chief judge.

Left to right: A soul's heart being weighed by Anubis, recorded by Thoth, and then standing before Osiris, who is sitting on the throne.

The *Book of the Dead* was also a script containing the words that the deceased were expected to recite at every stage of their journey. An example was the "Declaration of Innocence" before the forty-two judges. Other aspects of the *Book of the Dead* indicated what each soul was to wear in the afterlife, such as a "heavenly white garment and sandals."

The *Book of the Dead* was commonly written by scribes who were well versed in spells. Unlike the Coffin Texts, which personified the deceased with Osiris, the *Book of the Dead* could be custom written for an individual or family. This would require the scribe to be familiar with the individual's identity, life story, physical features, personality, and pedigree. So, if a person was gravely ill and near death, they would request a scribe to draft a *Book of the Dead* for them.

Producing a *Book of the Dead* cost a fortune because of its importance in the afterlife. It is estimated to have cost up to half the annual wages of a laborer in ancient Egypt or a little over three ounces of silver. This made the *Book of the Dead* affordable mostly to the Egyptian aristocratic class and were often used more by men than women. Lower nobles who could afford secondhand papyrus and prefabricated versions owned a few copies. Scribes and priests could write for themselves, paying only for the materials to be used, not the workmanship.

Later in history, scribes began to write cheaper versions for the common folk. These versions had fewer spells and instructions and were written on far less quality papyrus. The commoners in this era took advantage of this, as it gave them a better chance at making it to paradise. Scribes made a fortune from this demographic for thousands of years, and consequently, there were many variations of the *Book of the Dead.* The more standard versions were found in royal tombs and burial chambers of bureaucrats, while the abridged versions were found in the coffins of commoners.

The highlights of the *Book of the Dead* are the journey of the dead in the Duat, the judgment of a soul, and spells for the protection of souls from a second death.

Chapter 22:
The Books of Caverns, Gates, and the Heavenly Cow

The importance of funerary art from ancient Egypt as a source of history cannot be overemphasized. Much of what is known about the Egyptian afterlife was described on the walls, ceilings, and roofs of ancient necropolises, coffins, and royal tombs.

You know all about the Pyramid Texts from the Old Kingdom, as well as the *Book of the Dead* from the New Kingdom.

One day in 1903, two archaeologists named Margaret Murray and Flinders Petrie discovered another form of funerary text on a corridor wall of an ancient temple of Osiris located in Osireion. This text was different from the Coffin Texts or the *Book of the Dead* in that it gave more gory details about what befell the souls condemned to the Egyptian hell in the Duat.

Incomplete versions of this text were found in the royal tombs of Pharaohs Ramesses IV, Ramesses VI, Ramesses VII, and Ramesses IX—they were all from the Ramesside era of the Twentieth Dynasty. There were also fragments of these texts in other non-royal tombs, totaling thirteen versions altogether. These texts were translated in the early to mid-1900s and compiled into a document titled the Book of Caverns.

The Book of Caverns

The complete versions of the Book of Caverns were found in the temple of Osiris and the grand tomb of a wealthy royal scribe from the Twenty-sixth Dynasty named Pediamenopet. The complete version has two parts; each part has three vertical subparts or sections, making a total of six sections.

The Book of Caverns tells the story of the sun god's journey in the underworld, the reward of saintly souls who pass the judgment, and the terrible plight of the souls who do not. The sun god's journey through the Egyptian "hell" happened every night, and the Book of Caverns illustrates every step of it with pictorials and texts.

In the first section of the Book of Caverns, the sun god is about to enter the Duat, standing at its gates.

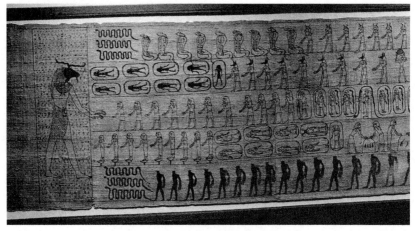

The first section of the Book of Caverns.

Waiting to receive him in the Duat is Osiris, the god of the underworld and judge of the dead. The first section also has five sub-parts called "caverns." The first cavern above the sun god is guarded by three snakes. These snakes protect the bodies of saintly souls in the first and second caverns, where they rest for eternity. The third cavern is where the sun god directly enters. Osiris sits there in two forms. The first form reaches out to the sun god, and the second form is in sarcophagus, facing the approaching sun god and guarded by snakes. The fourth cavern is of Osiris's followers, who are also in sarcophagi and guarded by snakes, ready to meet the sun god. The fifth cavern portrays the headless souls damned to hell. They are called "enemies of Osiris," and their cavern is a prison guarded by three snakes. The sun god will sentence them to a second death.

In the second section of the Book of Caverns, the sun god has entered the Duat. He asks for Osiris to receive him, and his request is granted. Other gods and goddesses in the underworld also receive him in their various forms. The last cavern shows the condemned souls on their way to the Place of Annihilation, the Egyptian concept of hell. Osiris is eager to lead the sun god farther into the cavern, especially where Aker, a gatekeeper of the underworld, is. Aker's gate leads back to Earth, where the sun god has to be by dawn to rise as the sun.

The sun god's journey progresses in the third section of the Book of Caverns. Here, he meets the gods of the sacred Ennead and other deities in the Duat. The condemned souls in the last cavern have reached their destination, the dreadful Place of Annihilation. The souls are hung upside down and are suffering immense punishment for their sins.

In the fourth section of the Book of Caverns, the sun god, Isis, Nephthys, Horus, and Anubis take care of Osiris and protect him. The condemned souls in the last cavern are still suffering at the hands of a ruthless demon, and they are eventually beheaded.

The fifth section portrays the sky goddess Nut, who receives the sun god and raises him up in her arms. Another part of the same section shows Osiris and other gods seeing the sun god off on the final stage of his journey. This is marked by depictions of the rebirth and rejuvenation of Ra. The languishing souls in the lowest caverns are introduced to the next stage of their punishment. Their heads and hearts are set ablaze, and two goddesses are with them in the Place of Annihilation, fanning the flames that slowly and painfully destroy them.

At the end of the sixth section is the sun god's divine barque, the Atet. It is rowed out of the underworld by his entourage with joy, and together, they prepare for the sun god's glorious ascension into the sky.

The Book of Caverns also mentions ten deities of the underworld apart from the known Ammit. These creatures, which are called "minor deities" or "demons," are charged with ensuring the punishment of condemned souls. These vicious demons were portrayed in different sections as fire-spitting snakes, catfish-headed gods, jackal-headed gods, and Ammit. They were all soul predators. A few sections have depictions of Osiris, Nut, and Anubis in the lower caverns, overseeing the punishment of the wicked.

Spine-chilling as the Book of Caverns might be, it represents the reasons why the people of the New Kingdom would have aligned their lives with Ma'at.

The Book of Gates

Just opposite the royal tomb wall of Pharoah Ramesses IV, where the Book of Caverns was discovered, there was a fragment of another ancient text dating to the Middle and New Kingdoms. This text was entitled the Book of Gates by a French Egyptologist named Gaston Maspero.

The Book of Gates portrays a journey through the underworld, but this time through the eyes of mortal souls. Discovered in tombs of kings, nobles, and other bureaucrats, some versions of the Book of Gates were incorrectly sequenced or woven into some content from the *Book of the Dead.*

Pharaoh Seti I's tomb had a colorful and detailed version of this text, showing four men, each of a distinct color of skin, entering the Duat. This representation of all the races on Earth reinforces the perception of the Duat by the Egyptians as a universal concept. Every human would live on after death, and the only way to get to paradise was to obey Ma'at.

The contents of the complete Book of Gates illustrate the soul's journey through several gates of the Duat and the guardians of each gate. The soul was required to know the name and attributes of each guardian to get past them and continue their journey. The Book of Gates has twelve chapters, each describing an hour of the night and what happens with the souls in each hour.

The first hour is titled "Ushemet-Hatu-Khefti-Ra." It opens with the sun god's arrival in the Duat through Amentet, the Hall of the Horizon. On his divine barque, Ra appears in the form of a scarab beetle, which comes from the creation story of Hermopolis, and he is protected by a snake and two companions named Sia and Hu. The gates of the Duat open, and all the souls of the dead join in welcoming Ra.

In the second hour, titled "Shesat-Makeb-Neb-S," the souls who obeyed Ma'at in their lifetime are separated from the wicked souls. The good souls are in the upper rows of the Book of Gates, and Ra blesses them, saying, "Your offerings are yours, you have power over your cool waters, your souls shall never be hacked to pieces, your meat shall never fail, [you who have] praised [me], and have vanquished Apep for me."

The wicked souls occupy the lower rows, depicted as laying on their backs in punishment. Atum, an aspect of Ra, acts as the son of the sun of god and curses the wicked, saying:

"The word of my father Ra is right (Maat) against you, and my word is right against you...Bound in fetters; your arms shall never more be opened...Your evil deeds [have turned] against you, your plotting [has come] upon you, your abominable acts [have returned] upon you, your destinies are for evil, and your doom has been decreed before Ra; your unjust and perverted judgments are upon yourselves, and the wickedness of your words of cursing are upon you."

The separated souls and the sun god continue down a narrow path until they reach twelve mummified guardian gods at the next entrance.

The third hour, titled "Thentent-Bau," is about crossing a foul-smelling fiery lake. The sun god's barque sails across it unscathed, as do the blessed souls. The wicked souls are burned and scorched by the fire as the beginning of their punishment. The serpent Apophis (Apep) appears at the end of the lake to attack Ra's barque, but Atum and two other gods defeat him.

The fourth hour in the Book of Gates is titled "Urt-Em-Sekhemu-Set." At this time, the traveling souls and the sun god meet the twelve jackal-headed gods guarding the next gates. These gates open to the Lake of Life and the Lake of Uraei. In this realm, the sun god resurrects more dead souls, including that of Osiris, who is protected by his son Horus. At the end of this scene, the souls of the wicked are punished in another bout of fire, and the sojourners arrive at a realm called Arit, whose gates are guarded by twelve gods.

"Sem-her-Ab-Uaa-As" is the name of the fifth hour in the sacred Book of Gates, and in this hour, the sun god and the traveling souls are depicted in a complex series of events. Notably, there is a portrayal of the Hall of Judgment, where the wicked are sent to the Place of Annihilation. In some versions, this sentence is pronounced by Osiris, who sits on his throne. The judgment of souls is linked to the sixth hour, which is titled "Mesperit-Ar-Maat." An array of mummified corpses await resurrection from Ra while armed gods restrain Apophis in this realm.

The seventh hour, "Khesef-Hai-Heseq-Neha-Hra," marks the time when every obstacle to the sun god's rejuvenation for the next dawn is destroyed. Midway through the realm, the sun god assents to the punishment of two of his captured enemies. The blessed souls continue their journey, with one group carrying baskets filled with stalks of grain on their heads. This is a reward for their commitment to Ma'at. The other group each bears the Feather of Truth, an aspect of Ma'at, as a symbol of blessing.

Hour eight is titled "Nesbt-Usha," where time as an infinite element is represented with an endless rope from Aken, the ferryman of the underworld. More blessings are given to the good souls in this realm, while the wicked receive more punishments. The mummies that had waited to be resurrected are gradually coming back to life, and the sun god continues on his barque to the next gate called Aat Shefsheft.

In the ninth hour, "Mak-Neb-S," the sojourners come to a chaotic river representing Nun, in which the souls of many mortals are floating. This does not allude to hopelessness or death. Instead, they will be nourished by the waters and set among the blessed souls to be fed vegetables and bread. The condemned remain in the lowest row; they are still languishing in the fires of destruction at the behest of Horus.

The tenth hour is "Tentenit-Hesq-Khakabu," and it portrays a fierce battle against Apophis, the enemy of Ra. The sun god battles Apophis in different forms, and he is joined by fourteen gods who hold magic-powered nets above their heads. This net is imbued with spells to weaken and defeat Apophis. At the end of this scene is text telling of an upward procession of the sky god. By this point, it is almost morning.

"Sebit-Neb-Uaa-Khesef-Sebiu-Em-Pert-F" is the title of the eleventh hour. Apophis has been defeated, captured, and dismembered. His mutilated body is held in place with a rope, and this time, the lowest row is occupied by gods and goddesses rowing the sun god's barque toward the east for his ascension. Souls of the dead are present to witness the glorious sight.

In the twelfth and final hour of the Book of Gates, the sun god advances to the gates of the final realm, where he is reborn as the bright morning sun. In his company are four gods holding sun disks in their right hands, four gods holding stars in their right hands, four hawk-headed gods holding scepters in their left hands, four ram-headed gods holding scepters in their left hands, one crocodile-headed god holding a serpent in his right hand and a scepter in his left hand, and eight female snake-like creatures holding stars in their left hands. Other details of this scene are the crowns of Ra, a chained Apophis, and four baboons celebrating the rebirth of the sun god.

While Osiris remains in the underworld, the sun god rises from the eastern horizon. The Book of Gates gives an engaging depiction of the Duat, and throughout the twelve hours, the souls traveling with the sun god are consistently enjoined to keep up with the divine barque. Every gate would close after the sun god's barque passed through it, and any soul left behind would be stranded for eternity.

The Book of the Heavenly Cow

A popular trope in mythology is the desecration of the world by mankind, leading their creator to be displeased and punish them. The story of Noah's ark and its destruction comes to mind from the Bible, but in Egyptian mythology, it is known as the tale of the Heavenly Cow.

The first version of this book was found in the tomb of the famous Pharaoh Tutankhamun, but it was incomplete. Subsequently, the tombs of Pharaohs Seti I, Ramesses II, and Ramesses III gave whole versions. Historians date this document to the Middle or New Kingdom, and unlike other funerary books, which offer spiritual guidance or depict the realms of the Duat, the

Book of the Heavenly Cow tells a fascinating story.

The first part, "The Destruction of Mankind," opens with a displeased Ra. He is described as "old, his bones being of silver, and his flesh of gold." Taking advantage of this, humankind has begun plotting a rebellion against their creator. The omniscient Ra summons a council of gods to deliberate on the next course of action. As suggested by Nun, the primordial waters that once covered the earth, Ra sends Hathor, the Eye of Ra, to punish the mortals for their insolence.

From here, the plot weaves into the story of Hathor, where she becomes the bloodthirsty Sekhmet and devours the earth with fire until she is stopped by a strong batch of wine from Ra. This part is called "The Withdrawal of Ra." It is the second part of the story of the Heavenly Cow, and it is linked to the crux of the story, which is titled "The Heavenly Cow."

Ra is determined to return to the sky, far away from his remaining creations. He seeks the help of Nut, the goddess of the sky, and asks to be placed on her back. Nut is confused by the sun god's request and seeks clarity. She then offers herself to be submerged in the magical waters of Nun and transforms into a celestial cow. The sun god mounts the cow and moves upward, just in time for the evil plans of humankind to hatch. In the morning, the people come out in droves, shooting arrows at the escaping sun god, who mocks them, saying, "O slaughterers, may your slaughtering be far removed from me!"

The sun god urges Nut to move faster. She goes higher, and the sun god summons more gods to join her.

Nut, the Heavenly Cow, being helped by the other gods with Ra on top of her.
https://commons.wikimedia.org/wiki/File:Nut1.JPG

Afterward, Ra establishes "The New World Order," which is also the name of the fourth part of the story. Nut becomes the sky and carries the sun (Ra), and Ra creates paradise (the Field of Reeds). Through the magic of Nut and Ra, in the final part, Ma'at is established, and it becomes the responsibility of humankind to uphold it.

The last part of the *Book of the Heavenly Cow* is very significant. In it, the sun god stops coddling his creation. Instead, they are tasked with maintaining the order of the world in exchange for a place in eternal paradise.

Conclusion

In Egyptian mythology, there is almost always a hint of the supernatural. The impact of this on ancient Egypt's history is immense. The people worshiped many gods and goddesses in the Egyptian pantheon. They performed sacred rituals and rites. They celebrated grand festivals, and they conducted elaborate funeral processes. All of these form a major part of Egyptian history.

So far, you have taken an enthralling adventure into the realms of the gods and have seen how their actions affected the humans on Earth and those in the underworld. Although we see myths as stories today, the people back then viewed them as being much more. Relics from the ancient eras of Egypt affirm this. Obelisks, pyramids, mummies, sacred texts, sphinxes, and temples are proof of the magnificent lives of the ancient Egyptian populace and their dedicated belief in something larger than themselves.

While most of them lived regular lives as commoners, they shared the same belief in the afterlife and the fate of all souls, whether they were good or evil. Thus, the people sought to live their lives in accordance with Ma'at in exchange for eternal bliss.

You have read of the ancient Egyptians' efforts and how much they persevered in their lives of worship. Apart from the intentionality of it, a laudable aspect of the ancient Egyptians was how they built those tombs, temples, and other monuments to last forever. Although they were focused on the afterlife, they also thought highly of the future and made sure to leave indestructible evidence of their rich culture behind.

Because of this, Egyptian mythology has been a major contributor to art, history, and popular culture. By the Graeco-Roman era, ancient Egypt had become a melting pot of cultures, with syncretized gods and the construction of new temples. Thousands of years later, Egypt would be occupied by Britain, and the surviving ancient monuments and artifacts would be unearthed.

Every piece of evidence tells stories of the ancient people as written by them. You have read about most of it: the lives of Egyptian gods and goddesses, the creation stories, their myths and folktales, and details of the sacred books. Museums, ancient sites, literature, and film have kept these stories alive for hundreds of years since their discovery. It is not too absurd to say that they will be remembered forever.

Here's another book by Enthralling History that you might like

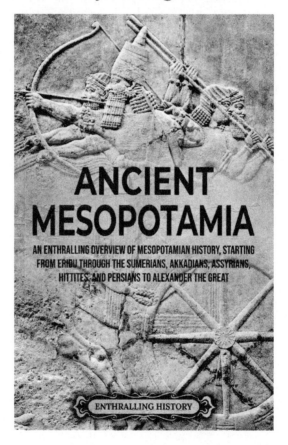

Free limited time bonus

Stop for a moment. We have a free bonus set up for you. The problem is this: we forget 90% of everything that we read after 7 days. Crazy fact, right? Here's the solution: we've created a printable, 1-page pdf summary for this book that you're reading now. All you have to do to get your free pdf summary is to go to the following website:

https://livetolearn.lpages.co/enthrallinghistory/

Once you do, it will be intuitive. Enjoy, and thank you!

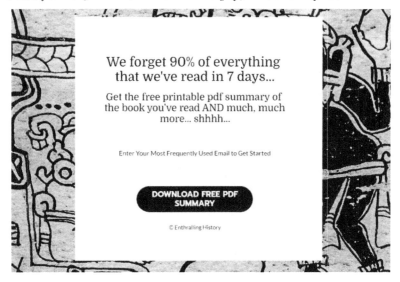

Bibliography

Title: Who were the mysterious Neolithic people that enabled the rise of ancient Egypt? Here's what we've learned on our digs
>
> Link: https://theconversation.com/who-were-the-mysterious-neolithic-people-that-enabled-the-rise-of-ancient-egypt-heres-what-weve-learned-on-our-digs-121070
>
> Date Accessed: 12/4/22

Title: Upper Egypt
>
> Link: https://www.britannica.com/place/Upper-Egypt
>
> Date Accessed: 12/4/22

Title: Lower Egypt
>
> Link: https://www.britannica.com/place/Lower-Egypt
>
> Date Accessed: 12/4/22

Title: Narmer
>
> Link: https://www.worldhistory.org/Narmer/
>
> Date Accessed: 12/4/22

Title: Old Kingdom of Egypt
>
> Link: https://www.worldhistory.org/Old_Kingdom_of_Egypt/
>
> Date Accessed: 12/4/22

Title: Djoser
>
> Link: https://www.worldhistory.org/Djoser/
>
> Date Accessed: 12/4/22

Title: First Intermediate Period of Egypt

Link: https://www.worldhistory.org/First_Intermediate_Period_of_Egypt/

Date Accessed: 12/4/22

Title: The Great Pyramids of Giza

Link: https://www.khanacademy.org/humanities/ap-art-history/ancient-mediterranean-ap/ancient-egypt-ap/a/old-kingdom-the-great-pyramids-of-giza

Date Accessed: 12/4/22

Title: Snefru

Link: https://www.britannica.com/biography/Snefru

Date Accessed: 12/4/22

Title: Imhotep

Link: https://www.worldhistory.org/imhotep/

Date Accessed: 12/4/22

Title: Horus

Link: https://www.britannica.com/topic/Horus

Date Accessed: 12/4/22

Title: Seth

Link: https://www.britannica.com/topic/Seth-Egyptian-god

Date Accessed: 15/4/22

Title: Isis

Link: https://www.britannica.com/topic/Isis-Egyptian-goddess

Date Accessed: 15/4/22

Title: Middle Kingdom of Egypt

Link: https://www.worldhistory.org/Middle_Kingdom_of_Egypt/

Date Accessed: 15/4/22

Title: Mentuhotep II

Link: https://www.britannica.com/biography/Mentuhotep-II

Date Accessed: 15/4/22

Title: Ancient Egypt's Middle Kingdom Period

Link: https://www.thoughtco.com/ancient-egypt-middle-kingdom-period-118155

Date Accessed: 15/4/22

Title: Amenemhet I

    Link: https://www.britannica.com/biography/Amenemhet-I

    Date Accessed: 15/4/22

Title: Senusret III

    Link: https://www.worldhistory.org/Senusret_III/

    Date Accessed: 15/4/22

Title: Amenemhet III

    Link: https://www.britannica.com/biography/Amenemhet-III

    Date Accessed: 15/4/22

Title: Sebeknefru

    Link: https://www.britannica.com/biography/Sebeknefru

    Date Accessed: 15/4/22

Title: Turin Papyrus

    Link: https://www.britannica.com/topic/Turin-Papyrus

    Date Accessed: 18/4/22

Title: New Kingdom of Egypt

    Link:
    https://www.worldhistory.org/New_Kingdom_of_Egypt/

    Date Accessed: 19/4/22

Title: Hyksos

    Link: https://www.worldhistory.org/Hyksos/

    Date Accessed: 19/4/22

Title: No one expected this pharaoh to found Egypt's most powerful dynasty

    Link:
    https://www.nationalgeographic.com/culture/article/ahmose-i

    Date Accessed: 19/4/22

Title: Hatshepsut

    Link: https://www.worldhistory.org/hatshepsut/

    Date Accessed: 19/4/22

Title: Thutmose III: The Napoleon of Ancient Egypt

    Link: https://discoveringegypt.com/ancient-egyptian-kings-queens/thutmose-iii-the-napoleon-of-ancient-egypt/

    Date Accessed: 19/4/22

Title: Amenhotep III
>
> Link: https://www.worldhistory.org/Amenhotep_III/
>
> Date Accessed: 19/4/22

Title: Akhenaten
>
> Link: https://www.livescience.com/39349-akhenaten.html
>
> Date Accessed: 19/4/22

Title: Tutankhamun
>
> Link: https://www.britannica.com/biography/Tutankhamun
>
> Date Accessed: 19/4/22

Title: Ramses I
>
> Link: https://www.britannica.com/biography/Ramses-I
>
> Date Accessed: 19/4/22

Title: Ramesses II
>
> Link: https://www.worldhistory.org/Ramesses_II/
>
> Date Accessed: 19/4/22

Title: Ramses III
>
> Link: https://www.britannica.com/biography/Ramses-III
>
> Date Accessed: 19/4/22

Title: The Rise of the Ramessides: How a Military Family from the Nile Delta Founded One of Egypt's Most Celebrated Dynasties
>
> Link: https://www.arce.org/resource/rise-ramessides-how-military-family-nile-delta-founded-one-egypts-most-celebrated
>
> Date Accessed: 19/4/22

Title: The Cult of Amun
>
> Link: https://www.archaeology.org/issues/174-1505/features/3146-sudan-nubia-dangeil-cult-of-amun-ra
>
> Date Accessed: 21/4/22

Title: Third Intermediate Period of Egypt
>
> Link: https://www.worldhistory.org/Third_Intermediate_Period_of_Egypt/
>
> Date Accessed: 21/4/22

Title: Egypt from 1075 BCE to Macedonian Invasion
>
> Link: https://www.britannica.com/place/ancient-Egypt/Egypt-from-1075-bce-to-the-Macedonian-invasion
>
> Date Accessed: 21/4/22

Title: Nubian Pharaohs of Twenty-Fifth Dynasty Egypt

Link: https://www.thoughtco.com/nubian-pharaohs-wenty-fifth-dynasty-egypt-3989880

Date Accessed: 21/4/22

Title: Late Period of Ancient Egypt

Link: https://www.worldhistory.org/Late_Period_of_Ancient_Egypt/

Date Accessed: 21/4/22

Title: Alexander in Egypt and Some Consequences

Link: https://www.jstor.org/stable/3853895?read-now=1&refreqid=excelsior%3Aa4de2b1b0f39bc3a48400199287264b9&seq=1

Date Accessed: 21/4/22

Title: Esarhaddon and Egypt: An Analysis of the First Invasion of Egypt

Link: https://www.jstor.org/stable/43074609?read-now=1&refreqid=excelsior%3A02412609704e33c923c78df7b5939f7d&seq=1

Date Accessed: 21/4/22

Title: Alexander the Great Egypt History

Link: https://www.journeytoegypt.com/en/blog/alexander-the-great

Date Accessed: 21/4/22

Title: The Battle of Pelusium: A Victory Decided by Cats

Link: https://www.worldhistory.org/article/43/the-battle-of-pelusium-a-victory-decided-by-cats/

Date Accessed: 21/4/22

Title: Ptolemaic Dynasty

Link: https://www.worldhistory.org/Ptolemaic_Dynasty/

Date Accessed: 21/4/22

Title: Ptolemy I

Link: https://www.worldhistory.org/Ptolemy_I/

Date Accessed: 21/4/22

Title: Hellenic Culture in Egypt

Link: https://www.jstor.org/stable/3853691

Date Accessed: 21/4/22

Title: Roman Egypt

    Link: https://www.worldhistory.org/Roman_Egypt/

    Date Accessed: 21/4/22

Title: Cleopatra

    Link: https://www.britannica.com/biography/Cleopatra-queen-of-Egypt

    Date Accessed: 21/4/22

Title: The Battle of Actium

    Link: https://www.history.com/this-day-in-history/the-battle-of-actium

    Date Accessed: 21/4/22

Title: Vespasian

    Link: https://www.britannica.com/biography/Vespasian

    Date Accessed: 21/4/22

Title: Diocletian

    Link: https://www.worldhistory.org/Diocletian/

    Date Accessed: 21/4/22

Title: Egypt's role in the Byzantine Empire

    Link: https://www.britannica.com/place/ancient-Egypt/Egypts-role-in-the-Byzantine-Empire

    Date Accessed: 21/4/22

Title: Bubonic Plague Traced to Ancient Egypt

    Link: https://www.nationalgeographic.com/science/article/bubonic-plague-traced-to-ancient-egypt

    Date Accessed: 29/4/22

Title: Egypt from the Islamic Conquest to 1250

    Link: https://www.britannica.com/place/Egypt/From-the-Islamic-conquest-to-1250

    Date Accessed: 29/4/22

Title: Rashidun

    Link: https://www.britannica.com/topic/Rashidun

    Date Accessed: 29/4/22

Title: Islamic Egypt Time-line

    Link: https://www.ucl.ac.uk/museums-static/digitalegypt/chronology/islamic.html

    Date Accessed: 29/4/22

Title: The Abbasid Empire

    Link: https://courses.lumenlearning.com/atd-herkimer-worldcivilization/chapter/the-abbasid-empire/

    Date Accessed: 29/4/22

Title: Fatimid Dynasty

    Link: https://www.britannica.com/topic/Fatimid-dynasty

    Date Accessed: 29/4/22

Title: The Ottoman Conquest of Egypt (1517) and the Beginning of the Sixteenth-Century World War

    Link: https://www.jstor.org/stable/162225?read-now=1&refreqid=excelsior%3Ae70bd594a54955011cfd60ba9e33c592&seq=1

    Date Accessed: 29/4/22

Title: Sasanian dynasty

    Link: https://www.britannica.com/topic/Sasanian-dynasty

    Date Accessed: 29/4/22

Title: Post- Byzantine Egypt

    Link: https://courses.lumenlearning.com/suny-hccc-worldcivilization/chapter/post-byzantine-egypt/

    Date Accessed: 2/5/22

Title: Mamluks

    Link: https://www.newworldencyclopedia.org/entry/Mamluks

    Date Accessed: 2/5/22

Title: Egyptian Views of Ottoman Rule: Five Historians and Their Works, 1820-1920

    Link: https://read.dukeupress.edu/cssaame/article-abstract/31/1/149/59700/Egyptian-Views-of-Ottoman-Rule-Five-Historians-and

    Date Accessed: 3/5/22

Title: The Ottomans (1517-1798)

    Link: https://www.britannica.com/place/Egypt/The-Ottomans-1517-1798

    Date Accessed: 3/5/22

Title: The Campaign in Egypt

Link: https://www.napoleon.org/en/history-of-the-two-empires/articles/the-campaign-in-egypt/

Date Accessed: 3/5/22

Title: Napoleon's military defeat in Egypt yielded a victory for history

Link: https://www.nationalgeographic.co.uk/history-and-civilisation/2021/01/napoleons-military-defeat-in-egypt-yielded-a-victory-for-history

Date Accessed: 3/5/22

Title: Battle of the Nile

Link: https://www.britannica.com/event/Battle-of-the-Nile

Date Accessed: 3/5/22

Title: Ottoman Empire

Link: https://www.history.com/topics/middle-east/ottoman-empire#:~:text=Decline%20of%20the%20Ottoman%20Empire,-Starting%20in%20the&text=In%201683%2C%20the%20Ottoman%20Turks,the%20Ottoman%20Empire%20in%201830.

Date Accessed: 3/5/22

Title: Biography of Suleiman the Magnificent, Sultan of the Ottoman Empire

Link: https://www.thoughtco.com/suleiman-the-magnificent-195757

Date Accessed: 3/5/22

Title: From the French to the British occupation (1798-1882)

Link: https://www.britannica.com/place/Egypt/From-the-French-to-the-British-occupation-1798-1882

Date Accessed: 3/5/22

Title: The Nature of Plague in Late-Eighteenth Century Egypt

Link: https://www.jstor.org/stable/44448549

Date Accessed: 3/5/22

Title: The Ottoman Response to the Egyptian Crisis of 1881-82

Link: https://www.jstor.org/stable/4283219

Date Accessed: 3/5/22

Title: Muhammed 'Ali

> Link: https://rpl.hds.harvard.edu/faq/muhammad-%E2%80%98ali
>
> Date Accessed: 3/5/22

Title: Icelandic Volcano Caused Historic Famine in Egypt, Study Shows

> Link: https://www.sciencedaily.com/releases/2006/11/061121232204.htm
>
> Date Accessed: 3/5/22

Title: Abbas II

> Link: https://www.britannica.com/biography/Abbas-II-khedive-of-Egypt
>
> Date Accessed: 3/5/22

Title: WWI in Egypt: A forgotten sacrifice for colonial powers

> Link: https://egyptindependent.com/wwi-egypt-forgotten-sacrifice-colonial-powers/#:~:text=Egypt%20was%20drawn%20in%20the,the%20residents%20of%20the%20city.
>
> Date Accessed: 3/5/22

Title: Egypt

> Link: https://courses.lumenlearning.com/boundless-worldhistory/chapter/egypt/
>
> Date Accessed: 3/5/22

Title: Wafd

> Link: https://www.encyclopedia.com/history/asia-and-africa/egyptian-history/wafd
>
> Date Accessed: 3/5/22

Title: Saad Zaghloul

> Link: https://www.britannica.com/biography/Saad-Zagloul
>
> Date Accessed: 3/5/22

Title: World War II and its aftermath

> Link: https://www.britannica.com/place/Egypt/World-War-II-and-its-aftermath
>
> Date Accessed: 3/5/22

Title: Gamal Abdel Nasser elected president of Egypt
> Link: https://www.history.com/this-day-in-history/nasser-elected-president
> Date Accessed: 3/5/22

Title: What is the Muslim Brotherhood
> Link: https://www.aljazeera.com/features/2017/6/18/what-is-the-muslim-brotherhood
> Date Accessed: 3/5/22

Title: Egypt: from revolution to coup to crisis, a timeline
> Link: https://www.trtworld.com/africa/egypt-from-revolution-to-coup-to-crisis-a-timeline-37581
> Date Accessed: 3/5/22

Title: Egypt President Abdul Fattah al-Sisi: Ruler with an iron grip
> Link: https://www.bbc.com/news/world-middle-east-19256730
> Date Accessed: 3/5/22

Title: Anwar Sadat
> Link: https://www.britannica.com/biography/Anwar-Sadat
> Date Accessed: 5/5/22

Title: Social Structure in Ancient Egypt
> Link: https://www.worldhistory.org/article/1123/social-structure-in-ancient-egypt/
> Date Accessed: 5/5/22

Title: Ottoman Cairo
> Link: https://www.laits.utexas.edu/cairo/history/ottoman/ottoman.html
> Date Accessed: 5/5/22

Title: Clothing and Adornment
> Link: https://www.historymuseum.ca/cmc/exhibitions/civil/egypt/egcl06e.html
> Date Accessed: 5/5/22

Title: Ancient Egyptian Law
> Link: https://www.worldhistory.org/Egyptian_Law/
> Date Accessed: 5/5/22

Title: Who were the Mamluks?

Link: https://www.historytoday.com/miscellanies/who-were-Mamluks

Date Accessed: 5/5/22

Title: Roman Egypt

Link: https://www.metmuseum.org/toah/hd/regy/hd_regy.htm

Date Accessed: 5/5/22

Title: Roman and Byzantine Egypt: background information

Link: https://www.ucl.ac.uk/museums-static/digitalegypt/roman/background.html

Date Accessed: 5/5/22

Title: The Ptolemaic Dynasty

Link: https://www.khanacademy.org/humanities/whp-origins/era-3-cities-societies-and-empires-6000-bce-to-700-c-e/36-the-growth-of-empires-betaa/a/read-the-ptolemaic-dynasty-beta

Date Accessed: 5/5/22

Title: Society in the Byzantine Empire

Link: https://www.worldhistory.org/article/1214/society-in-the-byzantine-empire/#:~:text=Byzantine%20society%2C%20as%20in%20that,were%20an%20even%20lower%20category).

Date Accessed: 5/5/22

Title: Social Structure of the Ottoman Empire

Link: https://www.thoughtco.com/social-structure-of-the-ottoman-empire-195766#:~:text=People%20associated%20with%20the%20Ottoman,members%20of%20the%20other%20professions.

Date Accessed: 5/5/22

Title: Christian Monks and Muslim Villagers in medieval Egypt: A Library of Congress Story

Link: https://blogs.loc.gov/kluge/2019/06/christian-monks-and-muslim-villagers-in-medieval-egypt-a-library-of-congress-story/

Date Accessed: 5/5/22

Title: Medieval Muslim Societies

> Link: https://www.khanacademy.org/humanities/world-history/medieval-times/social-institutions-in-the-islamic-world/a/medieval-muslim-societies#:~:text=Muslim%2Dmajority%20and%20Muslim%2Druled,by%20smaller%2C%20decentralized%20regional%20powers.
>
> Date Accessed: 5/5/22

Title: Why the Nile River Was So Important to Ancient Egypt

> Link: https://www.history.com/news/ancient-egypt-nile-river#:~:text=The%20Nile%2C%20which%20flows%20northward,the%20midst%20of%20a%20desert.
>
> Date Accessed: 6/5/22

Title: Impact of the Nile River on Ancient Egypt

> Link: https://pages.vassar.edu/realarchaeology/2017/04/09/impact-of-the-nile-river-on-ancient-egypt/
>
> Date Accessed: 6/5/22

Title: The Nile and Egyptian Religion

> Link: https://courses.lumenlearning.com/atd-fscj-earlyhumanities/chapter/the-nile-and-egyptian-religion/
>
> Date Accessed: 6/5/22

Title: Nilus

> Link: https://www.greekmythology.com/Other_Gods/Minor_Gods/Nilus/nilus.html
>
> Date Accessed: 6/5/22

Title: Ancient Egyptian Mythology

> Link: https://www.worldhistory.org/Egyptian_Mythology/
>
> Date Accessed: 6/5/22

Title: Hapi

> Link: https://www.britannica.com/topic/Hapi
>
> Date Accessed: 6/5/22

Title: Plant and Animal Life

> Link: https://www.britannica.com/place/Nile-River/Plant-and-animal-life
>
> Date Accessed: 6/5/22

Title: Quest for the Source of the Nile

Link: https://earthobservatory.nasa.gov/images/7236/quest-for-the-source-of-the-nile#:~:text=Beginning%20in%20the%20mid%2D1800s,the%20Nile's%20%E2%80%9Ctrue%E2%80%9D%20source.

Date Accessed: 6/5/22

Title: The Nile's Source Discovered

Link: https://www.historytoday.com/archive/nile%E2%80%99s-source-discovered#:~:text=John%20Hanning%20Speke%20discovered%20the,Nile%20on%20August%203rd%2C%201858.&text=John%20Hanning%20Speke%2C%20an%20army,at%20the%20age%20of%20seventeen.

Date Accessed: 6/5/22

Title: The Ancient Egyptian Economy

Link: https://rosenlearningcenter.com/article/689/the-ancient-egyptian-economy?username=rosensample&password=rosensample#:~:text=Agriculture%20made%20up%20a%20major,papyrus%2C%20stone%2C%20and%20gold.

Date Accessed: 6/5/22

Title: Oceanus' Family

Link: https://www.greekmythology.com/Titans/Oceanus/oceanus.html

Date Accessed: 6/5/22

Title: Khnum

Link: https://www.britannica.com/topic/Khnum

Date Accessed: 6/5/22

Title: Ancient Egyptian Religion

Link: https://courses.lumenlearning.com/suny-hccc-worldcivilization/chapter/ancient-egyptian-religion/#:~:text=The%20religion%20of%20Ancient%20Egypt,control%20the%20forces%20of%20nature.

Date Accessed: 6/5/22

Title: Egyptian Gods- The Complete List
> Link: https://www.worldhistory.org/article/885/egyptian-gods--the-complete-list/
> Date Accessed: 6/5/22

Title: The Emergence of Christianity in Egypt
> Link: https://dailynewsegypt.com/2013/06/19/the-emergence-of-christianity-in-egypt/
> Date Accessed: 6/5/22

Title: Christian Cairo
> Link: https://www.laits.utexas.edu/cairo/history/babylon/babylon.html
> Date Accessed: 6/5/22

Title: History of Egypt from the 7th Century
> Link: https://www.introducingegypt.com/modern-history
> Date Accessed: 6/5/22

Title: Jewish Life in Ancient Egypt
> Link: https://www.brooklynmuseum.org/opencollection/exhibitions/752#:~:text=Jews%20lived%20peacefully%20among%20the,its%20lack%20of%20ethnic%20tensions.
> Date Accessed: 6/5/22

Title: Serapis
> Link: https://www.worldhistory.org/Serapis/
> Date Accessed: 6/5/22

Title: The Cult of Alexander at Alexandria
> Link: https://www.jstor.org/stable/263514
> Date Accessed: 6/5/22

Title: Islam in Egypt
> Link: https://rpl.hds.harvard.edu/faq/islam-egypt
> Date Accessed: 6/5/22

Title: Diocletian, Persecution Of
> Link: https://www.encyclopedia.com/religion/encyclopedias-almanacs-transcripts-and-maps/diocletian-persecution
> Date Accessed: 6/5/22

Title: Fatimids Caliphate

Link:
https://www.newworldencyclopedia.org/entry/Fatimids_Caliphate

Date Accessed: 6/5/22

Title: What's The Difference Between Sunni and Shi'a Muslims

Link: https://crestresearch.ac.uk/comment/whats-difference-sunni-shia-muslims/#:~:text=Sunnis%20focus%20on%20following%20the,parts%20of%20the%20Middle%20East.

Date Accessed: 6/5/22

Title: Byzantine Egypt and the Coptic Period, an Introduction

Link: https://smarthistory.org/egypt-coptic-period-introduction/

Date Accessed: 7/5/22

Title: 8 Facts About Ancient Egypt's Hieroglyphic Writing

Link: https://www.history.com/news/hieroglyphics-facts-ancient-egypt

Date Accessed: 7/5/22

Title: Tombs

Link:
https://www.historymuseum.ca/cmc/exhibitions/civil/egypt/egca02e.html#:~:text=The%20first%20royal%20tombs%2C%20called,that%20have%20long%20since%20disappeared.

Date Accessed: 7/5/22

Title: Pyramids at Giza

Link:
https://www.nationalgeographic.com/history/article/giza-pyramids

Date Accessed: 7/5/22

Title: Inside the Tombs of Saqqara

Link: https://www.smithsonianmag.com/history/inside-tombs-saqqara-180977932/

Date Accessed: 7/5/22

Title: Uncovering Secrets of the Sphinx

Link: https://www.smithsonianmag.com/history/uncovering-secrets-of-the-sphinx-5053442/

Date Accessed: 7/5/22

Title: Ancient Egyptian Fortresses

Link: https://weaponsandwarfare.com/2018/09/20/ancient-egyptian-fortresses/

Date Accessed: 7/5/22

Title: The New Kingdom

Link: https://courses.lumenlearning.com/boundless-arthistory/chapter/the-new-kingdom/#:~:text=There%20are%20six%20great%20temples,sandstone%20from%20south%2Dwestern%20Egypt.

Date Accessed: 7/5/22

Title: Copt

Link: https://www.britannica.com/topic/Copt

Date Accessed: 7/5/22

Title: The Transition from Coptic to Arabic

Link: https://journals.openedition.org/ema/1920

Date Accessed: 7/5/22

Title: Discovering the wonder of Egypt's Islamic architecture

Link: https://www.arabnews.com/node/1044981/art-culture

Date Accessed: 7/5/22

Title: Akhenaten

Link: https://www.worldhistory.org/Akhenaten/

Date Accessed: 7/5/22

Title: Tutankhamun

Link: https://www.history.com/topics/ancient-history/tutankhamen

Date Accessed: 7/5/22

Title: How Did King Tut Die?

Link: https://www.history.com/news/king-tut-death-mystery

Date Accessed: 7/5/22

Title: Ay

> Link: https://www.britannica.com/biography/Ay-king-of-Egypt
>
> Date Accessed: 7/5/22

Title: Howard Carter

> Link: https://www.britannica.com/biography/Howard-Carter
>
> Date Accessed: 7/5/22

Title: The Discovery of King Tut's Tomb

> Link: https://www.thoughtco.com/tomb-of-king-tut-discovered-1779242
>
> Date Accessed: 7/5/22

Title: Archaeologist opens tomb of King Tut

> Link: https://www.history.com/this-day-in-history/archaeologist-opens-tomb-of-king-tut
>
> Date Accessed: 7/5/22

Title: Tutankhamun's Curse?

> Link: https://www.historytoday.com/archive/months-past/tutankhamuns-curse
>
> Date Accessed: 7/5/22

Title: Horemheb

> Link: https://www.britannica.com/biography/Horemheb
>
> Date Accessed: 9/5/22

Title: Tutankhamun

> Link: https://www.britannica.com/biography/Tutankhamun
>
> Date Accessed: 9/5/22

Title: Smenkhkare

> Link: https://www.britannica.com/biography/Smenkhkare
>
> Date Accessed: 9/5/22

Title: Ankhesenamun

> Link: https://www.britannica.com/biography/Ankhesenamen
>
> Date Accessed: 9/5/22

Title: Desperately Seeking Queen Nefertiti

> Link: https://www.nationalgeographic.com/adventure/article/150814-nefertiti-tomb-tutankhamun-tut-archaeology-egypt-dna
>
> Date Accessed: 9/5/22

Title: The Queen Who Would Be King

> Link: https://www.smithsonianmag.com/history/the-queen-who-would-be-king-130328511/
>
> Date Accessed: 9/5/22

Title: Who was Hatshepsut?

> Link: https://www.nationalgeographic.com/culture/article/hatshepsut
>
> Date Accessed: 9/5/22

Title: Hatshepsut

> Link: https://www.history.com/topics/ancient-history/hatshepsut
>
> Date Accessed: 9/5/22

Title: Hatshepsut

> Link: https://www.worldhistory.org/hatshepsut/#:~:text=Hatshepsut%20(r.,her%20stepson%20Thutmose%20III%20(r.
>
> Date Accessed: 9/5/22

Title: Cleopatra

> Link: https://www.history.com/topics/ancient-history/cleopatra
>
> Date Accessed: 9/5/22

Title: Arsinoe IV (D. 41 BCE)

> Link: https://www.encyclopedia.com/women/encyclopedias-almanacs-transcripts-and-maps/arsinoe-iv-d-41-bce
>
> Date Accessed: 9/5/22

Title: Cleopatra: Biography of the last pharaoh of ancient Egypt

> Link: https://www.livescience.com/44071-cleopatra-biography.html
>
> Date Accessed: 9/5/22

Title: Cleopatra

> Link: https://www.worldhistory.org/Cleopatra_VII/#:~:text=Cleopatra%20VII%20(l.%20c.%2069%2D30,of%20Alexander%20the%20Great%20(l.
>
> Date Accessed: 9/5/22

Title: Saladin
>Link: https://www.britannica.com/biography/Saladin
>Date Accessed: 10/5/22

Title: Saladin
>Link: https://www.history.com/topics/africa/saladin
>Date Accessed: 10/5/22

Title: Saladin
>Link: https://www.worldhistory.org/Saladin/
>Date Accessed: 10/5/22

Title: The Assassins
>Link: https://www.worldhistory.org/The_Assassins/
>Date Accessed: 10/5/22

Title: Why does Saladin have such good PR in the Medieval West?
>Link: https://www.medievalists.net/2014/09/saladin-good-pr-medieval-west/
>Date Accessed: 10/5/22

Title: Hosni Mubarak
>Link: https://www.britannica.com/biography/Hosni-Mubarak
>Date Accessed: 10/5/22

Title: Hosni Mubarak, Egyptian Leader Ousted in Arab Spring, Dies at 91
>Link: https://www.nytimes.com/2020/02/25/world/africa/hosni-mubarak-dead.html
>Date Accessed: 10/5/22

Title: Egypt's former President Hosni Mubarak dies at 91
>Link: https://www.aljazeera.com/news/2020/2/26/egypts-former-president-hosni-mubarak-dies-at-91
>Date Accessed: 10/5/22

Title: Mohamed Morsi
>Link: https://www.britannica.com/biography/Mohamed-Morsi
>Date Accessed: 10/5/22

Title: Mohamed Morsi, Who Brought the Muslim Brotherhood to the Egyptian Presidency

Link: https://www.newyorker.com/news/news-desk/mohamed-morsi-who-brought-the-muslim-brotherhood-to-the-egyptian-presidency

Date Accessed: 10/5/22

Title: Mohamed Morsi

Link: https://www.aljazeera.com/tag/mohamed-morsi/

Date Accessed: 10/5/22

Title: Mohamed Morsi's death: World Reaction

Link: https://www.aljazeera.com/news/2019/6/18/mohamed-morsis-death-world-reaction

Date Accessed: 10/5/22

Title: Italian Invasion of Egypt in WWII

Link: https://about-history.com/italian-invasion-of-egypt-in-wwii/

Date accessed: 28/6/22

Pinch, G. Egyptian Mythology: A Guide to the Gods, Goddesses, and Traditions of Ancient Egypt. Oxford University Press, 2004.

Bunson, M. *The Encyclopedia of Ancient Egypt*. Gramercy Books, London, 1991.

Shaw, I. *The Oxford History of Ancient Egypt*. Oxford University Press, 2004.

Ikram, S. *Death and Burial in Ancient Egypt*. Longman, 2003.

Leeming, David Adams (2010). *Creation Myths of the World*. Santa Barbaro: ABC-CLIO. p. 102. ISBN 978-1-59884-174-9.

Wallis Budge, E.A. *Egyptian Religion*. Cosimo Classics, 2005.

Wilkinson, R. *The Complete Gods and Goddesses of Ancient Egypt*. Thames & Hudson, 2003.

Hart, George (2004). *Egyptian Myths*. Austin, Texas: University of Texas.

David, R. *Religion and Magic in Ancient Egypt*. Penguin Books, 2002.

M.V., Seton-Williams (1999). *Egyptian Legends and Stories*. U.S.A: Barnes & Noble Publishing.

Nardo, D. *Living in Ancient Egypt*. Thompson/Gale, 2004.

Allen, James P. (2000). *Middle Egyptian: An Introduction to the*

Language and Culture of Hieroglyphs. Cambridge University Press.

Robins, G. *The Art of Ancient Egypt.* Harvard University Press, 2008.

Fleming, Fergus; Alan Lothian (1997). *The Way to Eternity: Egyptian Myth.* Amsterdam: Duncan Baird Publishers.

Goelet, O. et. al. *Egyptian Book of the Dead.* Chronicle Books, 2015.

Kemboly, Mpay. 2010. *The Question of Evil in Ancient Egypt.* London: Golden House Publications.

Van De Mieroop, M. *A History of Ancient Egypt.* Wiley-Blackwell, 2007.

Roberts, A. *Hathor Rising: The Power of the Goddess in Ancient Egypt.* Inner Traditions, 1997.

The One and the Many (translated by John Baines, Ithaca, NY: Cornell University Press, 1996).

Strudwick, H. *The Encyclopedia of Ancient Egypt.* Sterling Publishing, 2016.

The Crisis of Polytheism (London: Routledge, 2009).

Della-Piana, Patricia (2010). *Witch Daze, A Perennial Pagan Calendar.*

Quirke, S. (2001). *The Cult of Ra: Sun-worship in Ancient Egypt.* New York: Thames and Hudson, p.144.

"Book of the Dead of Nestanebetisheru."

https://www.britishmuseum.org/collection/object/Y_EA10554-66
"Book of the Dead of Djedkhonsiusankh."

https://www.britishmuseum.org/collection/object/Y_EA10328
Silverman, D. P. *Ancient Egypt.* Oxford University Press, 1997.

Bard, Kathryn (2008) *An Introduction to the Archaeology of Ancient Egypt.*

Herodotus (1920). The Histories with an English translation by A. D. Godley. Cambridge: Harvard University Press. At the Perseus Project of the Tufts University.

Printed in Great Britain
by Amazon